Picture Compositi
Film and Televisi

D0512768

However faithful an image that serves to convey visual information may be, the process of selection will always reveal the maker's interpretation of what he considers relevant.

E.H. Gombrich, *The Image and the Eye*

Picture Composition for Film and Television

Second edition

Peter Ward

Focal Press

OXFORD AMSTERDAM BOSTON LONDON NEW YORK PARIS
SAN DIEGO SAN FRANCISCO SINGAPORE SYDNEY TOKYO

Focal Press
An imprint of Elsevier Science
Linacre House, Jordan Hill, Oxford OX2 8DP
200 Wheeler Road, Burlington MA 01803

First published 1996
Second edition 2003

British Library Cataloguing in Publication Data
A catalogue record for this book is available from the British Library

Library of Congress Cataloguing in Publication Data
A catalogue record for this book is available from the Library of Congress

ISBN 0 240 51681 8

For more information on all Focal Press publications visit our website at
www.focalpress.com

Typeset by Keyword Typesetting Services Ltd, Wallington, Surrey
Printed and Bound in Great Britain by MPG Books Ltd, Bodmin, Cornwall

Contents

Preface

In the last years of the nineteenth century, moving pictures were viewed in penny arcades on Thomas Edison's Kinetoscope. This peepshow allowed the solo viewer to crank a handle, peer into a darkened box and watch in fascination the dim flickering silent representations of movement. This was quickly supplanted by projected images, but the mystery of a miniature world continued to have a strong attraction. After 45 years as a cameraman, I am still intrigued by a similar magic whenever I look through a viewfinder. There is a concentration of the field of view into a small intense, two-dimensional image that is quite unlike normal perception.

Moving the camera, lens and viewpoint creates a continuing kaleidoscope of changing images. Some images are attractive and pleasing whilst others are dull frames, a confused slice of passing reality. What makes the difference? What is the distinction between an image on the screen that delights the eye and the everyday, depiction of a commonplace 'window' on the world?

It may be the content of the picture that fixes the attention or it may be the technical quality of the image that is enjoyed. Frequently, however, it is the often unconscious pleasure derived from an arrangement of mass, line, tone and colour. The composition of the image appears to be one aspect of film and television production that attracts the audience and holds their attention.

Composition – the arrangement of all the visual elements within the frame – is at the heart of all visual communication. It is a subject that is seldom taught to broadcasting/film trainees who are expected to learn by example or to fall back on intuition or instinct. Many cameramen, in fact, insist that composition is intuitive and assume that framing decisions are based on personal and subjective opinion. Even a cursory examination of an evening's output of television will demonstrate the near uniformity of standard conventions in composition. There are original and innovative exceptions and this book aims to discuss the differences and the conventions of picture composition.

There is a huge diversity of film and television production techniques, ranging from a short 30-second news piece to a 2-hour blockbuster of a film. In general, they are all linked by a similar technique but there is a big variation among different types of production in the number of people involved when framing up a shot. I have attempted to give examples from both ends of the production spectrum but camerawork is shaped by production content and inevitably there will be incompatibilities between working methods.

Throughout the book I use the term 'cameraman' without wishing to imply that this craft is restricted to one gender. 'Cameraman' is the customary title to describe a job that is practised by both men and women and 'he', where it occurs, should be read as 'he/she'. Also, I often refer to the cameraman choosing visual options when in the majority of situations it will be a collaborative effort between director, designer, lighting, cameraman, etc.

This second edition has been extensively rewritten to take into account the impact of widescreen TV and the continuing growth of alternative camerawork styles to the classic Hollywood conventions.

Although there are enthusiasts in many crafts and professions, it is surprising, in such a competitive commercial activity as film making and television production, to find so many people who enjoy and are fascinated with the activity of picture making.

The British writer and stage director Jonathan Miller suggested that the rehearsal and performance of a film or theatre drama was literally 'play'. It is like the childhood absorption in pretence and make-believe. In a variety of film or television productions in studios or on location, large numbers of adults work together and take very seriously their individual task of perfecting an illusion. It is 'play' with a purpose.

One such film craftsman is Robert Kruger, film editor and director whose film making career began in the British documentary movement in the 1940s and moved to other types of factual films and European features. This book is dedicated to Robert whose enthusiasm for the art and craft of film making, even after a lifetime of working on over 1000 films, is undimmed.

My thanks to Robert, Alan Bermingham and Laurence Anthony for reading the manuscript and making many helpful and constructive suggestions. Needless to say, any errors or omissions in the book are mine. My thanks also to Margaret Denley of Focal Press and to John Rossetti and Mary Beresford-Williams for permission to reprint her photographs of television production. A special thanks to Patrick Caulfield for providing the drawing for the frontispiece of the book and to my wife, Sue, and my children, Sally and Edmund, for their help and encouragement in its production.

The cover picture is from 'The Big Combo', from the film library of Richard L. Rosenfeld, whose permission to reproduce it is gratefully acknowledged. It is a still from a film shot by the cinematographer John Alton, who was one of the first cameramen to write about his craft.

1
Invisible technique

Learning the ropes

There have been a number of boy-wonders and young prodigies in the history of film making but the most spectacular debut was when 25-year-old Orson Welles was summoned to RKO in 1939 to make his first movie. He had no experience of film making and Miriam Geiger, a researcher at RKO, explained camera angles to the young Welles by cutting out frame holes in pieces of paper and pasting over a selection of shot sizes taken from a reel of film. She added a short text description to remind Welles of the building blocks of film making.

Welles remembers that in the second week of shooting 'Citizen Kane',

an awful moment came when I didn't understand [screen] directions. That was because I had learnt how to make movies by running 'Stagecoach' [dir. John Ford, 1939] every night for a month. Because if you look at 'Stagecoach' you will see that the Indians attack [the stagecoach] left to right and then they attack right to left and so on. In other words, there is no direction followed – every rule is broken in the picture, and I sat and watched it forty five times, and so of course when I was suddenly told in an over-shoulder shot that I had to look camera left instead of camera right, I said no because I was standing here – that argument you know. And so we closed the picture down about two in the afternoon and went back to my house and Toland [the film's cinemato-grapher] showed me how that worked, and I said 'God there is a lot of stuff here I don't know', and he said 'There's nothing I can't teach you in three hours'.

('The Complete Citizen Kane', BBC TV)

Greg Toland was right. You can understand the visual grammar of film making in an afternoon. You can, in the same time, also learn the position of every letter of the alphabet in the 'qwerty' layout of a word processor keyboard. Knowing where each letter of the alphabet is positioned will not make you into a writer. How words are combined to make meaningful sentences will take longer. Creating vivid and memorable prose equal to the greatest novelists may never be achieved. If Welles was ignorant of film technique when he began shooting 'Citizen Kane', he must have been a prodigious high-speed trainee because, in the opinion of French film director François Truffaut, 'Citizen Kane' inspired more would-be directors than any other film.

Many newcomers to film and TV programme making often assume that as content and subject differs widely between programmes they must employ specific individual methods in their production. Film and television programmes are seen as one-off, custom-built entities. They may be surprised to find that there are significant links in technique, for example, between a 1930s musical, a 1940s crime film and a contemporary televised football match. The majority of productions (but not all – the exceptions will be discussed in the next chapter), share a common visual grammar. Like spoken language, this set of conventions was not originated by a group of academics laying down the law. The visual grammar evolved over time, through practical problem solving on a set, at a location or in an editing booth. This body of visual recipes is sometimes called invisible technique or continuity editing, and it evolved at the very beginning of film making.

It is important to understand the role composition plays in sustaining 'invisible technique', but it is equally important to remember that this is only one type of visual language. There are alternatives to this system, although 'invisible technique' is the predominant code used in nearly every type of film and television production. Its use is so widespread that many people in the industry believe that it is the only valid set of conventions. They suspect that anyone using alternative techniques is either ignorant of the standard conventions or is simply incompetent. To some extent they are correct if the production is aimed at a mass audience who usually anticipate and intuitively understand certain visual forms learnt over a lifetime of watching popular story telling on film and television. Unfamiliar codes of film making may confuse and 'switch-off' a mass audience.

A moving photograph

'Workers Leaving the Lumière Factory' is considered by many film historians to be the world's first moving picture. It was made by the Lumière brothers and, on 22 March 1895 in Paris, it was possibly the first film to be projected to an audience. Nine months later, on 28 December 1895, a paying audience watched a number of films made by the brothers including 'Arrival of a Train at a Station', 'Baby's Lunch' and 'The Sprinkler Sprinkled'.

These 'films' were single-shot, 'actualities' or documentary views with the camera framing a fixed viewpoint. They were considered as moving photographs and were unlike later developments in film making in both how they were made – a single uncut shot – and in how they were understood by their audience. Audiences were familiar with slide shows, some with mechanical moving images accompanied by a commentary and/or music. It has been suggested that early film was seen by audiences as a continuation of slide presentation and other serial projection of images. They were like the series of pictures, the

Rakes Progress, painted by William Hogarth in 1735. Each picture had individual interest but were linked by a common theme. The first moving pictures were discontinuous, animated photographs and in themselves did not form a continuous narrative. The images were not self-sufficient in telling a story and were possibly not conceived as telling a story by their producers or audience. The concept of film narrative and the required technique to create a convincing set of consecutive images had to be learnt by film makers and cinemagoers.

In a rudimentary form, basic film technology (except the recording of film sound) was invented by 1896, but the idea that film's primary purpose was to convince and persuade an audience they were watching a continuous event had to be recognized. During the 1890s, multi-shot views were shown, sometimes compiled by the exhibitor from different suppliers, and sometimes by the producers of film, without the concept that film could tell a story.

It has been suggested that Mèliès, in the 1890s, recognized the potential of film's ability to manipulate time and space when his camera jammed whilst shooting a bus leaving a tunnel. After clearing the camera jam he continued filming with the camera framed on exactly the same view and then found, when the film was developed, that the bus had miraculously turned from a bus into a hearse. This may be an apocryphal story, but it demonstrates the potential of film technique that Mèliès in a pioneering way was able to develop. He continued to shoot separate scenes containing no shot change and simply conceived the camera as the static eye of a privileged theatre spectator witnessing a series of magical illusions.

The claim that audiences for this primitive cinema saw the presentation differently from later cinemagoers is based on the conjecture that they were being shown views rather than being told a story. Film academic Tom Gunning proposed that cinema development split between story telling, which went on to dominate commercial cinema, and the cinema of attraction, which went underground and turned into avant-garde film. Primitive cinema in this sense was a series of visual displays providing spectator pleasure.

Continuity cinema

With magic lantern shows such as 'Fire', a rudimentary story was told, expanded by an accompanying commentary, of the start of a house on fire, raising the alarm at the fire station, the firemen journey to the fire, the fire raging in the interior, firemen with hoses and then climbing a ladder, followed by a rescue. Although there was a need for space relationships to be clear (e.g., interior fire station was distinct from interior burning house), there was really no need for time to follow a linear path.

There could be overlapping of time because as one slide followed another different events could be shown out of sequence and still be understood by the audience. Theatrical presentations such as Mèliès films are a series of scenes that the audience observe from their individual single viewpoint. Film storytelling gradually evolved a technique that allowed multiple perspectives or viewpoints without disrupting the audience's involvement with the story.

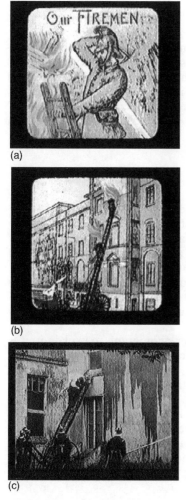

(a)

(b)

(c)

Figure 1.1 (a) The title slide of a series of Victorian coloured illustrations of scenes of a fire. Another drawing **(b)** depicts firemen rescuing the trapped inhabitants of the building on fire. As one slide followed another, often accompanied by an explanatory spoken commentary, different events could be shown out of sequence and still be understood by the audience. A shot from an early silent film **(c)** of the same subject. The shots in the film followed the conventions of the slide show and made little attempt to persuade the audience they were watching a continuous event in real time. The difference was that film provided a series of moving illustrations

Film added a time dimension, and a major problem for film makers was to establish linear continuity. They discovered that action could be made to seem continuous from shot to shot. Instead of each shot being seen as a different and distinct view, similar to turning the pages of a photo album, film makers learnt how to join the views together into a seamless flow of images.

In early film, action was played out to its end before moving to another piece of action. Unlike the single-shot actuality pioneering films, the director of 'The Great Train Robbery' (1903), Edwin S. Porter, cut away from action before it was concluded. Although he did not intercut during a scene this effectively was the invention of the shot.

The shot

The shot replaced the scene to become the unit of storytelling. In the period from the Lumière brothers' first public projection of film to the outbreak of war in 1914, film making moved from a series of tableaux scenes echoing Victorian slide shows and theatre presentations, to a unique method of narrative presentation. Theatre relies on scenes, staging action, movement, lighting and text to make the required dramatic point. Film invented the concept of multi-positioned viewpoints. These innovations occurred as the result of practical problem-solving rather than abstract theorizing.

A photograph does not need another photograph to explain it; it is self-contained. A film shot is a partial explanation – a piece of a jigsaw puzzle. The innovation in film making was to tell a story in individual images (shots) that did not disrupt the audience's attention by the methods used to produce the pictures. It was a coherent set of visual conventions and techniques that aimed to be invisible to the audience. The first film makers had to experiment and invent the grammar of editing, shot-size and the variety of camera movements that are now standard. The ability to find ways of shooting subjects and then editing the shots together without distracting the audience was learnt over a number of years.

The creation of 'invisible' technique

The ability to record an event on film was achieved in the latter part of the nineteenth century. During the following years, there was the transition from the practice of running the camera continuously to record an event, to the stop/start technique of separate shots where the camera was repositioned between each shot in order to film new material. The genesis of film narrative was established.

There was a moment of discovery when someone first had the idea of moving the camera closer, or using a closer lens, to provide an image of a person in close-up. Another had the idea of putting the camera in a car or train and filmed the first tracking shot. As early as 1897, a camera was placed in a gondola and provided camera movement in 'Le Grand Canal à Venice'. The panning shot was invented when someone moved the camera slowly across a landscape or street scene.

As well as camera movement came the problems involved in stopping the camera, moving to a new position and starting the camera again. The guiding concept that connected all these developing techniques of camera movement and shot change was the need to persuade the audience that they were watching continuous action in real time.

Standard camerawork conventions

The technique of changing shot without distracting the audience were discovered by a number of film pioneers. Several editing methods were evolved and became the standard conventions of film making and later television. These included continuity cutting and parallel action cutting, variation in shot size and not crossing 'the line', matching camera movement to action, lighting for mood, glamour and atmosphere, and editing for pace and variety.

Many film practises evolved from the need to stitch together a number of shots filmed out of sequence. A seamless string of images was designed to hide the methods of film production and to convince the spectator that the fabrication constructed by many weeks of film making had a believable reality. Camera and editing methods contrived to prevent the viewer becoming conscious that they were watching an elaborate replica.

Early film technique had the camera firmly fastened to a tripod, although some camera movement was achieved by mounting the camera on a moving vehicle or craft. Panning heads gradually came into use after 1900 and the standard horizontal lens angle appears to have been 25° or 17° (see Chapter 12, 'Composition styles' for a discussion on lens angle and the focal length of the lens). Framing was similar to contemporary still photography with staging similar to a theatre presentation.

Reverse angles, point-of-view shots and position matching on cuts were all discovered and became standard technique. The evolution of the grammar of film technique was not instantaneous or self-evident. Each visual technique, such as parallel tracking with the action, had to be invented, refined and accepted by other film makers before entering the repertoire of standard camera practice.

The thread that linked most of these innovations was the need to provide a variety of ways of presenting visual information coupled with the need for them to be unobtrusive in their transition from shot to shot. Expertly used, they were invisible and yet provided the narrative with pace, excitement and variety. These criteria are still valid and much of the pioneering work in the first decades of the last century remains intact in current camera technique. To tell a believable film story, the audience had to believe they were watching an unfolding event that was occurring 'now'. The technique that evolved ensured that the audience understood the action and were not distracted by the production methods.

This required the mechanics of film making to be hidden from the audience; that is, to be invisible. Invisible technique places the emphasis on the content of the shot rather than production technique in

(a)

Figure 1.2 (a) To cut from this shot...

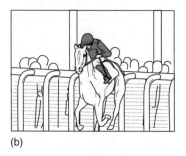

(b)

(b) to this shot...

(c)

you need this shot **(c)** to show change of direction, otherwise there would be a visual jump in the flow of shots.

Keeping the audience informed of the geography of the event is the mainstay of standard camera technique. Shots are structured to allow the audience to understand the space, time and logic of the action and each shot follows the line of action to maintain consistent screen direction so that the action is completely intelligible

order to achieve a seamless flow of images directing the viewer's attention to the narrative. It allows shot changes to be unobtrusive and emphasizes what is contained within the frame and to smoothly move the camera to a new viewpoint without distracting the audience. This is achieved by:

- unobtrusive intercutting (see Chapter 17 on editing);
- camera movement motivated by action or dialogue (see Chapter 16, Movement);
- camera movement synchronized with action;
- continuity of performance, lighting, atmosphere and action.

The development in storytelling in pictures required selection and choice of shot when recording. This included decisions on:

- size of shot;
- camera height;
- choice of lens and camera distance from main subject;
- camera angle relative to main subject.

Where to position the camera (camera angle), when intercutting on a scene created the convention of the 180° system. To avoid confusing the audience, it was found necessary to position the camera one side of an imaginary line drawn between two or more subjects when intercutting between them. If this is ignored and the camera 'crosses the line' when shooting a subsequent shot, it appears as if intercut faces are looking out of the same side of the frame and leaves the audience with the impression that the actors are not in conversation with each other (see Figure 1.3).

The same convention is applied to chase sequences and sports events where succeeding shots follow the line of action to maintain consistent screen direction so that the geography of the action is completely intelligible (e.g., camera positions at a football match). It is important that in each scene shots are structured to allow the audience to understand the space, time and logic of the action. This creates the illusion that distinct, separate shots (possibly recorded out of sequence and at different times) form part of a continuous event being witnessed by the audience.

Orson Welles' complaint of the lack consistent screen direction in 'Stagecoach' is correct, but John Ford, a great film director, may have deliberately 'broken the rules' and crossed the line in order to inject confusion and tension in the Indian attack on the stagecoach sequence.

In general, for invisible technique to succeed, careful thought must be given to how each shot is set up and how it will relate to the intended preceding and succeeding shots. Editing and shooting are inseparable.

Another convention – the 30° system, avoided distracting the audience by cutting between following shots of the same subject with a camera position of less than 30° relationship to the preceding shot. The audience was taught a visual convention that when a character looks out of frame, the subject of their observation – their point of view – was shown in the next shot. A variation of this is the eye line match when characters are in conversation. Individual shots of char-

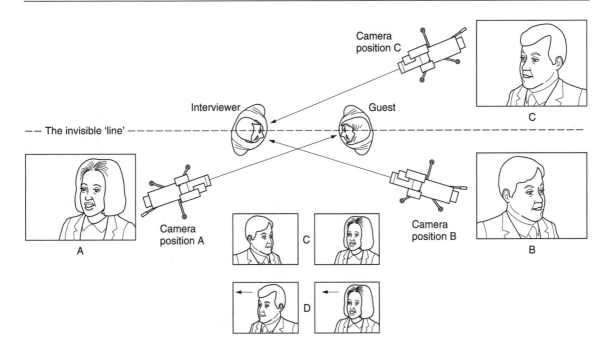

Figure 1.3 Crossing the line. If the camera is positioned at A to record the interviewee's comments and there is a need to capture the interviewer's questions or reactions, then the camera must be repositioned on the same side of an imaginary line drawn between the interviewee and the interviewer. This will result in two shots that will intercut and give the viewer the impression the participants are talking to each other (C). If the camera is repositioned to C, the shots, when intercut, will now give the impression that the people are looking in the same direction and that they are not making eye contact (D)

acters look out of frame at the anticipated position of their listener who will be seen in the subsequent shot. This convention is so well established that 'Vampyr' (1976), has a point-of-view shot from the camera position of a dead man in a coffin. It is a dead man's point-of-view!

The success of invisible technique in visual storytelling is that it is effective in engaging the audience and discretely moving them from one piece of action to the next. Variation in shot size in a scene and variation in shot length provide story emphasis and allow changes in pace and dramatic tension. Intercutting between parallel action of different events (e.g., the hero rushing to the rescue of the heroine intercut with shots of the heroine) increases dramatic intensity. The manipulation of space and time to serve the needs of the story allow shot structure to be pared down to storytelling essentials. Any shot or action that is not subservient to the main story direction is eliminated. In effect, the audience has learnt to place emphasis on any visual 'clue' they are shown because their movie-going experience has taught them that its relevance would be revealed as the story unfolded. This type of storytelling, as opposed to alternative technique discussed in the next chapter, aims to leave no loose ends in the resolution of the story both in the way it is shot and in the structure of the plot.

The methods of film making emerged in a remarkably short time compared with the history of other arts and crafts. It was and is a very practical craft emerging out of experiment, lucky accident or simply meeting the audience requirements of what was to become the most popular medium of mass entertainment. As each new technique was discovered it was quickly absorbed into the body of visual grammar that is still in use today, not only in dramatic/storytelling productions, but also in all forms of film and TV production. Documentary, news, comedy, sports broadcasting all attempt to hold their audience's attention by the use of invisible technique.

Realistic representation

Obviously there is deception in this technique. For example, a shot of an actor entering a train followed by another shot of a train leaving a station, and then continuing with a montage of shots until the train reaches its destination when the actor alights (in close-up), will be seen by the audience as a truthful account of the man's journey. In reality, the actor simply entered a train in one shot, and then left the train in another shot without journeying anywhere. It is the very essence of invisible technique for a production to convince the audience by a series of replications of 'real life'. The event never happened in the way portrayed but the audience must be convinced that it did.

Invisible technique is reinforced by a mistaken belief in the scientific accuracy of a photographic image. A nineteenth-century view of the history of art was that painters had struggled for many centuries in the quest for a convincing representation of the world but were finally beaten to the post by the invention of photography. The photographic image was thought to bring a new standard of objectivity in depicting a three-dimensional object in two dimensions. The fallacy of considering the photographic image as an impartial depiction of an event is matched by a common assumption that painting is primarily concerned with a convincing representation of a specific field of view.

There is a widespread belief that whereas a painter's preoccupations may influence his vision, the TV or film camera is a fairly straightforward device for converting an event into a two-dimensional image.

Mechanical reproduction

Photography in the nineteenth century was welcomed by many people as a new and objective way of recording the world, unhampered by the subjective mediation of the individual artist. It was some time before people realized that the camera was as partial in the image it produces as a painter. Whenever a camera converts a three-dimensional subject into a two-dimensional picture the imprint of the lens height, camera tilt, distance from subject and lens angle is present in the composition of the shot.

The cameraman therefore needs to understand all the elements of visual design if he is to convey precisely the idea or event that is intended to be communicated. If he or she ignores conscious compositional decisions, then 'auto composition' takes over and the camera provides images that are a product of the characteristics of the camera and lens rather than the creative choices of the manipulator of the camera. The camera is not a scientific instrument. It subjectively records an event either by design, that is the cameraman selectively exploits camera technique, or by default if the camera is simply pointed at a subject before recording. Visual imagery has its own version of grammar and syntax that requires the same discernment and application to achieve precise communication as that practised in the study of language.

The camera is never objective. There are a number of conditioning elements that convert the original image into a two-dimensional image, including loss of binocular vision, a selective frame that excludes as well includes, a change in perspective, and so on.

Even if these distortions could be kept to a minimum, there is still the problem that the image is a selected message that has to be decoded by the viewer. The camera stands between the viewer and the original subject and apart from the preconceived attitudes the viewer brings to the images presented to him, the cameraman also brings his assumptions and professional values (technique) to bear on the message. In art historian E.H. Gombrich's (1982) words:

However faithful an image that serves to convey visual information may be, the process of selection will always reveal the maker's interpretation of what he considers relevant.

(The Image and the Eye)

Any camera – still, film or video – cannot record an image without leaving an imprint of the optical properties of its lens, its position in space and some indication of the reasons for selecting that lens position. Camerawork is a highly subjective activity and both the methods of perception (viewer and cameraman) and the 'professional' values that the cameraman brings to the subject will affect what is communicated.

In general one can attempt to classify camerawork into two groups. There are the camera positions that are chosen to record an event. These include not only the obvious examples of sports broadcasts and news events but also many feature productions rely on the script and performance to tell the story while the camera records the action. The opposite to the camera as a 'neutral' observer is when the camerawork attempts to 'interpret' the event. One of the best-known examples is Walter Ruttmann's 'Berlin, Symphony of a Great City' (1927). There are often more productions that mix the two approaches than concentrate on one style. A sports broadcast will often throw in shots of the crowd's wild enthusiasm or a fan's despair to interpret the excitement of the event.

Framing a shot

Composition is an umbrella word to describe choosing which set of camera parameters to employ in any given situation. It need not imply a formal balance or academic design when framing a shot. Composing an image is the process of selecting which set of techniques to employ.

Every shot has to be composed. In general, cameramen and directors may not describe the process of framing up, staging or setting up a shot as shot 'composition'. The term may imply a formality that many programme makers wish to avoid. Contemporary productions aim for a freer, looser way of presenting visual information and tend to discard the formality of rigid balance of tone, shape and colour. And yet the process of choosing lens, lens height, camera angle, frame and positioning of subject and subject priorities are all elements that have been perennially used in image making.

Visual communication in painting, film or television have often shared similar visual conventions. In the fifteenth century Leon Alberti realized that the controlling design factor when creating a two-dimensional image was the distance of the eye from the scene and its height from the ground – considerations that a modern cameraman/director will take into account when choosing the camera distance from the subject and camera height. In the Renaissance period, Piero della Francesca wrote a book *Of the Perspective of Painting* where he detailed his ideas about the geometry of linear perspective. He included a recommendation that the angle of view of an event to be painted should be 60°. Today many film makers would consider that this 'wide-angled' shot would distort the appearance of the image but others would welcome the dynamic movement and images such an angle of view would create.

The appearance of a photographic image can be manipulated by many different camera techniques to suit the intended visual communication. Composition is the *portmanteau* word to describe these techniques. In image making, it has no formal aim other than to choose the most appropriate photographic style in order to effectively communicate.

Composition

Composition plays a central part in invisible technique. The intention within this style of production is to disguise the mechanics of production. To achieve this every shot must take into account:

- if the most important element in the frame is the most dominant – what other visual elements distract or compete?
- how does the size of shot and camera angle relate to the previous and succeeding shots?
- what motivates camera movement?
- does the framing keep the audience's attention to within the frame or are there indicators of activity beyond the frame?
- how visually dynamic does the shot need to be – what is its storytelling purpose?
- what part does colour play in the framing?
- what part do objects in focus and depth-of-field play in the composition?
- is the purpose of the shot clearly achieved?

Whatever genre of film making (with exceptions to be discussed) some or all of these conventions will be used. They are discussed in more detail in succeeding chapters.

What is composition?

Another definition of composition is arranging all the visual elements in the frame in a way that makes the image a satisfactory and a complete whole. Integration of the image is obtained by the positioning of mass, colour and light in the most pleasing arrangement.

This definition is a start in the examination of composition but it does prompt further questions. What counts as 'satisfactory and complete' and is 'pleasing arrangement' an objective or subjective judgement?

The definition also has a half-hidden assumption that the purpose of pictorial composition is always to provide an agreeable visual experience independent of the purpose of the shot. Film and TV productions obviously serve more purposes than simply providing a 'pleasing arrangement' of images. There appears to be other aspects of picture making to be examined before answering the question – what is good composition and what function does it serve?

This book will concentrate on how to arrange a given subject for maximum visual effect. The subject of the shot is the predominantly influential element but many cameramen, in devising solutions to visual problems (another definition of composition) have to work with a subject that has already been selected. The cameraman's role usually centres on deciding between a choice of techniques on how best to handle the given material. In everyday programme production, there may be opportunities for the cameraman to select material that provides good visual potential but frequently the subject is prescribed by script or brief and the cameraman has to devise the best shot that can be achieved with the available material.

Whether the composition of any photographic image has succeeded could be judged by a number of criteria. The chapter on perception (Chapter 3) looks at the way images attract and hold attention and the relationship between the nature of human perception and how visual elements can be grouped and arranged to maintain interest.

Perspective, the influence of the frame and the visual design elements available to the cameraman, are discussed in relation to defining the purpose of a shot, creating and controlling visual elements to facilitate the transmission of the intended message and what is needed to create and control the image to establish atmosphere. Does the image convey, by its presentation, the reason why the shot was recorded?

Light, colour, how action is staged and camera movement all influence decisions about composition but they are never self-contained elements in the final image. A dynamic forceful image is not adequately analysed by identifying the constituent parts and a shot never exists in isolation. Answers to questions such as 'is the image relevant to its context?', 'what is the relationship to the previous and succeeding shots?', 'what are the visual style and conventions of the programme genre and what is the influence of current fashions and styles?', all contribute to the structure of the composition.

There are many factors at work when framing up a shot and, in describing the general principles that influence compositional decisions, there is a need to set the current working practices and visual conventions in some sort of context. There are other conventions of presentation that intentionally draw attention to the means of production. Camera movement in this alternative technique is often restlessly on the move, panning abruptly from subject to subject, making no effort to disguise the transitions and deliberately drawing attention to the means by which the images are brought to the viewer. This technique may employ disruptive shot change, erratic camera movement and unexplained or puzzling events. Not all productions aim for clear, unambiguous storytelling. This breaking down or subverting the Hollywood convention of an 'invisible' seamless flow of images has a number of different forms or styles that require a separate treatment (see Chapter 2).

As there is a widespread emphasis on the 'Hollywood' model of 'invisible technique' of image making in mass entertainment and the majority of cameramen work within this convention, it would seem appropriate that it should be thoroughly understood and described. This analysis does not necessarily endorse these conventions over any other method of production but simply seeks to explain the principles of the techniques employed.

Composition involves a number of factors that at times interact and overlap. In attempting to tease out and describe constituent elements there is often the need to look again at basic compositional requirements by way of a new visual design. Pictorial unity is achieved by integrating all the visual elements within a frame but in attempting to describe the constituent parts it has not always been possible to keep these topics separated in watertight chapters.

Does the shot work?

Within the 'invisible technique' conventions, whether the cameraman's objective in composing the image has been achieved could be judged by answers to some of the following questions:

- Does the image (as well as the sound) attract and hold the attention?
- Is it accessible to normal human perception?
- What elements in the shot maintain visual interest?
- Does the image convey by its direct content, or by its mood, the intended information?
- Does it fulfil the purpose of the shot?
- Is the image relevant to its context?
- How does it relate to the previous and succeeding shots?
- Does it conform to the visual style and conventions of the programme genre?

Intuition

Can composition be taught? Can the ability to frame and light eye-catching images be learnt or is it all based on intuition? It is the folklore of film and TV cameramen that composition is intuitive and therefore almost inexplicable. Whereas trainees and juniors on camera crews have access to volumes of technical explanation about exposure, film stock, electronic image making and all the other technical descriptions of the tools of their trade, composition – the heart of visual communication – is considered a God-given talent that is either understood or not; if it is not, then the unfortunate individual who lacks compositional ability is seen to be similar to a tone-deaf person and would not know good composition if it jumped out of the viewfinder and hit them in the eye.

Johannes Itten, an art teacher, gave this advice to his students:

If you, unknowing, are able to create masterpieces in colour, then unknowledge is your way. But if you are unable to create masterpieces in colour out of your unknowledge, then you ought to look for knowledge.

Many of us working in film and TV know, through many years of experience, exactly how to reposition the lens in space or choose a different lens-angle in order to improve the appearance of the shot. We are either working to inherited craft values of what is 'good' composition or we are repositioning and juggling with the camera until we intuitively feel that we have solved that particular visual problem. Frequently there is no time to analyse a situation and the only thing to fall back on is experience. Compositional experience is the result of many years of solving visual problems. Good visual communication is not a gift from heaven but is learnt from finding out in practice what does and does not work.

The following chapters attempt to review and reveal why certain visual solutions to framing are considered acceptable and where and how these standards originated and developed. There are aspects of composition that are subjective and determined by individual taste but much of what is considered standard practice both in painting and in the creation of film and television images is conditioned by the innate requirements of human perception.

'I see what you mean!'

There is usually a reason why a shot is recorded on tape or film. The purpose may be simply to record an event or the image may play an important part in expressing a complex idea. Whatever the reasons that initiate the shot, the cameraman recording the shot should have an understanding of compositional technique if the idea to be expressed is to be clearly communicated to the intended audience.

The appearance as well as the content of the shot is an integral part of the process of communication. Often, as in painting, form and content of screen images are inseparable. It is accepted that in a drama production the composition of the shot will play a major part in the storytelling. The form, as well the content of the shot, is used to tell the story. But even in the hardest of 'hard news' stories where objectivity is striven for and the camera is intended to be a neutral observer, the effect of the image on the audience will depend on camera framing and camera position. Each time the record button is pressed, a number of crucial decisions affecting clear communication have been consciously or unconsciously made.

Why composition is important

A cameraman shows the audience where to look. His role is to solve visual problems usually in the shortest possible time. Although the cameraman's presence in factual programme making can influence or disrupt the subject matter, the bottom line is to get the best possible rendering of what is there.

An image should communicate in a simple, direct way and not have to rely on a 'voice over' to explain, reveal or argue its significance. The definitive shot has the relevant content with all the visual elements in the frame organized to achieve clear communication. The compositional design will condition how the image is perceived. There must be no confusion in the viewer's mind about the purpose for which the shot was taken.

Good composition reinforces the manner in which the mind organizes information. It emphasizes those elements such as grouping, pattern, shape and form that provide the viewer with the best method of 'reading' the image smoothly and efficiently. If there is friction in visual movement of the eye across the frame, if there are areas of the image that stop the eye dead, then an unsatisfactory feeling is unconsciously experienced and, in an extreme form, will end the attention of the viewer. There is a fine dividing line between 'teasing' the eye with visual ambiguities and losing the interest of the audience.

The cameraman must help the viewer to perceive what is intended to be communicated by providing design guidelines to channel the movement of the eye within the frame. The eye movement must be continuous and smooth and be led in a premeditated route across the relevant parts of the subject matter without any distracting detours to unimportant visual elements in the frame. It is part of the cameraman's craft to create shots that are well designed and engage the attention of the viewer. Simply putting a frame around a subject by a 'point and shoot' technique will often result in incoherent visual design that fails to connect.

The image produced by a camera has no memory, knowledge or experience of the content. If you, as the cameraman, have additional details about the subject that are not contained within the frame but this information helps you to understand the image, the audience will also need that knowledge or it will supply its own conjectures. If this extra knowledge is vital to the information that is intended to be conveyed, the shot is incomplete and partial communication can only be achieved. Can the image explain all that is required without additional explanation? For example, in a television feature item about traffic congestion, a doctor was shown driving to an emergency and then having great difficulty in finding a place to park. In one shot, his efforts to repeatedly reverse into a narrow parking space were seen by most of the audience as simply his inability to drive. The shot failed in communicating its intended purpose, which was that traffic congestion could be a hazard in an emergency.

To recap, control of visual communication requires:

- a clear understanding of the message to be communicated;
- an understanding of invisible technique to maximize the communication;
- an understanding of perception;
- employing the full range of visual grammar to achieve communication.

Control of composition

Control of composition is achieved by the ability to choose the appropriate camera technique such as viewpoint, focal length of lens, lighting, exposure, in addition to employing a range of visual design elements such as balance, colour contrast, perspective of mass/line, etc.

A well designed composition is one in which the visual elements have either been selectively included or excluded. The visual components of the composition must be organized to engage the viewer's attention. A starting point is often to follow the old advice to simplify by elimination, and to reduce to essentials in order to create an image that has strength and clarity.

Visual design techniques

Much of the technique employed in programme/film production is the result of subjective decisions made from a range of possible options in sympathy with the main narrative or programme requirements. Alongside subjective creative preferences there are also objective principles of design and specific ways of organizing the image to have predictable effects. Good visual design involves elements of individual creativity plus a knowledge of the role of a number of factors that affect the way an image is perceived. These will be dealt with in detail in the appropriate chapter and include light, figure/ground relationships, shape, frame, balance, light/dark relationships, line, perspective of mass and line, colour, content.

Cultural influences

Some aspects of compositional technique are timeless whilst others are fashionably of the moment. They both have a part to play in the well-designed shot. The image should be designed to satisfy an aesthetic appreciation as well as the quest for information. This aesthetic 'buzz' changes with culture and fashion over time. Attention can be captured by the new and the novel but, when dealing with a mass audience, attention can just as easily be lost if current conventions and the expectations of the audience are flouted and the shock of the new is used with the mistaken idea of grabbing attention. As will be seen in the psychology of perception (Chapter 3), people ignore what they cannot understand. Communication can only be achieved if you have the attention of the audience.

Changing fashions

Styles of film and TV camerawork change but the stylistic changes are usually elements of narrative presentation rather than in compositional form. Barry Salt in *Film Style and Technology* (1983) identified the first use of the 'over-the-shoulder two shot' as in about 1910. The reverse angle shot of faces intercut in dialogue appeared in 'The Loafer' (a silent western) in 1912. These basic compositional techniques have become part of the language of visual storytelling. Shot structures are refashioned, editing conventions in the presentation of time and space are re-worked, conventions of narrative continuity are challenged and replaced but many composition conventions have remained (Figure 1.4).

Figure 1.4 Over-the-shoulder two shot

Such compositional conventions are considered normal or standard and have been learnt over time by cinemagoers and TV viewers. These compositional stereotypes can be reinforced or confronted. Human perception functions by seeking to simplify complex forms and patterns but this can be frustrated by the cameraman if, in his choice of framing, he creates disorganized images. 'But what is it?', the viewer inquires when presented with an unfamiliar image. The search to classify is natural to the human mind and a perceptual 'puzzle' may engage the attention of an observer up to the point where he or she gives up the attempt to decode its significance. This point will vary with the individual but many people, anticipating a familiar and recognizable image on the screen, have an aversion to the unfamiliar. If the shot cannot immediately be categorized, they may mentally switch off if their image of visual reality is too severely challenged.

The American cinematographer William Fraker was setting up a shot for 'Rosemary's Baby' (1968). The director, Roman Polanski, requested a specific framing through a door to show a woman telephoning in the adjacent room, but had so staged the action that the woman's face was masked by the door frame. Fraker wanted to reposition the camera to bring her face into view. Polanski resisted. 'With my framing' he explained 'we will have every member of the audience craning to their right in an attempt to see the face behind the door-frame'. The function of this shot was to withhold information in order to feed the curiosity of the audience in the development of the story.

Summary

Good composition is the best arrangement of the subject matter in sympathy with the function of the shot.

It should have simplicity and intensity and achieve its objective with clarity, precision and economy.

2
Alternative technique

Jump cuts

You may have seen films or TV programmes where you become very conscious of the camerawork and continuity editing conventions are not followed. Music videos are often full of ambiguous images, rapid changes in location and an apparent complete disregard for the invisible technique tradition. Many commercials tell a 30-second story in a similar way.

Some filmmakers have consciously rejected the central philosophy of the invisible technique tradition and do not wish to disguise how the film was created. They appear to expose the mechanics of film making with obtrusive cutting and camera movement divorced from action.

'Breathless' (1959), directed by Jean-Luc Goddard, has a sequence of an open-topped car driving through Paris. The two main characters in the film (played by Jean Paul Belmondo and Jean Seberg) are shot from behind, with Belmondo driving. The shot of Jean Seberg is edited without cutaways causing the view through the windscreen to abruptly change. There is no attempt to disguise these rapid transitions to different locations. The standard continuity editing technique is abandoned.

Composition in this technique has obviously has a different function to the codes developed for invisible technique.

What are the characteristics of this alternative technique?

Figure 2.1 'Breathless' (1959; dir. Jean-Luc Goddard). A continuous shot with the same foreground framing is edited so that the background occasionally 'jumps' to a new locale

- Unsteady frame produced by the preference for hand-held camerawork;
- obtrusive camera movement that is constantly on the move or unrelated to action;
- a rejection of standard framing – a deliberate mispronunciation of standard visual conventions (e.g., faces squashed to one side of the frame; see Figure 2.2);
- a tendency to draw attention to the methods of production (e.g., camerawork, editing, etc.) rather than the content;

Figure 2.2 An offset framing deliberately squeezing the face to the edge of the screen

- form becomes content;
- jump cuts and a rejection of continuity editing;
- abrupt, unexplained changes in location or time;
- the open frame technique where the audience's attention is drawn to what is unseen and outside the frame;
- abrupt changes between monochrome and colour shots;
- the mixture of low tech and high tech formats (e.g., use of 8 mm film in flashbacks by Resnais in 'Muriel' (1993));
- deliberate degradation of the image using sub-standard formats or deliberately degrading the image by overexposure or marking the negative;
- lighting that is unconnected with action to produce images that are unlit, obscure or ambiguous;
- slow-motion sequences unmotivated by action.

Some of these characteristics were summarized by Andre Breton when he was commenting on surrealism:

The depiction of chance and 'marvellous' juxtapositions, creating an impression of randomness and irrationality for the viewer and thus rejection of the idea that art must cling to the representation of an everyday reality.

(Hill and Gibson, 1998: 400)

Alternatives

Invisible technique was developed to keep the audience involved with the story, for example in action films and suspense thrillers, and for the viewer to identify with the main characters until the story's resolution. Essentially the camerawork that evolved sought to avoid distracting the audience with detail or shots that did not serve these ends. These production methods encouraged the audience to enter a 'dream' state eliminating any annoying interruptions to their 'sleep' that would cause them to become aware that they were watching a fabrication, a fiction put together by a group of people.

Many of the audience did wish to 'lose themselves in the story' and escape from their own lives, and ignore or suspend judgement on the wider political and social issues that surrounded the story. For some film makers, this technique and this type of story construction that enforced these aims robbed the audience of critical judgement. They sought production methods that provoked the audience to 'wake up' and examine what they were being told, how they were being told and why they were being told that particular story.

The major influence on this alternative method of storytelling was Bertolt Brecht, a writer, poet and theatre director working in Germany during the rise of the Nazi party. He wanted the audience to think about the wider political context of the story they were witnessing, and not simply identify with the stage characters.

It's magic

If the aim of a magician or illusionist is to convince the observer that the impossible has happened he must not reveal his methods of achieving the 'magic'. If he does, the illusion will simply be seen as a 'trick' and will be without fascination or awe. His skill is his invisible technique, which convinces the audience they are seeing everything whereas their attention is deliberately misdirected so that they miss the most important part of the action. Standard film and TV techniques have the same objective. The technique must be sufficiently skilful to hide the fabrication of reality from the audience.

A British comedy magician, Tommy Cooper, deliberately subverted this magical deceit by failing to perform the trick or by revealing the shallow deception that was being practised. In a sense he was performing in a Brechtian way by making the audience aware of the illusion. He was making them think of the nature of 'magic'. Another comedy act, Morecambe and Wise, used the same technique of revealing the mechanics of melodrama and by looking at the camera and the viewer, they acknowledged their 'play' was a piece of fiction, a make believe. They were inviting the audience to join them in watching themselves perform.

In film, this alternative technique rejects the notion of a set of sleep-inducing 'invisible' conventions. The aim of some avant-garde film makers is to constantly remind the viewer that they are watching a fabrication, and therefore any conventions that render technique 'invisible' and encourage the audience to suspend criticism are to be avoided. Often they wish the audience to be uncertain of the outcome of events described, and therefore these film makers deliberately avoid narrative conventions that provide structured explanations. It requires an audience response that is at ease with uncertainty.

It challenges the 'realism' of Hollywood continuity editing and aims for uncertainty, ambiguity and unresolved narrative. This type of randomness and irrationality may cause an audience conditioned by the language of standard film making conventions to be confused and unresponsive. The film language is simply not one to which they are accustomed. In the words of film academic Jonas Mekas, 'more than 90 per cent of people do not like films, they like stories'. This leaves the remaining 10 per cent a minority audience who may enjoy a visual challenge and are prepared to watch types of film making other than standard Hollywood conventions.

Extreme alternative technique are those productions that reject storytelling and may consist of unrelated, impressionistic shots or even one static eight-hour shot of the Empire State Building. Andy Warhol, who made this particular film called 'Empire' (1965), had a very idiosyncratic way of making films. Paul Morrissey, another independent filmmaker, described him at work.

There were about 30 people on one side of the room and the camera was on the other side in front of them and I said 'what kind of film are you making?'. He said 'I don't know. What shall we do?'. Then he said 'but you know, I don't like to move the camera'. I said 'really, well then the camera will be on the other side of the loft and there will only be little tiny people on the other end', and he said 'I know, I don't know what to do'. Also he said 'and I don't like to stop the camera'. Well when he said 'I don't like to move it and I don't like to stop it', I realized that he needed somebody to figure out what to do with the film and the camera. He couldn't direct, therefore he said let's not direct. All right, let's see. He was hoping that somehow, without doing anything, something would get made. Basically I was contracted as his manager with the distinction being that when you manage somebody usually they do something.

('Andy Warhol' documentary, Channel 4, 3 February 2002)

In one sense, a book about picture composition can only deal with standard visual conventions. Alternative styles of production up to the most radical avant-garde films have no requirement for formal visual structures to communicate a story or idea. Composition as a technique for communication assumes that there will only be one reading of the events depicted. A suitable composition will be chosen to most accurately communicate that point. But communication, like perception, does not always provide one infallible reading.

Realism and imagination

Film historians often trace the two traditions of realism and imagination in film technique back to the early French film pioneers, Lumière and Mèliès. Lumière's 1895 single shot of a train entering a station suggests the factual style of film making – a straightforward depiction that will be understood in a similar way by the whole audience. In effect there could have been a number of positions selected for the camera to film this event. The cameraman, however, selected a position that had the engine approaching the lens. The shot allowed the dynamic depiction of movement, relationship with passengers and people on the platform without panning because the fixed position of the camera on its tripod did not allow such a camera movement. The first pan/tilt head was not in use until 1897. The shot had a visual impact on its first audiences, unused to movement of a projected image, and alarmed and frightened some of them. It was factual, but had the power to move and affect the audience more than the event would have done in reality.

The alternative strand of film making is to use the camera to suggest fantasy, imagination and subjective experience. Mèliès, as an ex-stage magician, sought to create images that caused wonder and amazement in his audience. 'A Trip to the Moon' (1902) was a science fiction romp that used camera tricks and creative imagination to entertain and enthral his audience.

The film moment is always now

A film story often has a predictable future. Characters follow the path created for them in the plot and the audience's curiosity is heightened by plot construction and character identification. What happens next holds the audiences attention.

An audience may feel the enjoyment of a film is exhausted once the mystery of the plot has been resolved. The hook of their attention is fastened on wanting to find out how the story ends. The construction or the aesthetics of the film form has little attraction for the majority of the audience. What happens to their favourite star overrides all other considerations.

Figure 2.3 The Lumière brothers, 'Arrival of a Train at a Station' (1895), contains one static shot of the train arriving and passengers disembarking

In reality, many people's lives are not as predictable as a film story, especially to the individual. With hindsight, an individual may be able to see a pattern of cause and effect but, in the present, the future is neither predictable nor, to the individual, inevitable. A standard film story resolves problems, explains misunderstandings and eliminates any ambiguity of the action. Only action that is pertinent to the main story is included. Any inconsequential events or activities to the main story are usually omitted.

Sidney Lumet's 'Twelve Angry Men' (1957), uses the standard technique to cover twelve men attempting to reach a decision in a jury room. At all times the geography of the room is provided by the shot structure. Important plot points are made with an appropriate close-up. The pace and tension of the story is controlled by the performance and shifts in shot size.

Contrast this with a short film located in a bar where a group of people seated around a table are in discussion. The camera frequently circles the table, panning across faces but not consistently on the person who is talking. Sometimes, by accident, a speaker comes into frame but often the speaker would be out of frame. To many viewers, the camerawork would be intrusive and would frustrate their natural curiosity to see who is talking. There is no change of tempo or interpretation of the discussion. The film ends with a speaker in mid-sentence.

There is a distinct difference in the compositional conventions used in the two films because the aims of the film makers were different.

Avant-garde film makers often feel that the 'Twelve Angry Men' treatment of reality is misleading and incomplete. They may be motivated by political aims to reveal what they feel is the true structure of society or they may feel conventional story telling ignores a large part of human experience. Individuals do not see their life as a rounded story-line limited to meaningful activity. There is a great deal of ambiguous and confusing activity that at the time fits no apparent pattern. Avant-garde productions therefore seek to reject the standard visual conventions and are often ambiguous and incomplete, like the example of the discussion in the bar. The talk is rambling, unstructured and reaches no conclusion. There are no tidy endings and explanations, no characters to drive the story along, in fact there is no story.

Without a story there is no requirement to structure the images with a continuity understandable to the audience. In this alternative film form there is no simple explanation of events, no one reading of reality bundled up in a 90-minute segment that neatly explains the action depicted. The majority, if not all, of the visual conventions developed by the commercial cinema to attract, hold and entertain an audience can be discarded. This free form artefact can often cause confusion, puzzlement and even annoyance because it does not conform to the standard set of visual conventions audiences have been educated to follow. Audiences often assume that a film can only have one set of conventions. But not only audiences. Many film/TV programme makers assess the competence of a production by how well it employs standard visual conventions.

Why people dislike the rejection of standard conventions

Camerawork that appears to ignore traditional invisible technique may be thought of as either lacking in knowledge or ability or wilfully ignoring such technique out of a perverse desire to be 'different'. The same criticisms have been levelled in other art and craft forms. A popular response when examining a Picasso painting is that the observer's child could produce the same or a better image. The inference is that Picasso lacks the skill and expertise to create a 'proper' illusion of reality. He lacks the knowledge of Renaissance perspective and the mastery of eye/hand coordination that would allow him to compete with better works that provide a complete illusion of three-dimensional space on a two-dimensional surface. There is obviously an assumption by such an observer that the aim of all painting is to create a recognizable illusion of their concept of reality. The same unexamined assumptions can operate when people are faced with forms of contemporary dance that do not incorporate the conventions of classical ballet, drama that appears to have no storyline and music without melody.

People hold similar strong assumptions about film. They believe it should have recognizable characters in a dramatic situation that is resolved before the end. A series of images that evoke, for example, an ambiguity and uncertainty without character or plot is not only unacceptable, it often annoys or even enrages the viewer. They feel that it is not a 'proper' film and the maker of the film is either incompetent or naive, but most often a charlatan for attempting to pass off bad work for the real article – a properly constructed film.

Many cameramen believe that visual conventions of storytelling (e.g., linear continuity in shots, camera movement motivated by action, matched shots and eye lines, etc.) are ignored out of ignorance. They feel a practitioner employing an alternative visual language does not understand the conventions. They believe there is only one acceptable set of camerawork conventions because all their experience in production is grounded in storytelling either in fiction, documentary or news. The aim of their craft is to attract and hold the attention of the audience. In the words of Orson Welles, perhaps they should consider 'God, there is a lot of stuff here I don't know'.

One of the paradoxes of radical or avant-garde technique is the speed with which it is absorbed to serve commercial ends. The French Impressionist painting style was dismissed as 'mere daubs' by contemporaries but was later recycled into chocolate box labels to be sold back to their hostile critics. The radical images of German expressionist experimental 1920s films reappeared again in mass market music videos in the 1980s.

Storytelling

A story is a commercial imperative as most people demand what they are used to – a beginning, a middle and an end. Avant-garde practitioners reject this presentation of reality when it is understood as a linear revelation of facts. There may be plot twists and red herrings but a standard film story usually in the end has an explanation of all that has been presented.

Camerawork that is intrusive and erratic (e.g., news coverage of unrehearsed incidents) has a specific authenticating credibility even when it is replicated. For some people, music without a melody is difficult to enjoy, just as a series of images without a story is incomprehensible. What does it mean? How are the images connected?

One of the seminal avant-garde films was Luis Buñuel's 'Un Chien Andalou' (1928). It contains a sequence where an eye is sliced by a razor. The image is alarming and frightening. It is a radical assault on the viewer who may require a film that tells a story. It is a visual assault on the eye of the viewer's preconceptions of what a film should be.

Don't wake me up

Most viewers dislike any technique that distracts them from being fully immersed in the story. They require a stream of images that, without distraction, allow them to follow the action and become identified with the participants. The camera style that achieves this is unobtrusive, and only presents images and action that are relevant to the story.

Lumière's 'Arrival of a Train at a Station' has a rudimentary story. The train arrives, passengers are moving on the platform. In cultures that are familiar with trains the information in the image can easily be interpreted. They may even surmise the motivation of individual people on the platform. Are they waiting for friends, relatives? Are they going on a journey, etc.? A culture without trains or people not familiar with the dress codes in the image may make completely different deductions. Are these people involved in some kind of religious or ceremonial activity? Is that large black moving shape (the train) benevolent or threatening?

The relevance of an image, like perception, is dependent on what the observer brings to their understanding of the shot as well as its factual content. It is often erroneously believed by film makers that all audiences will understand their chosen visual storytelling methods.

Antonioni's film 'Chung Kuo Cina' (1972) contained a shot of a Chinese bridge taken from a low angle with wide-angle distortion to provide a dynamic and imposing image. This was considered insulting by the Chinese because, in their eyes, it inferred that the bridge was unstable and distorted. They considered it should have been shot from a square-on position to provide a symmetrical, imposing, stable image.

Definition of alternative conventions

In general, invisible technique is more consistent than alternative technique that does not form a recognized standard visual grammar. There is not one alternative technique; there are many. Different elements are employed in individual avant-garde or art house films. They can be loosely summarized as the story might not be structured by logical cause and effect. For example, an event is depicted and then another event, which appears to be unconnected, follows. There might never be an explanation of the connection. Yasujiro Ozu's 'Tokyo Story' (1953), is the story of an elderly couple gradually becoming estranged from their adult children. The clear linear narrative is occasionally interspersed with shots of washing on a line, empty urban landscapes, a clump of factory chimneys. Each shot is visually attractive and there is the subjective impression that these depictions of an empty, hostile environment are part of the old people's gradual alienation from their family but there is no linear connection as occurs in conventional shot structure. Although these locations are near where the story takes place, they do not directly connect with the story. Unlike standard visual technique, the connection is made obliquely. The existence of these non-essential narrative shots appears to give greater depth to our understanding of the characters and story. In the majority of commercial, mass market productions, this type of shot would be judged to slow the pace, interrupt the action, be irrelevant to the plot and eliminated from the final cut.

Avant-garde productions, or 'art house' films as they are sometimes termed, often suggest conflict or story lines that are left unresolved. This 'open-endedness' may be intended to suggest the lack of meaning or form to everyday living. Whereas invisible technique attempts to provide guidelines of the geography of the action – the space/time relationships of the story, alternative technique will often ignore linear continuity and have abrupt changes in place or time without explanation.

Many mass-entertainment films/programmes are built around charismatic artistes – the star system of promoting a new film. These celebrities require close attention from the cinematographer/cameraman to ensure they remain attractive (and commercially in demand) in the way they are shot and presented. Alternative productions may feature unattractive, difficult, disturbed people with whom it is difficult to identify.

Some types of alternative productions appear to be seeking a different technique to express those themes that are not normally commercially acceptable. Others attempt to dispense with central 'charismatic' characters and rely on montage to provoke feeling, emotion or discussion. A third category is the attempt to subvert standard Hollywood visual conventions and invent visual structures that remind the audience they are watching an illusion – a replication of reality. These avoid any disguise of technique and deliberately expose the mechanics of film making with jump cuts, subjective camerawork and constant reminders to the audience that they are watching an artefact. This can be too successful and a mass audience may reject the production. Many people found the swerving and constantly moving camerawork in the American TV crime series 'NYPD Blue' an irritant and, although they may have been interested in the story, the form in which it was presented (see Chapter 12) was, to them, objectionable.

Conventions

I want to make a distinction between 'commandment' and 'convention'. Photographically speaking, I understand a commandment to be a rule, axiom, or principle, an incontrovertible fact of photographic procedure

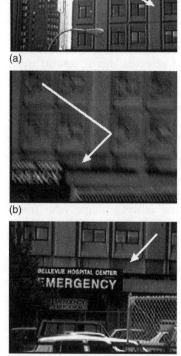

Figure 2.4 For an experienced cameraman, it would be no problem to pan from a tenth floor hospital window **(a)** down to the main entrance **(c)** timed to meet the arrival of the main characters. Instead, to fabricate the camera 'surprised by events' style the camera starts unsteadily on its travel, misses the entrance **(b)**, and hurriedly pans back to hold an unsteady frame of the entrance. This jittery camerawork is there by design

which is unchangeable for physical and chemical reasons. On the other hand, a convention to me, is a usage which has become acceptable through repetition. It is a tradition rather than a rule. With time the convention becomes a commandment, through force of habit. I feel the limiting effect is both obvious and unfortunate.

('How I broke the rules in "Citizen Kane" ', by Greg Toland, *Popular Photography*, Vol. 8, June 1941)

Greg Toland, an outstanding Hollywood cinematographer, identifies one of the fundamental problems when discussing composition of the moving image. What aspects of standard composition are conventions accepted by repetition – 'a tradition rather than a rule' and what aspects of composition are an 'incontrovertible fact' indispensable in visual communication?

Like spoken language, the language of standard visual conventions that grew up and was developed in the first decades of film making is always in the process of change. Techniques once universal, such as perfect studio portrait lighting to glamorize the star of the film, have been modified to serve the fashion for a more spontaneous and realistic look, although the concept of what is 'realistic' tends to change with every decade – see Chapter 11, 'News and documentary'.

An alternative camerawork and editing language may create a sense of randomness and a lack of purpose compared with standard invisible technique but it still has to share a common ancestry. The use of lenses, camera movement, shot size and cutting points cannot stray too far from standard practice before the images become so disjointed there is no communication. This objective is sometimes striven for and is similar to the punk movement's attempt to destroy the existent conventional performance of pop music. Non-communication carried to extreme must eventually lose the attention of all but a tiny minority of its audience.

Summary

Some filmmakers reject invisible technique tradition and do not wish to disguise how the film is created. They expose the mechanics of film making with obtrusive cutting and camera movement divorced from action.

This technique and some types of story construction provoke the audience to 'wake up' and examine what they are being told, how they are being told and why they are being told that particular story. The aim is to constantly remind the viewer that they are watching a fabrication.

3

The lens, the eye and perception

Introduction

A useful ability when framing up a shot is having the experience to predict how a particular subject or view will translate into a two-dimensional recorded image. A beginner without this skill may have to wander around the subject looking through the viewfinder at various set-ups, and with various choices of lens angle and camera distance, in order to see how these variables affect the shot. Cameramen and directors often have the developed visual ability to mentally predict the effect of mass, line and size relationships and how they will impact on the shot for any specific lens angle and camera position chosen. Viewpoint can be decided before a camera is taken out of its case. This is often called having a photographic eye and in one sense it is learning to see like a lens. How do we learn to see like a camera and why is it necessary?

Composing a shot involves the translation of a three-dimensional subject into a two-dimensional image. The eye and the lens are both used in this activity but the two imaging devices differ in their interpretation.

The lens of the eye focuses a two-dimensional image onto the retina of the eye and somehow the mind interprets the image. That 'somehow' is known as perception and has a significant influence on how an individual understands what he or she is looking at. There is always a subjective element in any individual's interpretation of their senses.

The lens of a camera focuses an image onto a recording medium but it is not an objective scientific instrument precisely translating the field-of-view of the lens into an image. The conversion of the original subject into an image viewed on a screen is conditioned by what is chosen from a number of variables associated with the conversion at the moment of recording, and its later method of two-dimensional presentation. The variables include:

- the lens – *f*no, focal length, camera height, camera distance, etc.;
- the recording medium characteristics – film, tape and method of processing;
- detail and resolution of lens and recording/transmission medium;
- colour rendition;
- lighting conditions;
- filters;
- the image size when viewed;
- viewing conditions;
- the subjective influence of context;
- cultural influences.

These topics are discussed in more detail in later chapters.

The imprint of the lens

When a camera converts a three-dimensional scene into a film or TV picture, it leaves an imprint of lens height, camera tilt, distance from subject and lens angle. We can detect these decisions in any image by examining the position of the horizon line and where it cuts similar sized figures. This will reveal camera height and tilt. Lens height and tilt will be revealed by any parallel converging lines in the image such as the edges of buildings or roads. The size relationship between foreground and background objects, particularly the human figure, will gives clues to camera distance from objects and lens angle. Camera distance from subject will be revealed by the change in object size when moving towards or away from the lens.

For any specific lens angle and camera position there will be a unique set of the above parameters. The 'perspective' of the picture is created by the camera distance except, of course, where false perspective has been deliberately created.

Developing a photographic eye is learning how to manipulate these variables to achieve a particular image. These are the basic tools of visual design for the cameraman and they are discussed in more detail in the following chapters. The choices made can create style, mood or emphasize a significant element of the shot. Ignoring these lens/camera factors in an unthinking point-and-shoot technique will still control the appearance of the image because the lens/camera will be left to produce an image customized by whatever set of default characteristics are engaged.

The eye and a lens

There are similarities and differences between how we perceive the world and how the camera lens translates the world into images. What is often overlooked when making the comparison is the influence of the mind on the image produced by the eye.

Most people believe that seeing is a straightforward activity – just open your eyes and see what's there. But the component parts of seeing such as movement, depth, shape, colour and size, etc., are constructed in our heads and have to be pieced together by the brain.

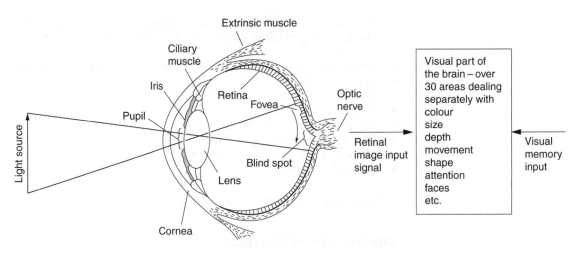

Figure 3.1 The contemporary theory about the brain and perception is that the visual brain has two systems:

There is part of the brain that generates images from the eyes (front projection); there is also a part of the brain that uses visual memories (back projection)

There is no adequate explanation of how these two parts of the brain are combined in perception. Perception is an active process by the brain that invents, ignores, distorts what is coming through the eyes

Visual information coming into our eyes is dismantled and then reassembled. Different aspects of seeing are dealt with by sub-sections of the brain; each area decoding one aspect of visual information. There is parallel processing by over 30 areas of the brain such as motion, colour, depth, etc. It is the brain that turns seeing into understanding. Like a film or TV frame, our eyes only capture static images: they are transmitted to the back of the brain where they are incorporated into seeing movement.

There are a number of facets of the brain's involvement in seeing that need to be taken into account when framing up a shot that may only be on the screen for a few seconds.

Size constancy

A shot, if taken with an appropriate lens angle, camera distance and viewed with a specified screen size and viewing distance (see next chapter), will replicate the retinal image, but this image will not necessarily be the same as how an observer views the same field of view.

With the above conditions, the camera will provide true geometrical perspective, but because we do not see the world as it is projected on the retina, the perspective of the shot may look wrong. For example, a holidaymaker takes a photograph of an impressive range of mountains. Looking at the print, the holidaymaker may be disappointed because the mountains look very small compared with their memory of the landscape (see Figure 3.2).

The mismatch between how we think we see a subject and how the camera records the same subject is due to a perceptual distortion called size constancy. This is the tendency for the perceptual system to compensate for changes in the retinal image with viewing distance. As a retinal image, a person walking away from a static observer halves in size as their distance from the observer doubles. The relationship between image size and distance from the observer is a constant, but in normal perception it is not seen as a constant. Perception adjusts the perceived size to match our knowledge of the size of the receding subject.

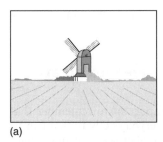

(a)

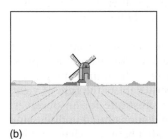

(b)

Figure 3.2 The mismatch between how we think we see a subject **(a)** and how the camera records the same subject **(b)** is due to a perceptual distortion called size constancy. This is the tendency for the perceptual system to compensate for changes in the retinal image with viewing distance

We habitually underestimate the change in size of a person walking towards or away from us and mentally picture them modified in size but only with a slight alteration to their 'normal' size. An audience will appear from the front to have similar size faces and yet, to an observer, the retinal image of the faces of the people in the back rows will probably be a tenth of the size of the faces of the people in the front row. We never recognize that the image of our face in the mirror is always much smaller than its actual size. These are all depth indicators we habitually ignore or make the necessary adjustment for, as in the phenomenon of the 'upside down' image that is focused on the retina of the eye. We 'mentally' correct this inversion of our field of view as we subconsciously 'correct' the change in size. Size constancy is what the brain does and the camera does not do and therefore when planning a shot we should not be misled by this habitual distortion.

A simple experiment demonstrating this phenomena is described by R.L. Gregory in *Eye and Brain* (1967):

Look at your two hands, one placed at arm's length the other at half the distance – they will look almost exactly the same size, and yet the image of the further hand will be only half the (linear) size of the nearer. If the nearer hand is brought to overlap the further, then they will look quite different in size.

To 'see' like a camera obviously requires overcoming this everyday mental adjustment in the perceptual process. Many artists have trained themselves to accurately draw their perceptual image whereas most of us are trapped, particularly when taking photographs, in the perceptual misconception of size constancy. In essence we see what we think is there, not what is actually there.

This characteristic of perception in habitually making adjustments to the size of a subjects at various distances from the viewer provoked a heated debate in the mid-nineteenth century when artists began basing painting on photographs. Always assuming that a lens/camera distance provided 'normal' perspective in a photograph (see Chapter 4, 'The lens and perspective'), there was fierce criticism on what many people thought was the gross distortion in the painting depiction of size relationships. People were for the first time confronted with their adjustment of optical size as presented on the retina and the optical truth of a photograph transcribed into a painting (e.g., the holiday-maker disappointed with his photograph of a diminutive mountain range).

In 1858, Mrs Jane Carlyle complained about a Robert Tait painting of herself and husband in their drawing room, claiming that it was bad enough to be recorded for posterity with a frightful table cover, but what was worse was that their dog Nero, in the lower right foreground, was as big as a sheep. What was called the 'false and ugly perspective of a "photographic" painting' was in fact the true optical perspective showing size relationships as they were, not how we imagined they were.

Manipulating size relationships and the perspective depth of the shot is one of the principal compositional devices in film and TV productions. Seeing as a camera does requires not only retraining our habitual way of discounting the actual size of objects in a field

Figure 3.3 Perception is making sense of an image – searching for the best interpretation of the available data. The mind sees patterns and searches for the best interpretation. A perceived object is therefore a hypothesis to be tested instantaneously against previous experience. If it looks like a duck then it is a duck. That is, until we see it as a rabbit

of view, but also mentally conceiving the visual effect of choosing different lens angles and camera distances.

How do we understand what we are looking at?

In setting up shots for film and TV it is important to remember that perception is not a simple common sense everyday activity that can be ignored. Understanding how the audience makes sense of the images presented to them, often in rapid succession, will ensure the required visual communication is effective. Unfortunately there are many competing theories about human perception.

The 'perspectivist' theory proposes that our understanding of a visual field is simply determined by the laws of geometric optics. There is no need to invoke mental processes. The retinal image, if it obeys the laws of linear perspective, correctly depicts the field of view. With this theory, a camera is an accurate substitute for an observer. The weakness with this theory, as has been demonstrated in discussing size constancy, is that there is often a mismatch between what we think we see and what the camera 'sees'.

The Gestaltist theory suggests that mental operations play a much larger role in perception. There are a number of visual concepts the mind employs in the act of perception, which is much more complex than the simple mechanical process suggested by the perspectivist theory. A third theory, the constructivist, suggests that perception is an active process by the observer, who is constantly making assumptions and testing out visual phenomena until he is satisfied he has made the correct interpretation. These are not compatible ideas but there are elements of each that can be combined to suggest guidelines when attempting to compose a shot.

Characteristics of perception

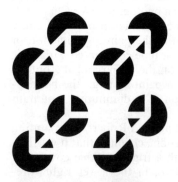

Figure 3.4 Searching for coherent shapes in a complex image, human perception will look for and, if necessary, create simple shapes. Straight lines will be continued by visual projection (cube shape from 'Organisational determinants of subjective contours', Bradley and Perry, 1977)

Most theorists agree that perception is instantaneous and not subject to extended judgement. It is an active exploration rather than a passive recording of the visual elements in the field of view and is selective and personal.

The mind makes sense of visual elements by grouping elements into patterns. Any stimulus pattern tends to be seen in such a way that the resulting structure is as simple as the given conditions. Making sense of visual stimuli involves testing by hypothesis. An unfamiliar or ambiguous image may be assigned a tentative definition until further information becomes available (Figure 3.3).

An American law lecturer once tested the accuracy of his students' ability to witness an event by staging a fake crime in his lecture hall. A man ran into the hall disrupting his lecture and brandished a weapon of some kind and then left. The law teacher immediately asked his students to accurately describe what they had seen. Needless to say every student 'witness' had a different version and a different description of the bogus criminal. The simple point was made that most people are selective in their viewpoint. They see what they expect to see or what they can understand.

What a person perceives is dependent on personal factors as well as the visual elements in their field of view. Their understanding of an image reflects past experiences as well as their present state of mind. Although it is probable that no two observers may observe a given scene in the same way and may disagree considerably as to its nature and contents, much of our perceptual experience shares common characteristics.

How the mind responds to visual information

Much of the theory of perceptual characteristics has been influenced by Gestalt psychologists. Gestalt is the German word for 'form' and these psychologists held the view that it is the overall form of an image that we respond to, not the isolated visual elements it contains. In general, we do not attempt to perceive accurately every detail of the shapes and objects perceived but select only as much as will enable us to identify what we see. This may depend on the probability of appearance of a particular type of object but the precision of our perception is sufficient only for our immediate need.

We may increase our visual concentration if we feel it is warranted but this enhanced visual attention may be of short duration. The tendency is for the perceptual system to group things into simple units.

The minimum amount of time needed to recognize an object (possibly 1/100 second) will depend on the familiarity and expectation of that specific image. An observer can perceive a large and complex picture that is seen everyday and is anticipated in a time that would be quite inadequate for the perception and understanding of a complex meaningless shape.

In searching for the best interpretation of the available visual data we utilize a number of perceptual 'shorthand' techniques that include organization of similar shapes and similar sizes. Shapes that are similar are grouped and form a pattern that creates eye motion. A 'good' form, one that is striking and easy to perceive, is simple, regular, symmetrical and may have continuity in time. A 'bad' form, without these qualities, is modified by the perceiver to conform to 'good' form qualities.

Perceptual steps

Perception is extraordinarily fast. This can be demonstrated by the deductions and judgements made when driving a car or, as a pedestrian, the perceptual calculations made when crossing a busy city street. Each element of the perceptual steps may operate instantaneously or occur in an order conditioned by the visual situation.

First, there is the need to separate figure from ground. Figure describes the shape that is immediately observable whilst ground defines that shape by giving it a context. A chess piece is a figure with the chess board as its ground. Identifying the shape of the figure – that it is a pawn – may provide complete recognition. Other subject recognition may involve colour, brightness, texture, movement or spatial position. Instantaneous classification and identification occur continuously but the perceptual process can be helped or hindered by the presentation of the subject (Figure 3.5(a) and (b)).

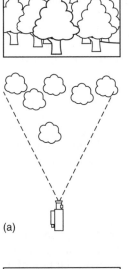

(a)

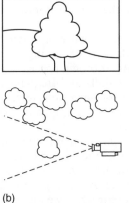

(b)

Figure 3.5 (a) (b) Sometimes you cannot see the tree for the wood. A shift in camera position may establish figure/ground priorities and allow the dominant subject to be emphasized

If the image is familiar, recognition may be instantaneous and therefore there is a redundancy of information. If the image is unrecognized then there may be a rapid search and match through memory to find similarities in mental images. When an unexpected image cannot be identified then either a guess is made or it is ignored.

People habitually overlook things they cannot understand. For example, a foreign news story in a TV news bulletin in which the political context or geographic situation is unknown to the viewer, ceases to be information and is ignored unless a connection can be established with an existing frame of reference. The reporter, who may have lived with the story for days, weeks or even months, may have an abundance of background knowledge to the specific two-minute item he files that day. This may cause him to overestimate the background information the viewer brings to the story. A similar extended preparation and filming of a narrative sequence may involve the production group investigating and discussing every nuance and significance of a 10-second shot. The first-time viewer of the shot has to extract all this days/weeks of considered deliberations during the 10-second running time of the shot. If a shot is viewed many times in editing, its visual impact can appear limited and easily understood. It is often tempting to shorten its screen time in order to inject pace and visual vitality into a sequence that has grown stale with repeated viewing in the edit suite. The audience, however, usually only see the shot once amidst a montage of other shots.

We predict what is likely to happen next from our experience of the past and rely on these assumptions to forecast the future. Shot structure and shot composition have to take into account this habit of searching for the cause of an effect.

Problems with perception

There is a basic distinction between 'reading' the space in a two-dimensional image, where a hypothesis of shape, depth, etc., has to be estimated by viewing from a fixed position; compared with the potential, in a three-dimensional situation, to move within the space to confirm a hypothesis. We cannot walk around a picture.

Our perceptual knowledge is gained from our experience of moving in a three-dimensional world. An essential element of testing and checking perceptual information is by moving through space. We use these acquired three-dimensional perceptual skills and frequently apply them to a very reduced image depicted in two-dimensions (e.g., a television screen) where we have no opportunity of testing out our depth 'guesses' by moving into the picture space.

Although the image created by a video or film camera may be similar to the image focused on the retina of the eye, there is the crucial difference of being unable to test out the depth indicators of a two-dimensional image by moving into its picture space. A moving camera can reproduce some of the image changes that occur when we move in space but not the visual depth checks achieved by binocular vision and head movement.

There is a considerable amount of visual information that is used in perception that is usually unacknowledged until an attempt is made to reproduce three-dimensions on a two-dimensional plane. If an untrained person attempts to draw a townscape they will soon realize

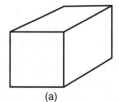

(a)

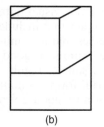

(b)

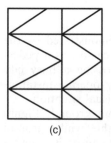

(c)

Figure 3.6 A simple shape such as a cube is easily seen in isolation but is camouflaged when swallowed up in a more complex figure. The centre of interest of a composition requires visual emphasis (Gollschadt diagram)

that there are many aspects of visual representation of which they may never have been consciously aware. Although information about perspective of line and mass and vanishing points are present in the eye they are unexamined, even though they help us to determine distance.

As we move our viewpoint in space, so the appearance of objects alters. A plate may have the shape of a circle seen from above but viewed from any other angle its shape is never circular, but we persist with a mental image of a plate as a circle. We know that objects have an identity and a permanent form and ignore perceptual problems with the continuity of form produced by a changing viewpoint.

The two-dimensional representations of film and video provide image dimensions or size relationships of which we may not be aware. Sometimes the appearance of everyday objects are altered when lit from an unfamiliar angle or seen in extreme close-up. A low-angle, close shot of a golf ball against the sky in 'Murder by Contract' (1960), accompanied by the murmur of out-of-frame golfers, established an expectation of the normal object size, until the camera pulled back and disclosed that the normal two-inch golf ball was in fact a four-foot-high structure identifying the entrance to a golf course.

An unfamiliar setting or the absence of a field of reference to an object frequently creates difficulties in identifying what normally is instantly recognized. 'It looks like an "x" but I must look at it longer to make quite sure' can be caused by unexpected lighting or shot size. The meaning of a familiar image can be understood without conscious thought whereas intelligent interest is required to understand unfamiliar subjects. Recognition of images may be easily accomplished if the observer is favourably disposed towards them. That which tends to arouse the observer's hostility or antipathy may be either forgotten or ignored.

A tight shot of a woman feeding her baby with the woman's face looking down to the baby at her breast will engender, in most people, a feeling of warmth and human empathy. It is universal and timeless and will, in general, produce a feeling of uncritical endorsement. The same activity, if framed in a wider shot now showing mother and child in an exterior that includes shabby and broken coaches and caravans, dirty and half clothed children and a few mangy dogs roaming around a wood fire, will set up a completely different set of responses. Putting the original subject in a social context will provoke the viewer into bringing preconceived attitudes and social judgements to bear on the activity. It may even provoke anger that a woman should bring a child into the world in such an inhospitable and alien (to the viewer's frame of reference) world. What is *included* and *excluded* from the frame alters the way the central subject is understood.

Attention and perception

Perception is dependent on attention. If attention is concentrated on a small part of the field of view, little will be perceived of the rest of the scene. If attention is spread over a large area, no one part will be very clearly and accurately perceived. The total amount that can be attended to at any one moment is constant.

There is selective perception in everyday life, with people unable to attend to two different visual events; they either combine the two or

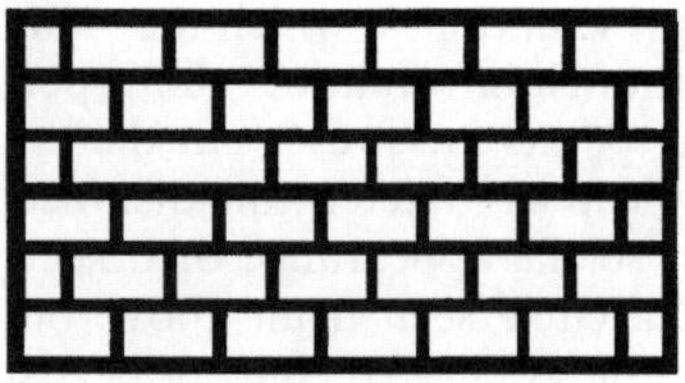

Figure 3.7 Our attention is almost immediately captured by the 'one' that is different. The repetition of the brick shape provides an overall image unity whilst at the same time emphasizing the one exception

their attention ends. It is not possible to continually attend to even one part of an image. After a short period, attention wanders, but by directing perception understanding improves.

Attention can be split three ways even when watching a familiar TV event such as a weather forecast. The physical appearance of the forecaster, as well as their spoken commentary, will split the attention and to this is added a third part of the image that requires attention – the changing graphics of the weather chart. It is difficult to attend to all three elements even in this simple display without loss of attention to one part of the information presented.

Change blindness

Two psychologists at Harvard University devised an experiment to measure how attentive people are in an everyday situation. They were attempting to demonstrate how little we see of what comes through our eyes.

They set up a reception counter staffed by a young man to hand out forms. Individuals who were the subjects of the experiment approached the counter in turn. They were unaware at this stage that they were part of an experiment. When they handed the form back, the young man ducked down to get more information for them. While he was briefly out of their sight he was immediately replaced below the counter by another young man of different appearance including a different coloured shirt. The duplicate young man stood up and presented the material and gave directions to a room.

More than 75 per cent of the subjects, when debriefed, did not notice that the young man had changed between them receiving their first and second form. The 25 per cent who did notice may have been concentrating on a specific part of the young man and therefore noticed his appearance had changed when he re-emerged from behind the counter. Because our attention system allows us to actively select what to look at, we often miss large changes to our visual world that appear to be perfectly obvious to someone who knows what is going to change.

The brain fills in the gaps

The eyes are the slaves of our attention system. In film making this can be exploited and directed by subject emphasis in a shot, for example, a shadow behind a door or a face specially lit in a group of faces.

Viewing a horror film demonstrates the power of the viewer's imagination. It is not what is on the screen but what we think we see on the screen (e.g., the shadow behind the door). The less we see the more we imagine. There is nothing more vivid than the pictures we generate in our head.

Research suggests that our brains are constantly distorting what we see. We guess what is out there from past experience rather than having to build up images instantaneously. The brain fills in a vast amount of additional information. The brain just doesn't see – it invents much of it. Perception is a highly personal inner world.

Neuro scientists suggest that although the world appears to be visually high resolution and photographically sharp, a lot of this is filled in from memory. In recent years perceptual research has suggested the visual brain relies as much on information from our memory as from our eyes. We are using information from the past to imagine what is out there.

Vision is not a one-way transfer of information from eye to brain. There is also an exchange between the 30 known areas of the visual brain and the use of stored visual information. Our perception of the world is as much what we expect to see as it is about what we actually see. When composing images this aspect of perception can be exploited.

Summary

There is a mismatch between how we think we see a subject and how the camera records the same subject due to a perceptual distortion called size constancy.

The mind tends to group objects together into one single comprehensive image. The mind sees patterns and composition can enhance or facilitate this tendency or it can prevent it. A knowledge of how the mind groups visual elements is a valuable tool for good communication.

Test the strength of a composition by examining the individual visual elements it contains and check if they separately or collectively strengthen or weaken the overall form.

Although all these perceptual habits may seem obvious and unremarkable they often play a significant part in shot composition and cannot be overlooked when seeking to maximize visual communication.

4
The lens and perspective

Perception and depth

The eye/brain judges depth by binocular cues (available to two eyes) and monocular cues (available to one eye). Because the eyes are about 6 cm apart the retinas of the eyes receive slightly different images. It is the comparison of these two images and by movement of the head that information about depth is achieved with binocular vision. The short fashion for three-dimensional films in the 1950s replicated stereoscopic vision by having two overlapping images forming the projected image that were separated when viewed by green and red spectacles. Apart from this fashion, a television or film shot is a 'one-eyed' system and indications of depth are achieved by:

- *relative size* of known objects or same size objects;
- *linear perspective* – parallel lines converge in the distance (e.g., looking along railway lines);
- *overlap* – any subject that obscures another subject is perceived as being closer to the lens;
- *relative brightness* – subjects that are clearer and brighter are perceived as being closer to the lens than subjects at a distance;
- *motion parallax* – as the camera's viewpoint changes, more distant objects will move more slowly than objects close to the lens;
- *texture gradient* – regular size objects (e.g., blades of grass, fabric weave) will diminish in size as they recede from the lens;
- *height in the frame* – a subject that is higher in the frame (and smaller) than a similar foreground subject is perceived as being further away.

Depth indicators and their relationship to the lens

The mathematical laws by which objects appear to diminish in size as they recede from us, the way parallel lines appear to converge and

Figure 4.1 A detail from *The Profanation of the Host* (1465), a painting by the Florentine artist Paolo Uccello where he explores the newly discovered linear perspective indicators to represent depth on a two-dimensional surface.

The artist David Hockney suggests that some paintings of the fifteenth century and later were created with the aid of mirrors or lenses. If his theory is correct, artists who worked on a projected image may have faced similar lens problems to those contemporary cameramen are involved with

vanish at the horizon, were introduced to Western art in the fifteenth century.

The Profanation of the Host (Figure 4.1), is a detail of a painting by the Florentine artist Paolo Uccello. As you can see, he has used all the newly discovered linear perspective indicators to represent depth on a two-dimensional surface. They include converging parallel lines such as the timbers in the ceiling, the tiles on the floor and the walls, and a reduction in the size of the tiles as they recede.

So what are the laws of perspective that need to be understood? Unlike the Renaissance artist, the cameraman does not have to puzzle over how to represent a two-dimensional plan of a three-dimensional view before he produces a realistic picture. He does not have to analyse how the eye perceives depth. He simply presses the record button and the camera does the rest. Or does it?

The cameraman has to decide at what distance and with what lens angle he will shoot the scene. That will make a difference to the size relationships within the frame – he will control the perspective of mass.

He has to decide the lens height. Shooting low with a level camera will produce one type of line perspective. Shooting from a high vantage point tilted down will produce another set of line relationships in the frame.

The camera doesn't lie – much. It simply reproduces an image conditioned by one of the four parameters mentioned above – lens height, camera tilt, distance from subject and lens angle.

In identifying how the two-dimensional depiction of space is created, there are a number of lens characteristics that play an important part. In order to control and manipulate these variables in the visual

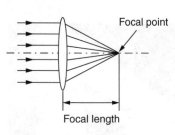

Focal point

Focal length

Focal length of a single lens
(a)

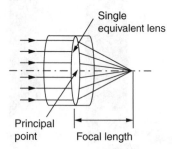

Single
equivalent lens

Principal
point   Focal length

Focal length of a compound lens
(b)

Figure 4.2 (a) single element lens;
(b) multi-element lens

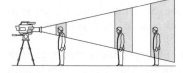

Figure 4.3 Depth-of-field: the three
variables that affect depth-of-field
are camera distance, ƒno and lens
angle

design of a composition, it is necessary to understand how the lens
creates depth indicators.

Focal length

When parallel rays of light pass through a convex lens, they will converge to one point on the optical axis (see Figure 4.2). This point is
called the focal point of the lens. The focal length of the lens is indicated by the distance from the centre of the lens or the principal point
of a compound lens (e.g., a zoom lens) to the focal point. The longer
the focal length of a lens, the smaller its angle of view will be; and the
shorter the focal length of a lens, the wider its angle of view.

Focal length (lens angle) and the distance of the camera from the
subject(s) of a shot play a crucial part in the two-dimensional depiction of space.

Angle of view

The focal length of a prime lens has a specified angle of view. A zoom
lens has a variable focal length and therefore a variable angle of view.
The approximate horizontal angle of view of a fixed focal length lens
can be calculated by using its focal length and the size of the recording
format frame of the camera. Because the horizontal angle of view of
the lens is proportional to the width of the recording format (e.g.,
35 mm film, 2/3″ CCD video, etc.), lenses with the same focal length
will produce different angles of view depending on the format in use
(see Chapter 12, 'Composition styles').

For example, a video camera fitted with 2/3″ CCDs the formula
would be:

$$\text{Angle of view} = \frac{2 \tan -1.8 \, \text{mm (width of CCD)}}{2 \times \text{focal length (mm)}}$$

Depth-of-field

The depth-of-field, how much of the scene in shot is in acceptable
focus, is another important element in shot composition and in controlling how the viewer responds to the image. Cinemagraphic fashion
has alternated between deep focus shots (Greg Toland's work on
'Citizen Kane' (1941)), to the use of long focal lenses with a very
limited depth-of-field only allowing the principal subject in the
frame to be sharp. Changing the ƒno alters the depth-of-field – the
portion of the field of view that appears sharply in focus.

This zone extends in front and behind the subject in focus and will
increase as the ƒno increases. The greater the distance of the subject in
focus from the camera, the greater the depth-of-field. The depth-of-
field is greater behind the subject in focus than in front and is dependent on the focal length of the lens and ƒno. For a correctly exposed
picture, the depth-of-field can be adjusted by altering light levels or by
the use of neutral density filters that will then require an adjustment to
the aperture (ƒno) to return to a correct exposure.

*f*no

The *f*no of a lens is a method of indicating how much light can pass through the lens. It is inversely proportional to the focal length of the lens and directly proportional to the diameter of the effective aperture of the lens. For a given focal length, the larger the aperture of the lens the smaller its *f*no and the brighter the image it produces. *f*nos are arranged in a scale where each increment is multiplied by $\sqrt{2}$ (1.414). Each time the *f*no is increased by one stop (e.g., *f*2.8 to *f*4), the exposure is decreased by half:

*f*1.4   *f*2   *f*2.8   *f*4   *f*5.6   *f*8   *f*11   *f*16   *f*22

Zoom

The majority of video cameras are fitted with a zoom lens that can alter its focal length and therefore the angle of view over a certain range. This is achieved by moving one part of the lens system (the variator) to change the size of the image, and by automatically gearing another part of the lens system (the compensator) to simultaneously move and maintain focus. This alters the image size and therefore the effective focal length of the lens. To zoom into a subject, the lens must first be fully zoomed in on the subject and focused. Then zoom out to the wider angle. The zoom will now stay in focus for the whole range of its travel.

Readjustment on shot

In live television productions, the zoom lens angle is often altered to trim or adjust the shot to improve the composition when the content of the shot changes. Someone joining a person 'in shot' is provided with space in the frame by zooming out. The reverse may happen when they leave shot – the camera zooms in to recompose the original shot. Trimming the shot 'in vision' may be unavoidable in the coverage of spontaneous or unknown content but it quickly becomes an irritant if repeatedly used. Fidgeting with the framing by altering the zoom angle should be avoided during a take.

Zoom ratio

A zoom lens can vary its focal length. The ratio of the longest focal length it can achieve (the telephoto end) with the shortest focal length obtainable (its wide-angle end) is its zoom ratio. A broadcast zoom lens will state zoom ratio and the wide-angle focal length in one figure. A popular zoom ratio is a 14 × 8.5. This describes a zoom with a 14:1 ratio starting at 8.5 mm focal length (angle of view = 54° 44′) with the longest focal length of 14 × 8.5 mm = 119 mm (angle of view = 4° 14′).

Extender

A zoom lens can be fitted with an internal extender lens system that allows the zoom to be used on a different set of focal lengths. A 2× extender on the 14 × 8.5 zoom mentioned above would transform the range from 8.5 mm–119 mm to 17 mm–238 mm but it will lose approximately two stops of sensitivity.

Focus

Focusing is the act of adjusting the lens elements to achieve a sharp image at the focal plane. Objects either side of this focus zone may still look reasonably sharp depending on their distance from the lens, the lens aperture and lens angle. The area covering the objects that are in acceptable focus is called the depth-of-field.

The depth-of-field can be considerable if the widest angle of the zoom is selected and, whilst working with a small aperture, a subject is selected for focus at some distance from the lens. When zooming into this subject, the depth-of-field or zone of acceptable sharpness will decrease.

Follow focus

Film and television often have a high proportion of shots of faces and the eyes need to be in sharp focus. Focus on a video camera is determined and adjusted with reference to the viewfinder picture. Sharpest focus can be checked 'off-shot' by rocking the focus zone behind and then in front of the eyes. As camera or subject moves there will be a loss of focus that needs to be corrected. The art of focusing is to know which way to focus and not to overshoot. The peaking control (if fitted) on the viewfinder emphasizes the electronic edges and is an aid to focusing and does not affect the recorded image. In setting a film shot, the principal subject distance is measured and any change of focus is calibrated and marked.

Zoom lens and focus

A zoom lens is designed to keep the same focal plane throughout the whole of its range (provided the back focus has been correctly adjusted). Pre-focus whenever possible on the tightest shot of the subject. This is the best way of checking focus because of the small depth-of-field and it also prepares for a zoom-in if required.

Pulling focus

Within a composition, visual attention is directed to the subject in sharpest focus. Attention can be transferred to another part of the frame by throwing focus onto that subject. Match the speed of the focus pull to the motivating action.

If the focus is on a foreground person facing camera with a defocused background figure and the foreground subject turns away from camera, focus can be instantly thrown back to the background. A slower focus pull would be more appropriate in music coverage, for example, moving off the hands of a foreground musician to a background instrumentalist.

Differential focus

Differential focus is deliberately using a narrow depth-of-field to emphasize the principle subject in the frame in sharp focus that is contrasted with a heavily out-of-focus background.

The structural skeleton of a shot

Although a television or film image is viewed as a two-dimensional picture, most shots will contain depth indicators that allows the audience to understand the two-dimensional representation of space that contains the action. Text on a blank background has no depth indicators but the text is still perceptually seen as 'in front' of the page.

The audience will be looking at the surface of the screen, a two-dimensional plane covered by a series of lines, shapes, brightness points, contrasts, colour, etc., and will respond to any indication of recognizable form and space contained in the shot. They will read into the two-dimensional image an impression of a three-dimensional space.

There are therefore two aspects of the composition. The content – a house, horse or face – and the front surface arrangements of lines, shapes, contrasts, etc., that form the recognizable images. The majority of the audience may only remember the content of the shot – the house, horse or face – but they will also be affected by the series of lines, shapes, brightness points and contrasts, colour, etc., which construct the front surface plane of the image. This 'abstract' element of the shot may be crucial to the way the viewer responds to the image.

Each visual element in a shot can therefore serve two functions:

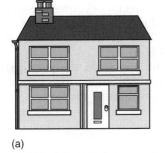

(a)

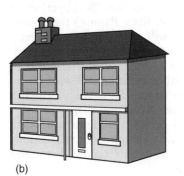

(b)

Figure 4.4 Diagonal arrangements of lines in a composition produce a greater impression of vitality than either vertical or horizontal lines. The square-on shot of a house **(a)** is visually static because it maximizes the number of horizontal lines in the frame. Angling the camera position to show two sides of a building **(b)** converts the horizontal lines into diagonals. A line at an angle is perceptually seen as a line that is in motion. Compositions with a strong diagonal element imply movement or vitality (see Chapter 5, 'Visual design').

Although the subject of the shot remains the same – a house – the structural skeleton of the shot has been rearranged to increase the viewer's perceptual attention independent of their interest in the specific content of the shot

1. as *content* – that part of the composition that provides depth indicators and information about the physical subject of the shot;
2. as *form* – part of the design that lies on the surface plane of the screen and forms an overall abstract design that can produce a reaction in the viewer independent of any response to the content of the shot.

The reduction of this aspect of the shot, its form, to a simplified diagram of line and shape has been termed the structural skeleton of the image. It reveals the perceptual elements that potentially can hold the viewer's attention over and above the interest in the content of the shot.

The construction of the structural skeleton of the plane of the shot does not simply rely on content. For example, every cameraman knows that a shot of a building can be made more interesting if the camera is moved from a square-on symmetrical viewpoint to an angle of view favouring more than one side or surface, and/or if the height of the lens is varied. Repositioning the camera is altering the structural skeleton for, while the content of the shot remains and is recognizable as 'a building', converging lines of rooftop, windows, doors, etc., have been altered and restructured to provide a more pleasing 'front surface' design (Figures 4.4(a) and (b)).

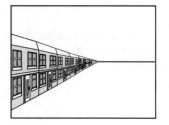

Figure 4.5 All parallel horizontal lines that recede into the distance appear to converge towards the horizon at one point known as the vanishing point. If the camera is level (i.e., without tilt), the horizon line will bisect the frame at midpoint. A line projected from the camera to the vanishing point will intersect all objects at a height equivalent to the lens

Vanishing point

All parallel horizontal lines that recede into the distance appear to converge towards the horizon line. Receding parallel lines above eye-line slope down, receding lines below eye-level appear to slope up towards the horizon (Figure 4.5) The position of the vanishing point in the frame will control the degree of convergence of any parallel lines to the line of the lens axis.

A single vanishing point in the centre of the frame (e.g., level camera positioned in the centre of a street looking along the street with lens at half house height) will produce a very centralized composition with all the parallel lines of the houses meeting in the centre of frame. It could emphasize, for example, the conformity and rigidity in the planning of a housing estate but the shot may have little or no compositional elements that hold the attention (Figure 4.6(a)).

A very popular compositional device to emphasize the principal subject in the frame by focusing the strongly convergent lines behind the subject is to place the vanishing point just outside the frame.

Tilting the camera

Panning the camera up will move the horizon line down and redistribute the proportion of the converging lines so that the upper set of lines will have a steeper angle than the lower lines. Panning the camera down will move the horizon line up and will have the reverse effect.

A third influence on the degree of convergence will be camera position. Moving the camera back and using a longer focal length lens to keep in frame the original houses will reduce the angle of convergence. Moving the camera forward and using a shorter focal length lens will increase the angle of convergence (Figures 4.7(a) and (b)).

The final influence on the structural skeleton of lines will be to increase or decrease the camera height. Craning up and panning down will produce one set of converging lines. Craning down and panning up will create another set of lines.

These four camera parameters – camera height, tilt, lens-angle and camera position – in combination or singularly, all influence the structural skeleton of the shot without altering content.

Two-point vanishing perspective

A camera positioned at the corner of a building with a lens positioned at half building height will produce a shot with two vanishing points. Depending on the framing and content, the vanishing points may be inside or outside the frame.

Again the four camera parameters listed above will have a significant effect on the convergence of lines. Using a very wide-angle lens combined with a camera position close to the building will create the greatest angles of convergence.

Three-point linear perspective

If a camera is looking at the corner of a very tall building at lens position of eye height and is panned up to include the whole building, a third set of converging vertical lines is added to the two sets of

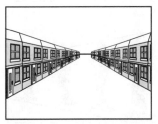

(a)

(b)

(c)

Figure 4.6 (a) A single vanishing point in the centre of the frame (e.g., level camera positioned in the centre of a street looking along the street) will produce a very centralized composition, with all the parallel lines of the houses meeting in the centre of the frame. **(b)** Panning the camera right will push the vanishing point to the left of the frame and produce a different set of converging lines. **(c)** A common compositional device to emphasize the principal subject in the frame is to place the vanishing point just outside the frame so that the strongly converging lines draw the eye to the main subject.

Panning the camera right will push the vanishing point to the left of the frame and produce a different set of converging lines **(b)**. Continuing to pan the camera right will position the vanishing point outside the frame **(c)** and progressively reduce the angle of convergence of parallel lines until they become horizontal at the point when the lens axis is at 90° to them

horizontal converging lines. There are now three vanishing points in or out of the frame with the additional flexibility of altering all the angles of convergences with camera height, lens angle, camera distance from building and angle of tilt (Figure 4.8).

Multiple vanishing points

Any number of vanishing points are created depending on the variety and position of parallel horizontal and vertical lines in relationship to the camera lens. For example, a high camera angle looking down on the rooftops of a village has little control over the structural skeleton of the shot apart from adjustment in framing. This becomes unimportant because the variety and interaction of the lines usually gives the shot sufficient visual interest without the need to control the angle of convergence.

Horizon line and camera height as a compositional device

Our normal perceptual experience of someone of our own size moving on flat ground towards us is that the horizon line will always intersect behind them at eye level.

As was mentioned in Chapter 1, it was a fifteenth-century writer/architect, Leon Alberti, who realized that the controlling design factor when creating a two-dimensional image was the distance of the eye from the scene and its height from the ground. The crucial element in his construct was the horizon line. This illusionary line where the ground plane meets the sky is also the point where all orthogonals, that is, parallel lines running at right angles to the horizon line, meet. This point is called the vanishing point.

We are usually most aware of the horizon line when we are by the sea. If we set up a horizontally level camera at eye level beside the sea it follows from Alberti's reasoning that as only horizontal lines can ever reach the horizon, the horizon line will appear to be at mid-point vertically in the frame. It will bisect the frame at its mid-point because only the centre axis of the vertical lens-angle is horizontal.

If the camera is level, the centre axis of the lens will always be the only horizontal line that meets the horizon therefore increasing or decreasing the lens height has no effect on the position of the horizon line in the frame.

Of course, Alberti's explanation of our normal perception of linear perspective does involve two visual illusions. The first illusion is that the sky meets the sea when it obviously does not; second, that a visual sight line parallel to the sea would eventually meet this illusionary line at what is termed the vanishing point.

Looking from behind the camera, we will see that the horizon line will intersect the camera at lens height. If the lens height is 1.5 m then all 1.5-m objects in front of the lens will be cut at the same point by the horizon line in the frame.

If we tilt the camera down, the horizon line moves up the frame. If we tilt up, the line moves down. But if we crane the camera up, keeping it level, the horizon line follows and continues to bisect the frame.

Figure 4.7 A significant influence on the degree of linear convergence is the distance of the camera from the main subject. Moving the camera back **(a)** and using a longer focal length lens to keep in frame the foreground chess pieces will reduce the angle of convergence of a projected line at the top and at the base of the other chess pieces. Moving the camera forward **(b)** and using a shorter focal length lens will increase the angle of convergence

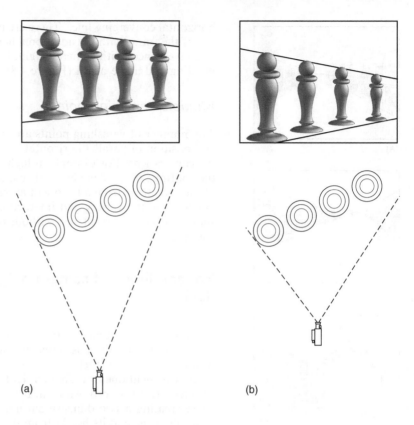

(a)   (b)

If the camera is level, any object between the lens and the illusionary vanishing point on the horizon will be intersected by the horizon line at the same height as the lens.

American silent film production at the turn of the twentieth century used a convention of a 50 mm lens at eye level and actor movement was restricted to being no closer to the lens than 12 ft. With an actor standing 12 ft from the lens, the bottom of the frame cuts him at knee height. By 1910, the Vitagraph company allowed the actors to play up to 9 ft from the lens and the camera was lowered to chest height.

Lens at eye level

From these static camera positions there developed a Hollywood convention of frequently placing the camera at eye level, which in turn allowed the horizon line to cut the foreground actors at eye level. It is particularly noticeable in exteriors in westerns made before the 1960s. Whether the artistes are standing or sitting, the camera is often positioned at eye height, which places the horizon behind the eyes. This emphasizes the main subject of the frame – the face – and the main area of interest of the face – the eyes (Figure 4.10).

In television production, a more prosaic factor controlling lens height is the need to avoid shooting off the top of studio sets. Keeping the camera at eye level speeds up production as actor movement to camera can be accommodated without panning up and shooting off the top of the set or without the need to relight.

Figure 4.8 If a camera is looking
at the corner of a very tall building
and is panned up to include the
whole building, a third set of
converging lines is added to the
two sets of horizontal lines

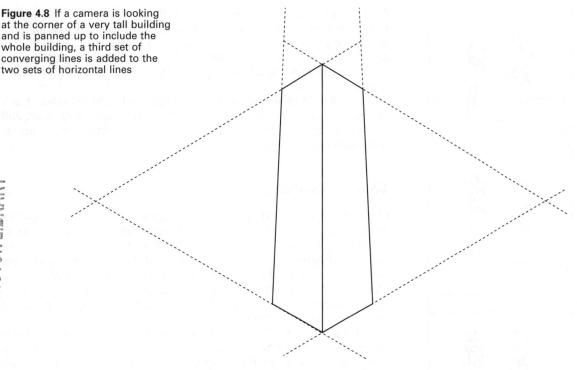

Lens height

The height at which the lens is set will also control the way the audience identifies with the subject. Orson Welles, in the film 'Touch of Evil' (1958), played a fat corrupt detective in a Mexican border town. He directed the film and, by using a wide-angle lens and placing the camera at a low height looking up at this character, he created a brooding dominant personality who appeared to be towering over the audience and almost falling forwards on to them. The impression produced by this lens height and angle was of an unstable but powerful figure.

Moving the horizon down below a person makes them more dominant because the viewer is forced to adopt a lower eye line viewpoint. We are in the size relationship of children looking up to adults. Leni Riefenstahl's film 'Triumph of the Will' (1934) about the 1934 Nazi Party Nuremberg Rally has frequent low-angle shots of Adolf Hitler. It increases his height and status and is contrasted with the high-angle 'bird's eye views' of the massed ranks of his followers.

A low lens height may also de-emphasize floor or ground-level detail because we are looking along at ground level and reducing or eliminating indications of ground space between objects. This concentrates the viewer's interest on the vertical subjects. A high position lens height has the reverse effect. The many planes of the scene are emphasized like a scale model. The viewer is in a 'God-like' privileged position observing more than the participants in the scene. We are now adults looking down on children.

Usually it is better to divide the frame into unequal parts by positioning the horizon line above or below the mid-point of the frame.

(a)

(b)

(c)

Figure 4.9 On a flat surface, the horizon line cuts similar size figures at the same point. The height of that point is the height of the lens. The position of the horizon line is controlled by the degree of camera tilt. **(a)** Low angle; **(b)** lens at eye height; **(c)** high angle

Figure 4.10 If the camera is at eye level, the horizon line (if it is in the frame) will pass behind the foreground actors at eye level. This emphasizes the main subject of the frame – the face, and the main area of interest of the face – the eyes

Many cameramen intuitively use the Rule of Thirds (see Chapter 10) to position the horizon. A composition can evoke space by panning up and placing the line low in frame. Placing a high horizon in the frame can balance a darker foreground land mass or subject with the more attention-grabbing detail of a high key sky. It also helps with contrast range and exposure.

A lens height of slightly above presenter eye height (whether standing or sitting) is usually kinder to the face, provides a more alert and positive body posture and often improves the lighting on an artiste with deep set eyes, etc.

Camera distance

Our normal perceptual experience of someone of our own size moving on flat ground towards us is that the horizon line will always intersect behind them at eye level. Looking at *The Profanation of the Host* painting (Figure 4.1) one can observe that Uccello has reduced the size of the tiles as they recede from the observer. The ratio of size change puzzled many painters until Alberti showed the common-sense arithmetic of how the reduction in size is directly proportional to the distance from the eye.

A 1.5-m woman, 2 m from the lens, will produce an image that is twice as large as a 1.5-m woman, 4 m from the camera (Figure 4.11).

Size relationships or the perspective of mass can be confused with the wide angle effect and the narrow angle effect. By this I mean that to increase the size of a background figure to a foreground figure it is common practice to reposition the camera back and zoom in to return to the original framing. The size relationships have now altered. It is not the narrower angle that produced this effect but the increased distance from the camera (Figure 4.12(a)–(c)).

By tracking away from the two figures we have altered the ratio between lens and first figure and lens and second figure. It is a much smaller ratio and therefore the difference in size between the two is now not so great. When we zoom in and revert to the original full frame for the foreground figure we keep the new size relationships that have been formed by camera distance. The two figures appear to be closer in size.

As part of our perception of depth depends on judging size relationships (the further away the subject is, the smaller it appears), our perception of this new size relationship produced by tracking out and zooming in leads us to believe that the distance between equal height figures is not so great as the first framing.

Possibly, the narrow angle and the wide angle effect is misnamed. It should be called the distant viewing effect. Our eyes cannot zoom and therefore we are not so conscious of size relationships changing in normal perception.

The important point to remember is that subject size relationship is a product of camera distance. How the subject fills the frame is a product of lens angle. This, of course, is the crucial distinction between tracking and zooming. Tracking the camera towards or away from the subject alters size relationships – the perspective of mass. Zooming the lens preserves the existing size relationships and magnifies or diminishes a portion of the shot (see Chapter 16, 'Movement').

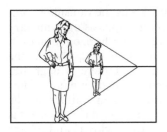

Figure 4.11 Size relationships are proportional to the distance of the subjects from the camera. The image of a 1.5-m subject 2 m from the lens will be twice as large as the image of a 1.5-m subject 4 m from the camera, whatever lens-angle is used

Lens angle

The choice of lens angle and camera distance from the subject is the controlling factor in the way that depth is depicted in the image. This subject is treated in more detail in 'Staging' (Chapter 15) but the 'internal' space of a shot often plays a crucial part in setting up the atmosphere of a shot.

A long focal length lens positioned at a distance from a cramped interior will heighten the claustrophobia of the setting. Subject size ratios will be evened out from foreground to background and movement to and away from camera will show no significant change in size and therefore give a subjective impression that no distance has been traversed.

Controlling space with choice of lens angle/camera distance

Both compression of space and the reduction of apparent movement caused problems in the editing of an 'all action' film, where a shot of two people struggling on a railway line with a train in the distance was shot with a long focal length lens. The visual impression, because of the compression of space, was that the train was nearly upon them, whereas the narrative required a great deal more action before that point was reached. Secondly, because the train appeared to have little change in size over the duration of the shot, it had the appearance of moving slowly. This negated its threat to the protagonists and reduced the build-up of tension. A wide-angle lens close to the subject will increase space, emphasize movement and, depending on shot content, emphasize convergence of line and contrast of mass.

Placement of vanishing points

Control of convergence becomes important when it is used to focus attention on the main subject of the shot. Converging lines can be used to bring this foreground subject into prominence (see Figure 4.6(c)). The positioning of the vanishing point controls the convergence angles of receding parallel lines. By tilting or panning the camera the vanishing points can be placed within or outside the frame. Where the vanishing point is positioned will have a considerable influence on the composition.

Figure 4.14(b) shows that Leonardo chose a central vanishing point where all orthogonals (receding parallels perpendicular to the picture plane) converge on the head of Christ. This 'implosion' of converging lines is in contrast to the square-on table position that in general tends to reduce the dynamic impact of an image. Placing the vanishing point at the central subject emphasizes the subject as being the centre of the view and therefore psychologically in this viewpoint, the centre of the world. If the vanishing point of these strong converging lines was placed outside the frame or at the edge of the frame, the main subject of the painting could be seen as just another element in the frame.

Many cameramen, in framing up a shot, will seek to maximize the convergence of lines by choice of lens angle and camera height/posi-

(a)

(b)

(c)

Figure 4.12 The distance between the two figures remains unchanged in all three illustrations. The distance between foreground figure and camera has altered. With each camera reposition, lens-angle of zoom is adjusted to keep the foreground figure the same size in the frame. The 'wide angle' effect and the 'narrow angle' effect is a product of the camera distance from subjects. **(a)** Mid-range; **(b)** wide angle; **(c)** narrow angle

tion. Shooting square-on to a subject usually keeps the vanishing point within the frame and often results in a strong emphasis on symmetry and simple balance, particularly if there are strong horizontal lines in the frame at 90° to the lens axis. By shooting at an oblique angle, the vanishing point is moved out of the frame and there is a greater emphasis of converging orthogonals. These form dominant groups of receding wedge shapes and give a greater dynamic attack to the image compared with strong level horizontal lines. Visual excitement is created by neighbouring parallel lines getting closer and closer together.

'Normal' perspective

If an observer looks at a field of view through an empty picture frame held at arms length, he will require the frame to be progressively increased in size the greater the distance the frame is positioned away from him in order that the same field of view is contained within the frame at all times (Figure 4.16).

As we have discussed, the perspective of mass and the perspective of line are created by the distance of the subjects from the observer.

Size relationships and convergence of line in his field of view will depend on their distance from him. Therefore if he does not change his position, the perspective appearance of the 'image' within the frame will remain unchanged. The frame will simply get larger and larger the further it is from the observer's position.

If a photograph was substituted for the frame and increasingly enlarged to match frame size, the two factors that control the exact replication of perspective characteristics in an image are revealed as image size and the distance of the image from the observer.

No lens produces a 'wrong' perspective provided the viewer views the correct size image at the taking distance. A wide-angle shot taken close to the principal subject would require the viewer almost to press their nose to the screen in order to experience the perspective characteristics of the image that they would experience if they had been the camera.

The calculation of which lens-angle provides 'correct' perspective (i.e., equivalent to an observer replacing the camera) must include image size of reproduction and the distance the viewer is to the screen. A person sitting in the back row of a cinema may be viewing a screen size that is a tenth of the size the audience in the front is experiencing. There is no lens-angle that can provide both viewing distances with 'correct' perspective. The audience in the front row will experience wide-angle shots as having 'correct' perspective whilst the audience in the back row may judge narrower angle shots as having more 'correct' perspective.

Often a script requires interpretation rather than precise replication of 'correct' perspective. Interpretative compositions can therefore be created using perspective characteristics that expand or flatten space.

To visually represent the sensation of vertigo, Alfred Hitchcock, in a famous shot in 'Vertigo' (1958), had the camera tracking in matched to a zoom-out to keep the visual elements at the edge of the frame static (see Figure 4.16). Because the camera was moving closer to the subject, the image size relationships and line convergence in the frame changed and gave a greater impression of depth to the shot. The zoom-out

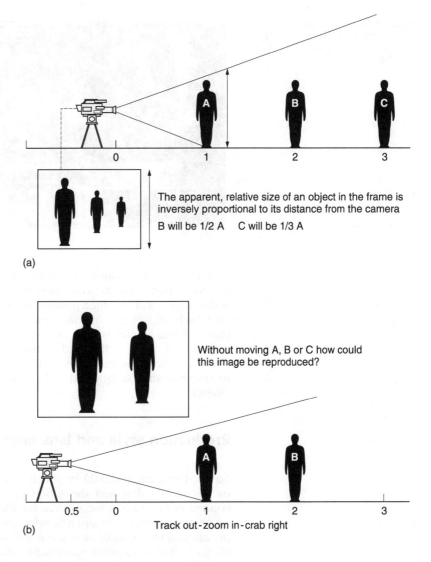

(a)

The apparent, relative size of an object in the frame is inversely proportional to its distance from the camera

B will be 1/2 A   C will be 1/3 A

Without moving A, B or C how could this image be reproduced?

Figure 4.13

(b)

Track out - zoom in - crab right

compensated by keeping the same size image of the foreground subject producing an effect of space expanding without movement. This zoom effect has been used subsequently by Steven Spielberg in 'Jaws' (1975) and Martin Scorsese's 'GoodFellas' (1990) and many others.

The internal space of a shot

The internal space of a shot is a subtle but important part of the look, mood and atmosphere of the shot. As we have seen, when three-dimensional objects are converted into a flat two-dimensional image, size relationships will be controlled by camera distance to subject and lens angle. A small room can appear large using a wide-angle lens and a large room can appear cramped and condensed using a long focal length lens.

A medium shot of an actor can be achieved using a zoom lens with a lens angle that varies between more than 75° down to less than 5°. The wider angles will produce possible distortion of features or exaggerated body movement but the crucial distinction between using this range of lens angles is that to keep the same size medium shot, the camera will move further and further back from the main subject as the lens angle is decreased. This will alter the size relationship between foreground and background – the internal space of the shot will be altered.

Production style and lens angle

So what lens angle should be selected? This will depend on the mood or feel of the shot and the action that it is to contain. For visual continuity during a scene, or even for the whole production, a limited range of lens angles are often decided upon. For example, one style of production may consistently use a wide-angle lens producing a series of shots that emphasize movement towards or away from the lens giving a great deal of internal space to the shots. This is often accompanied by a low camera height emphasizing ceilings and dynamic converging lines of walls, buildings, etc.

Another 'internal space' style is to use long focal length lenses to produce compressed space, extended movement towards and away from the camera and a general mood of claustrophobia. Frequently this style is accompanied by a lack of 'geography' shots (e.g., shots that provide information about setting or locale). Shot in tight close-up, the action is followed without revealing the location, resulting in a series of images with swirling backgrounds that generate pace without information. The viewer is sucked into the mystery and teased with a lack of precise visual clues as to the surroundings.

The choice of the lens angle is therefore dependent on how the action is to be staged and the visual style that is required. The narrower the lens angle the more difficult it becomes to achieve smooth and fluid camera development and movement. The camera has to travel further to achieve size change or movement on a narrow lens

Figure 4.14 (b) The 'implosion' of
the projected converging lines of
the ceiling and side panels
meeting behind the head of Christ
emphasize his central importance
in the composition

Figure 4.15 The screen size of the
reproduced image will increase
proportionally to the viewing
distance if the original perspective
experienced by the observer at
distance Z from the subject is to
be duplicated.

The viewing distance Z of
screen A is too close to reproduce
a 'natural' perspective and would
simulate a 'wide angle' look at
that viewing distance.

Screen B would simulate a
'narrow angle' viewpoint because
the screen size is too small for
viewing distance Z

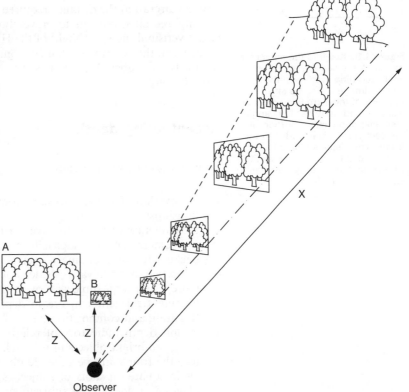

(a)

(b)

(c)

Figure 4.16 Keeping the subject in mid-shot, the camera tracks out while zooming in to keep the subject image the same size. Because of the increasing camera distance and narrower lens angle, a smaller and smaller portion of the background is included in the frame. The visual effect is to freeze the subject in space as the background apparently flows out either side of the frame

than on a wide angle; is more prone to movement vibration or unsteadiness on very narrow angles; and requires larger and more precise focus pulls.

Estimating distance

There are a number of perceptual clues that are used to estimate distance or space. The depth indicators include binocular vision, which allows convergent and divergent movement to be estimated by the use of 'two' viewpoints. Subjects moving towards or away from the observer alter the size of the image focused on the retina of the eye. This change in size may not be accurately appreciated, as perception often involves deductions from what is known rather than what is seen (see Chapter 3). Objects that overlap and their size relationship, if they are similar sized objects, indicate their relative position in space. Colour change due to atmospheric haze and hazy outline at long distance also aid depth perception. Similar objects moving at different velocities also indicate their spatial relationship.

All these depth indicators can be used in film and television composition not only to replicate normal perceptual experiences but also to create atmosphere or to interpret narrative requirements. The decrease in size of objects as they recede from us is used continuously to check on distance. In can also help to create a false distance. The final scene in 'Casablanca' is set inside an aircraft hanger with the doors open, revealing an aeroplane. There was insufficient space in the studio to have an aircraft at the distance required so a scale model was built and 'casting' recruited midgets to move about close to the scale model to give it verisimilitude. In 'Night of the Hunter' (1955), during the chase sequence in the swamp, a silhouette figure on a horseback crossing the skyline is not Robert Mitchum as implied in the story but a midget on a small pony.

Accentuating depth

To emphasize depth in a shot:

- use overlap of subjects to show foreground and background relationships;
- use camera movement to cover or uncover objects in the frame;
- use camera movement past foreground subjects and a changing background on crabbing movements;
- subjects moving towards the lens or away from the lens will create more depth than subjects moving across the frame;
- lighting treatment can create depth indicators (see Chapter 13 'Lighting and composition');
- exploit depth indicators of relative brightness. By making dark close and bright objects in the background, the eye will be carried into the frame and perceive depth in the shot;
- avoid square-on shots of subject (see Figure 4.4). Show as many planes and sides of the subject as possible to emphasize depth;

- accentuate line convergence by the choice of lens angle and focal length.

Summary

No camera – still, film or video – can record an image without leaving an imprint of the optical properties of its lens, its position in space and some indication of the reasons for selecting that lens position. One of the crucial factors that condition the 'look' of the shot concerns perspective.

The form ('structural skeleton') of a shot, its dominant lines and shapes, can potentially hold the viewer's attention over and above the interest in the content of the shot. The construction of this 'structural skeleton' is dependent on the distance of the camera from the subject and the lens angle, which control the size relationships within the frame – the perspective of mass.

The choice of lens angle and camera distance from the subject is the controlling factor in the way that depth is depicted in the image. Lens height and camera tilt will control line perspective. Shooting low with a level camera will produce one type of line perspective; shooting from a high vantage point tilted down will produce another set of line relationships in the frame.

The important point to remember is that subject size relationship is a product of camera distance. How the subject fills the frame is a product of lens angle. This is the crucial distinction between tracking and zooming.

5
Visual design

Introduction

An unbalanced composition appears accidental and incomplete. There is no structure to the image and any part of the frame could be masked with no loss of meaning. There is insufficient arrangement of shapes to assist in grasping the reason for the image. It is ambiguous and unable to hold visual attention beyond the initial search for understanding.

This style of 'non-composition', although sometimes used in alternative technique productions, is seldom the preferred practice in mainstream broadcasting and film making where it is customary, when framing up a shot, to employ various visual design techniques to emphasize one aspect of picture content. This may be one person amongst a group or one object amongst a number of objects.

The need to guide the attention of the audience is usually part of the overall aim of a production which, by selectively structuring its material, communicates the intended meaning. Composition is part of film-making technique employed to solve the perennial questions of what does the audience need to know, how will they be told and at what point in the production should they be told?

Visual design is another way of describing this process. It is the selection and control of a number of competing elements for the audience's attention within the frame. A shot of a railway terminus, for example, may provide information about train times, train types or feature a perplexed traveller who has lost his luggage, as well as the main storytelling reason for the shot, which may be to show that a railway employee is carrying a gun. Apart from this essential element, the rest of the visual information is superfluous to the storyline and must be subdued or eliminated. How the shot is set up will reveal the film maker's priorities but frequently the audience's interest in the location or setting will intrude and compete with the main subject unless all competing visual elements are unobtrusive.

One of the aims of good composition is to find and emphasize structural patterns that the mind/eye can easily grasp. One of the

(a)

(b)

Figure 5.1 Changing size relationships in the frame is a simple way of eliminating competing visual interest **(a)**. Moving the camera left and either changing lens angle or camera distance will establish one subject's dominance in the composition **(b)**

problems in compiling a 'flow chart' of how the mind perceives an image is the speed at which the perceptual process functions. There are rarely discrete steps that can be listed in order, as frequently the mind/ eye instantaneously uses all the component parts of perception to grasp the relevance of an image. The speed at which visual information is absorbed and often unconsciously acted upon is an everyday activity. Visual deductions, evaluations and decisions flow through the mind/eye at a rapid rate without pause to consciously analyse or deliberate on the continually changing visual 'cacophony'. Television and film images frequently have the same complexity. The difficulty in describing how effective composition works is that no one ingredient acts in isolation. Each of the different groupings by shape, light/dark contrasts, line, colour, etc., can be individually part of perception or they can, depending on the content of the shot, be the dominant element.

It is worth stressing the flexible nature of composition 'rules' for film and television productions before we discuss the variety of visual design techniques that can be employed. Think of the various visual design components as a list of cooking ingredients that can be combined in numerous different recipes. What ingredients are used will depend on what meal is being cooked. All of the visual design 'ingredients' cannot be used in the same shot.

There is also the compositional effect of pleasing the eye. Should all shots be aesthetically pleasing? Should slum shots be beautifully composed? Obviously every shot need not be a 'Rembrandt' but essentially it should be subservient to the overall purpose of the production. Like any aspect of invisible technique, if a shot is so striking that it disrupts the flow of images, it may draw attention to itself and defeat its main purpose of advancing the story or factual explanation. A visually dynamic shot is sometimes deliberately placed by the director (for example the shots of Monumental Valley in a John Ford western), to create atmosphere or location identity.

Two aspects of a film/TV production often dominate and cancel the deployment of any visual design principles. Movement takes precedence over compositional balance and also sound will frequently direct attention to a part of the frame and create atmosphere and space beyond the visual aspects of the shot. However effective a composition is in emphasizing the principal subject in the frame, movement or sound will often distract attention and override the visual design of the shot.

The 'movies' have always emphasized this unique selling point. By staging spectacular action, and by means of story structure, camerawork and editing, the audience is given a roller-coaster ride of non-stop movement. Even news camerawork often gives a priority to movement over a static frame.

Movement

There are many visual design generalizations that can be applied to art, photography, graphics, film and television compositions but with one significant and influential exception; as well as considerations of space, tone, mass, colour and line when creating an image, film and TV compositions also have to accommodate movement. Human perception is invariably attracted by movement. At one stage in human history, survival may have relied on instantly being aware of change in the environment and movement indicates change. It may have tilted the balance between successfully gathering food or being 'gathered' as food by a predator.

In many ways this is an advantage, as movement is a strong attention grabber. Film and TV images can hold the audience's attention simply by movement, but there is a compositional price to pay. A well composed static shot is easily unbalanced by subject or camera movement. Either attention is switched to the element in motion or the frame becomes unbalanced.

Camera and subject movement interact and there are customary ways of dealing with the compositional problems this involves. Through long experience, film and TV practitioners have evolved a number of visual conventions to accommodate and to maximize the value of movement within the frame. These techniques are discussed in Chapter 16, 'Movement'.

Frequently a shot will have to be set up for a constantly changing image pattern. All the following comments about the variety of visual design techniques available should be read with the understanding that movement will always interact and upset the dynamics of a static composition.

There is a further composition distinction between how movement can be dealt with in the separate shot technique of film and video productions and the limitation imposed by multicamera 'real time' television productions. This latter type of programme has to deal with movement as it occurs with no opportunity to smooth out compositional difficulties that occur from shot to shot in the timescale of the action. With thought and subtle editing technique, movement can be rearranged in the 'screen time' of the single shot film/video technique to eliminate distracting movement between shots and still maintain continuity.

In multicamera 'real time' productions, for example, every step and every arm movement will remain through succeeding shots only modified by the director's ability to stage movement of camera and artistes to avoid the most conspicuous disruption. In film, an actor can leave shot and can be cut to immediately in the following shot seven paces away. In multicamera productions every step has to be accommodated in the camera coverage.

In general, movement within the frame usually takes precedence over all other compositional devices in attracting attention.

Sound

Dialogue or other elements of a soundtrack will often control which subject in a frame is dominant, overriding any visual balance/compositional design of a shot. The design of a soundtrack is a large subject, comparable with composition. Sound and pictures complement each other and the influence of sound on how an audience will understand an image must often be taken into consideration when framing up a shot.

It is a well-worn truism that radio drama has the best pictures. Sound so often breaks the boundaries of the literalism of images. With many images there is no added value to the depiction of the subject. Sound is frequently a much more creative medium than image, working on the senses without being obvious. Sound can achieve very strong effects and yet remain quite unnoticeable. The production contribution of sound is usually the most unobtrusive and difficult for the audience to evaluate – until it is badly done. Visual awareness appears to take precedence over audible awareness and yet intelligibility, space and atmosphere are often created by sound. The selection and treatment of audio shapes our perception and can be used to focus our attention just as effectively as the selection of images. It therefore needs as much thought and technique as the equivalent camerawork technique of structuring and framing shots for editing.

A soundtrack foghorn, a church bell or a car driving away off-screen can save a great deal of footage that would otherwise be needed to create the required information or atmosphere. The opposite is the case in actuality coverage where an intrusive out-of-frame sound, for example, of children, animals or traffic, is swamping an interview. An additional shot may be required to inform the audience of the source of the problem in order for it to become partially acceptable. Sound, like movement, will nearly always take precedence over visual design.

Controlling composition

There may be a number of reasons why the composition of a shot needs to be organized. These include:

- a need to direct the audience's attention to one part of the frame in order to emphasize one important element, e.g., one person within a group or one feature of a complex subject;
- a production need to compose a shot that will create atmosphere, mood or a location identity;
- to provide essential or new information.

Primary decisions

To achieve any one of these objectives, the first consideration is to decide the position of the lens in relation to the subject. The choice of lens position will determine:

- *Camera angle*: camera angle describes the camera's position relative to the subject. A three-dimensional subject will display different facets of its design according to the viewpoint of its observer. Moving the camera's position left or right, up or down, will substantially change the appearance of the image.
- *Lens angle*: varying the angle of view of the lens includes or excludes additional information. It can magnify subject size and emphasize the principle subject.
- *Camera distance*: the distance of the lens from the principle subject controls the linear perspective of the shot and this can have a significant influence on composition through the variation in con-

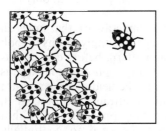

Figure 5.2 Perceptual grouping by size and proximity can emphasize the 'odd one out' that does not fit the pattern. This is a straightforward compositional method of emphasizing the main subject in the frame

verging lines. Often the camera distance and the lens angle are adjusted simultaneously to produce changes to size relationships in shot.

- *Camera height*: changing the height of the camera alters the relationship between foreground and background. A low camera height emphasizes foreground and condenses or eliminates receding horizontal planes. A high camera position allows a 'plan view' and shows position relationships over a wide area. There is also a subjective aspect of lens height that influences how the image is perceived.
- *Camera tilt*: camera tilt is often used in combination with lens height and shifts the horizon (real or unseen) in the frame and adds emphasis to ground or sky.
- *Frame or aspect ratio* (see Chapter 6), *subject in focus* and *depth-of-field* will also have a significant effect on visual design and are discussed later.

Control of composition

Control of composition is achieved by the ability to choose the appropriate camera technique such as viewpoint, focal length of lens, lighting and exposure, in addition to employing a range of visual design elements such as balance, colour contrast, perspective of mass/line, etc.

A well designed composition is one in which the visual elements have either been selectively included or excluded. The visual components of the composition must be organized to engage the viewer's attention. A starting point, as mentioned in Chapter 1, is often to follow the old advice to simplify by elimination, and to reduce to essentials in order to create an image that has strength and clarity.

Emphasizing the most important element

Composition involves drawing attention to the main subject and then making it meaningful, but often a shot can be selected on a visual decision that ignores all but one part of the image. The poor compositional relationship between this area and the total frame may only become apparent after the event has been recorded. One of the more obvious mistakes therefore is not to see the whole picture but only that part which has initially attracted interest.

There is a puzzling piece of advice about camerawork that urges all students to 'Look before you see'. In essence this simply means to look at the overall image, and at its underlying pattern, before concentrating too much on the main subject. Developing a photographic eye is giving attention to all visual elements within the field of view and not simply selecting those elements that initially attract attention. With experience comes the ability to visualize the appearance of a shot wherever the lens is positioned, without the need to continually move the camera in order to look through the viewfinder to see what the shot will look like. Before deciding camera position, lens angle, framing, etc., it is worth considering the following questions:

- What is the purpose of the shot?
- Is the shot fact or feeling? Will the image attempt to be factual and objective and allow the viewer to draw their own conclusions or is

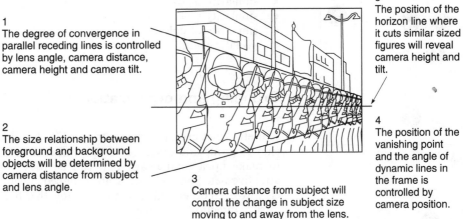

1
The degree of convergence in
parallel receding lines is controlled
by lens angle, camera distance,
camera height and camera tilt.

5
The position of the
horizon line where
it cuts similar sized
figures will reveal
camera height and
tilt.

2
The size relationship between
foreground and background
objects will be determined by
camera distance from subject
and lens angle.

4
The position of the
vanishing point
and the angle of
dynamic lines in
the frame is
controlled by
camera position.

3
Camera distance from subject will
control the change in subject size
moving to and away from the lens.

Figure 5.3

it the intention to persuade or create an atmosphere by careful selection?
- In what context will the shot be seen? What precedes – what follows?
- What will be the most important visual element in the shot?

The best viewpoint is the lens position in space that emphasizes the main subject. Make certain that the eye is attracted to the part of the frame that is significant and avoid conflict with other elements in the frame.

Check:

- that the purpose of the shot is understood;
- that the main subject is identified;
- that the camera parameters (lens position, angle, height, etc.) emphasize the principal interest;
- that any leading lines point to the main subject;
- that any supporting visual interest within the frame maximizes its support for the main subject and use framing and lens position to eliminate or subdue competing areas of interest;
- that the dominant interest is offset and balance this with less important elements;
- that attention is kept within the picture space and avoid placing principal information in the corner of the frame;
- if the image can be simplified by reducing to essentials.

Design techniques

In addition to the choice of the lens position, there are a number of visual design techniques that can be applied to a subject or subjects that will allow the cameraman to control the attention of the viewer. Showing the audience where to look is a significant part of framing a shot. This can be achieved by:

- grouping and organization
- similarity by proximity

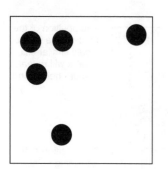

(a)

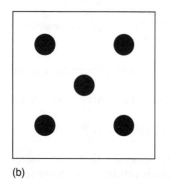

(b)

Figure 5.4 Wherever it is practical, it is better to arrange the subjects in a shot so that they are linked by grouping and organization. The scattered five dots on the side of a dice are instantly seen as '5' if they are arranged in a pattern. The pattern need not be as geometrically rigid as **(b)** but loosely form part of a shape that the eye can easily perceive

Figure 5.5 From *Language of Vision*, Gyorgy Kepes (1961)

- similarity of size
- similarity by closure
- similarity of colour
- visual weight.

Grouping and organization

A useful characteristic when setting up a shot is the perceptual tendency to group and organize items together to form a cluster of shapes to make up a total image that can be fully comprehended in one attentive act. Some elements are grouped together because they are close to each other. Others are bound together because they are similar in size, direction or shape.

'Seeing' is not simply a mechanical recording by the eye. Understanding the nature of an image is initially accomplished by the perceptual grouping of significant structural patterns. One of the aims of good composition is to find and emphasize structural patterns that the mind/eye can easily grasp.

One theory that attempts to explain the brain/eye's tendency to group and simplify, is that the images formed by the lenses of the eyes are picked up point by point by millions of small receptor organs that are largely isolated from each other. Rudolph Arnheim in *Art and Visual Perception* (1967) suggests that the brain, at the receiving end of a mosaic of millions of individual messages, pieces them together by the rules of similarity and simplicity. Similar size, direction of movement or shape are instantly grouped together and a complex image can then be understood by a few clusters of shapes.

Composition must therefore aim to create a unifying relationship between the visual elements of an image in order to feed the perceptual system with patterns that can be easily assimilated by the observer.

Similarity by proximity

Grouping objects together because they are near to each other in the frame is the simplest method of visual organization. One of mankind's oldest examples of perceptual grouping is probably the patterns imposed on isolated and unconnected stars to form the signs of the zodiac (see Figure 5.4). Grouping a foreground and a background object by proximity can achieve a coherent design in a composition.

'sp ati l org anisati on isthe vit alfacto rin a nopticalm essage'

'spatial organisation is the vital factor in an optical message'

Proximity of objects in the frame can also create relationships that are unwanted (e.g., the example of objects behind people's heads that appear on the screen as 'head wear').

Similarity of size

Same size objects in a frame will be grouped together to form one shape or pattern. The most common example of this principle is the grouping and staging of crowd scenes.

This grouping by size and proximity can be used in a reverse way to emphasize one person in a crowd scene by isolating the individual so that they cannot be visually grouped with the crowd (Figure 5.2).

Because of the assumed similarity of size between individual people, staging people in the foreground and in the background of a shot allows visual unity in the perception of similar shapes and also an effective impression of depth indicated by the diminished image size of the background figure.

Similarity by closure

Searching for coherent shapes in a complex image, human perception will look for and, if necessary, create simple shapes. The more consistent the shape of a group of visual elements the more easily it can be detached from a confusing background. Straight lines will be continued by visual projection (see Figure 3.4), curved lines that almost form a circle will be mentally completed.

A popular use of this principle is the high angle shot looking down on a seething crowd moving in one direction whilst the principal figure makes a desperate journey through the crowd in the opposite direction. We are able to keep our attention on the figure because of the opposing movements and also because we mentally project their straight-line movement through the crowd. The principal figure would soon be absorbed within the crowd if they frequently changed direction.

Similarity of colour

Objects grouped by colour is another effective method of compositional organization. Uniforms and a team's sportswear are linked together even if they are scattered across the frame. Identically coloured dance costumes for the chorus in musicals are used to structure movement and to emphasize the principals dressed in a contrasting colour scheme. But the opposite can also be effective. In a dance sequence in 'Top Hat' (1935), Fred Astaire in white tie and tails is backed by a chorus of identically costumed male dancers. Their unity as a group is held together by proximity, size and lighting. His separation and emphasis is achieved by being in the foreground and therefore a more dominant figure and by choreography which emphasizes the principal dancer.

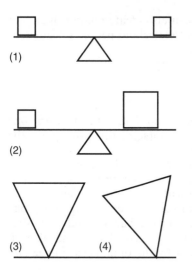

Figure 5.6 (I) Symmetrical balance; **(2)** balance by mass; **(3)** stable figure; **(4)** unstable figure

Balance

Because of the effect of perceptual 'reorganization', no visual element can exist in isolation within the frame. Within the act of perception, the eye/mind groups and forms relationships of the shapes it has organized (see Figure 3.4).

One relationship is balance: the relative visual weight of one clump of visual elements compared with another and their individual relationships to the whole.

A technological definition of balance is the state of a body in which the forces that act upon it compensate each other. Camera operators will know that when they mount a large lens on the camera there is the need to pull the body of the camera back on the pan/tilt head until the point of balance has been achieved – the seesaw principle where a small child at the extreme end can be balanced by an adult sitting opposite but much closer to the pivot point. There is also another aspect of balance connected with a combined group of objects such as lens, matte box, camera, pan bar, viewfinder, etc., which is connected to their overall centre of gravity and the physical position of that point of balance. This is the centre of balance of the combined mass.

Balance in a composition is distributing the visual elements across the frame so that a state of equilibrium is achieved for the whole. Equilibrium need not mean at rest for, as in the seesaw analogy, balance can still allow movement and therefore visual interest.

As with a camera mass, a visual pattern has a centre around which the visual elements are grouped. The pivot point need not be and frequently is not the centre of the frame. Balance can be achieved by visual weight determined by size, shape (a regular shape is heavier than an irregular shape), colour, light/dark relationships, isolation of a pictorial element, direction and the intrinsic interest of content. For example, the observer's wishes and fears induced by the image may outweigh any perceptual considerations of balance. For many people, a snake moving in any part of the frame will capture their attention irrespective of any other compositional design. Pictorial balance is often achieved with this type of psychological weight.

The content or objective of the image will determine which type of visual weight will be chosen to be pictorially reorganized when composing and staging the shot. Balance helps to emphasize the most important visual element.

Only the content can determine which pattern can be created by balancing out colour, mass, direction, etc., and which aspect of visual design is to be chosen and subjected to the business of pictorial organization. The function of visual design can be shown only by pointing out the meaning it helps to make visible.

The resolution of balance

Figure 5.7 A square-on two shot with equal emphasis, but one person can dominate by dialogue, positioning, lighting, etc. ('Breathless', 1959, dir. Jean-Luc Goddard)

The two factors that determine balance are visual weight and the direction of movement of the visual pattern. Visual weight is conditioned by its position in the frame. A visual element at the centre or close to the central vertical axis has less weight than one at the edge of the composition. An object higher in the frame is heavier than the

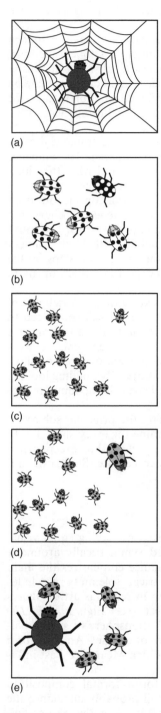

Figure 5.8 Five ways of concentrating attention on the main subject: **(a)** convergence of background lines; **(b)** contrast of tone; **(c)** contrast of position; **(d)** contrast of size; **(e)** contrast of form

same size object in the lower part of the frame. An object in the right of the frame (for most Western observers) will have less compositional weight than if it was positioned in the left of the frame.

Similar to the seesaw principle (see Figure 5.6 (1)), visual weight increases proportionally the further it is from its point of balance. A small significant object in the background will balance out a larger object in foreground.

The resolution of balance in a composition therefore requires small to be weighted against large with reference to the centre and outside edges of the frame in order to achieve unity of the total image. A small 'weight' in the composition can be placed a long way from the centre if a balancing large weight is placed close to the centre (Figure 5.6 (2)).

'Weight' need not only be differences in the physical size of balancing visual elements. Balance can be resolved with line, mass, light/dark, colour, etc.

Balance and ambiguity

Balance is a means of eliminating ambiguity and visual confusion. Without visual organization the message becomes confused, as the observer is stuck with a visual hypothesis with insufficient information to form a conclusion.

But a visual intention to confuse, discomfort or even disorientate the viewer also has a pedigree in mass entertainment. It is a popular style in television pop programmes where flashing and moving lights, star filters and extreme flare degrade the image to produce an impression of the atmosphere of a club.

Music videos, with a great deal of post-production work, elaborate this style and often aim to tease and invoke visual excitement by a string of unstructured shots, subliminal cuts and multi-images. Exploiting changes in technology, many youth programmes use continuously moving hand-held cameras overlaid with moving graphics in an attempt to emulate the rave experience of a 'drug'-induced buzz of disorientating images. As very little information can be assimilated with such a confusion of images, the style becomes the content that is being communicated.

Dynamic balance

Finding a dynamic balance requires not only positioning small with large or light with dark, etc., but also finding linking patterns to the main balancing duality.

Our experience of the physical properties of objects provides us with the knowledge that an object that is very large at the top and tapers to a very small base is likely to be unstable and easily toppled. The equivalent visual weight is attached to a large object at the top of the frame and a smaller object at the base. The composition appears to be unstable and transient (see Figure 5.6 (4)).

A dynamic balance that provides plenty of audience interest or visual excitement can be created either by the use of converging lines (see Chapter 4) or the competing contrasts between different masses, light/dark relationships, colour or the use of a wide-angle lens working close to the main subject in movement. A wide angle on a camera

moving between equal-sized objects (e.g., trees, buildings, etc.) produces images with rapid changes in size.

Balance can be disrupted by a visual element that makes a sudden
appearance in the frame. If the audience anticipates that something,
for example, maybe behind the door, the delay in satisfying this suspicion will heighten the suspense. The audience is invited to speculate on
where the 'ambush' will come from. The usual convention is to let the
audience down quietly, assuaging their fears before hitting them with a
surprise element from a totally new direction.

The invisible narrative element that is outside the frame can carry
strong visual weight when composing for the unseen. The audience
connects the dots between what they are shown and what they imagine. Leaving a blank part of the frame invites the audience to anticipate something will fill that pregnant space just as a conspicuous door
in the background of a shot will condition the audience to believe that
it will soon be opened. Other 'unseen' elements can be used to motivate a pan. In David Lean's 'Ryan's Daughter' (1969), the camera
pans across a schoolroom wall following the unseen footsteps on the
other side of the wall until the shot reaches a door which opens to
reveal the invisible 'walker'.

Strong visual film/TV images are often used sparingly. A rich diet of
dynamic images that zap the eyeball every second will soon need to
accelerate to greater and greater extremes to hold the attention of a
visually exhausted audience. Greater impact is often achieved by a
single high-impact shot placed amongst a conventional set of shots
(e.g., the high shot from the top of the New York UN building looking
down on the film's central character as he leaves the building in 'The
Man Who Knew Too Much' (1956).

Avoid the visual monotony of positioning the principal subject of
the composition in the same part of the frame for every shot. Try to
achieve variation and variety in composing each shot except when
intercutting on dialogue between two people (see Standard shot
sizes, Chapter 12).

Formal balance

Formal balance in a composition is achieved by having equal visual
weight on either side of the frame placed symmetrically around a
central main subject. Although formal balance emphasizes the main
central subject's importance, its symmetrical solemnity precludes
visual excitement. Many examples are seen in religious art of figures
grouped either side of the main subject (see Figure 13.1 *The
Martyrdom of San Sebastian*). The overall atmosphere of such a balance is to suggest peace, harmony or a lack of conflict. Another form
of classical balance is by the use of the Golden Mean (see Past influences, Chapter 10).

The type of artiste staging required for a formal composition
requires static grouping. Any movement will probably unbalance the
formality and disturb the emphasis on serenity. It is the type of balance used in religious themes or a critical moment of someone on their
death bed with relations or friends placed either side of a square-on
shot from the foot of the bed.

To hold visual attention, it is necessary to provide greater visual
complexity. A formal central grouping of figures balanced around the

centre of the frame, although assimilated, instantly fails to provoke further curiosity. Once the eye has swept around the central shape it has visually 'consumed' all that has been provided. To entice the eye to take a second tour, less obvious visual relationships need to be discovered. The eye and mind must be fed with visual variations embedded within the basic dominant pattern, although it must always be remembered that the eye takes the visual path of least resistance. Unravelling a very complex set of visual variations may mean a 'switch off' for the majority until easier shots come along. But visual variety provides the stimulation necessary for holding the attention.

The formality of such compositions are almost like a freeze frame and their necessary static quality has a limited screen time before the need for movement to reinvigorate the audience attention becomes essential.

The square-on two shot of Figure 5.7, staged to give equal weighting to the two artistes, would provide audience interest if the dialogue switched between the two presenters. Sound, as we have mentioned, attracts attention and this breaks up the static quality of the formal staging.

Dissonance

Whereas a balanced composition aims to promote a sense of equilibrium or stability, dissonance in a compositional grouping induces a feeling of discord or of resolution still to be realized.

Effective dissonance in music is not created (except by accident) by a non-musician aimlessly pressing groups of notes on a piano. It is based on the application of the theory of harmony. Dissonance in visual composition requires the same understanding of technique in order to achieve controlled disharmony.

For many centuries, the aim of composition in Western painting was to weld all the elements of the painting into a pictorial unity to achieve balance. The concept of dissonance – compositional elements deliberately offset in order to create visual tension – only entered compositional technique to any extent in the nineteenth century.

With the advent of 'snapshot' photography in the 1860s when exposures of 1/50 second were possible, many artists were influenced by the random photographic compositions of people in motion. Degas was one of the first artists to use decentralized compositions with the main subject offset to the edge of the frame (see Figure 10.3, the Degas reproduction in Chapter 10, 'Past influences').

A new pictorial convention emerged of cutting off part of an object by the frame to imply that the action continued outside the frame. If the observer is led out of the picture frame, there is set up an expectation or curiosity in the viewer that is not satisfied by the framed image. The composition is unresolved (see 'A hard cut-off', Chapter 6).

Dissonant compositions are therefore deliberately structured to evoke a sense of incompleteness. Just as there is a strong wish to straighten a picture hung crookedly on a wall, a well-structured dissonant shot will evoke the same feeling of a composition seeking to achieve balance. The friction and conflict that is set up can convey a strong sense of unresolved tension as well as creating interest and involvement.

Figure 5.9 Dissonance in a compositional grouping induces a feeling of discord. The offset framing and the eye line out of frame unbalances the shot and sets up a sense of visual disquiet

Dissonant arrangement of subject matter creates a dynamic tension. But increasing the degree of unbalance to an extreme might collapse into visual anarchy and produce a composition of random items that have no relationship.

Dissonance is as necessary to good composition as balance. Offsetting balance creates interest. Achieving balance can satisfy the urge for symmetry but quickly becomes uninteresting. If balance is a full stomach, then dissonance is an appetite that needs to be satisfied.

A modern reason for using visual dissonance is the wish to suggest that an unbalanced composition reflects the disorganized unsettled contemporary world – the fragmented uncertainty of existence. This embraces the view that there is no certainty – no consensus on a single viewpoint. All values are relative.

Divided interest

A composition with divided interest, where the eye flicks back and forth between two equal subjects, is a composition that will cause the audience a problem of deciding what they should be looking at. One subject must be made subservient to the other by placement, size, focus, colour or contrast (see Figure 5.1).

Mirror reverse/stage left

It has often been demonstrated with Western art that images are habitually scanned from left to right – the normal reading process. Theatre staging often takes account of this fact in the knowledge that the audience will automatically look to the left, the 'strong' side of the stage, as the curtain rises. Another consequence of a 'left/right' bias is that many formal balanced compositions can be destroyed if mirror reversed.

The normal scanning of an image from left to right appears to give less weight to an object on the left than if it is placed on the right of the frame. A theatrical convention of the 'strong' left side and 'weak' right side is that traditionally the Fairy Queen enters stage left whilst the Demon King enters prompt (right) side.

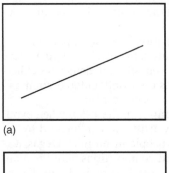

(a)

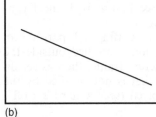

(b)

Figure 5.10 Because of the Western tradition of scanning text from left to right, the movement of the line in **(a)** appears to be travelling uphill whereas the movement of the line in **(b)** appears to be going downhill

Figure and ground

The relationship between 'figure' and 'ground' is fundamental to an understanding of perception and composition. Figure describes the shape that is immediately observable whilst ground defines that shape by giving it a context in which to exist. Figure is the prime visual element that is being communicated but can only be transmitted in a relationship with a ground (Figure 5.11(a) and (b)).

This may sound a rather academic analysis when setting up a shot but many heated arguments about production budgets often revolve around the cost of shooting at special locations in order to stage action against an appropriate background. Film financiers consider the foreground artistes to be where the money is – the background is dressing or atmosphere. The small piece of 'scenery' seen over the shoulder of a medium close-up (MCU) requires the expense of a large unit on location, but apart from all the other visual value of an appropriate loca-

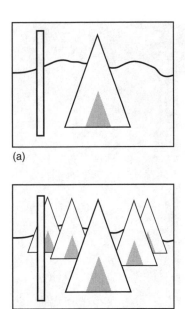

(a)

(b)

Figure 5.11 Figure describes the shape that is immediately observable whilst ground defines that shape by giving it a context in which to exist. A ground can be visually simple or complex but still remain subservient to the figure

Figure 5.12 With some subjects, there is indecision as to what is figure and what is ground. Figure/ground flip is when different visual elements reverse their role. The vase shape disappears when two profiles are recognized

tion, backgrounds are essential to tell the story. It is surprising how many documentaries/factual programmes stage a piece to camera against a bland featureless background and throw away the atmosphere of the location.

In composing a shot there needs to be an integration of subject (figure) and background (ground). There needs to be control between foreground and background so that the background does not dominate the main subject in frame.

Figure need not be physically closer to the lens than ground, although that part of the image that is seen as figure is often perceived as being closer to the viewer regardless of its position in the frame. Figure is usually smaller in area than ground and figure/ground cannot be seen simultaneously. They are viewed sequentially. Figure is seen as having form, contour or shape whilst ground is seen as having none of these characteristics.

Any visual element in the frame that stands out and achieves prominence will be considered by the observer as figure even if this object has been assessed of no visual importance by the cameraman. Hence the infamous background object that sits neatly on a subject's head, totally ignored by the snapshotter whose concentration is wholly centred on what he considers is the only 'figure' in frame. When two or more objects are grouped together they are perceived as one 'figure' even though the cameraman may have mentally marked out one of them as 'background'.

Figure/ground flip

A characteristic of ground is that it visually recedes and its detail is not noticed. There may be a number of figures in a frame and the visual elements that make up figure and ground can change their role as attention moves from one subject to another (Figure 5.12). This is termed figure/ground flip.

Figure/ground flip occurs when shape, tone or contour of ground becomes more dominant or is perceived as more dominant in the image. This can happen with a frame-within-a-frame shot, such as an entrance in a wall. The entrance and the visual detail it frames function as the figure with the wall as a featureless ground. If the observer's attention is allowed to switch to the wall, which is now perceived to have texture and contrast, this becomes the figure with the entrance becoming ground. The shot will quickly lose impact as the two 'figures' fight for attention (Figure 5.1(a)).

Control

Controlling the figure/ground relationship requires emphasizing the importance of the selected figure by light, brightness, colour, differential focus, texture, position, etc., whilst removing sufficient visual detail from the ground to avoid it competing with the figure (Figure 5.13).

The cameraman's craft is directed towards controlling the viewer's attention on figure whilst remembering that ground is equally important as it defines foreground. They are separate yet they work together.

The use of a very narrow-angle lens can blur the distinction between figure and ground. As the focal length of the lens increases, with the camera further from the subject, size relationships between objects at

Figure 5.13 The window and the visual detail it frames functions as the figure with the interior wall as a featureless ground. If the observer's attention is allowed to switch to the interior, this is now perceived to be the figure with the window becoming the ground

different distances from the lens are not so marked as in 'normal' eye perspective and all visual elements in the frame may achieve equal importance. The accompanying narrower zone of focus of objects at a great distance from the lens helps to discriminate between the intended figure and its out-of-focus ground.

Camouflage deliberately intends to deceive the observer in deciding what is figure and what is ground. Living creatures confuse their adversaries by attempting to 'break up' their overall shape and form by a fragmented, unsymmetrical pattern similar to their background habitat. Poor visualization by a cameraman of what is figure and what is ground in an image can achieve the same confusion.

It is easy to overestimate the psychological or narrative importance of one element when setting up a shot and underestimate its actual visual dominance within the frame. It may well have strong narrative importance but does it look visually significant? Many snapshots fail because the attention, when the photograph was taken, was wholly concentrated on one element of the field of view usually because it had strong personal significance. Even though it fails to hold the attention of a wider audience, the print may still have a strong subjective interest to one or two individuals because they will continue to ignore all but the main subject in the frame when looking at the image.

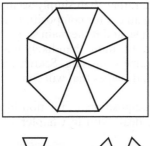

Figure 5.14 Although there are two Maltese crosses displayed, the cross whose main axes corresponds to the vertical and horizontal edges of the frame is usually selected as the figure with the other cross becoming the ground. The frame edge reference is very influential in determining the subject priority

Shape

One of the basic Gestalt theories of perception is that we tend to simplify visual patterns as much as the image will allow in order to grasp the significance of the image. The shape or outside boundary of an object is perceived as one dimensional, even though our knowledge and experience of the world demonstrates that the majority of objects exist in three dimensions.

This outside boundary, the shape of an object, plays a significant part in visual composition because of the ease and speed of grasping its simple pattern and relationships. If shapes become too abstract and ambiguous, however, then, as the wide variety of responses to the same Rorschach ink blob test demonstrates, individual states of mind and memory will control interpretation.

Simplicity and economy have always been valued in visual communication in the search to reduce to essentials in order to clearly communicate. Shape is a simple, visually easily 'digestible' element in a composition and, when setting up a shot, a few similar shapes should be looked for that can be grouped to reinforce the overall impact of the image. The space between forms also create shapes and can play a part in the design of a shot. It is said that Mozart was not so interested in the notes as the spaces in between. But whereas a painter has complete flexibility on where to position shapes and forms on a two-dimensional surface for maximum design potential, the director and cameraman have to deal with a three-dimensional world of solid objects that are usually not amenable to rapid resizing or relocation.

Grouping visual elements by overall shape

Similar shape is an effective way of unifying an image in order to make it easily comprehensible. The three basic regular shapes of oval, triangle and circle can be used in a variety of ways, such as in the grouping of people or objects. A shot can be strengthened if the visual elements are structured so that the eye follows one of the basic shapes around the frame.

Triangle and oval forms are the most flexible and accommodating in enclosing shapes and many cameramen, when they run their eye around a potential shot, are seeking this kind of relational shape to bind the composition together. A triangle composition is a closed form from which the eye cannot escape.

The overall shape of a composition also indicates mood or character. The triangle with a broad base is considered to have strength and stability. A popular, if unconscious, reflection of this is the shot of the newsreader who sits with elbows on the news desk making a 'trustworthy' triangle.

The triangle is a very flexible shape as a design element in a composition. The cameraman can control the shape and impact of a triangle by choice of lens-angle, camera distance and height. The line convergence forming the boundary of a triangle within a composition can be altered and arranged to provide the precise control of the compositional elements. The inverted triangle is weaker but can be useful.

The ability to analyse shapes in an image rather than simply seeing the content is an essential step in developing an eye for composition. If there appears to be a lack of unity in the image, and if the main subject appears to be fighting the background, then it is more than likely that an overall leading shape line around the frame is missing. Search for background shapes or re-light for background shapes that will connect and relate to foreground.

Light/dark relationships and the compositional relationship between a bright spot and its location are dealt with in Chapter 13, 'Lighting and composition'.

Line

As well as the physical lines within a shot that channel eye movement, there can also be invisible lines (e.g., eye line), that directs visual attention. The movement of the observer's eyes may create curved lines in its journey around the shot. Avoid lines that divide the frame into equal parts (split screen) and dominant lines at the edge of frame that may alter the aspect ratio and appear as if the image is cropped. Some lines lie flat on the surface of the image whilst other lines recede into the distance and add depth to the shot.

Line is a powerful picture-making design component and can be used to structure the attention of the observer. Within the frame, any visual elements that can be perceptually grouped into lines can be used to direct the eye around the image from one part of the picture to another to end, preferably, on the main subject of interest. Attention is attracted to where two lines cross or one line abruptly changes direction. The eye is attracted to the point of convergence of the lines or the implied point of crossing. In practice, a line need not be visible to act as a strong compositional element but it can be implied, such as the line of a person's gaze.

The vertical line

An isolated vertical subject such as a tree or a tower has directness and rigidity. It is immediately seen and takes visual precedence over any horizontal or other lines in the frame. The human figure in a landscape immediately attracts attention, not only because of its psychological importance but also because of this vertical aspect. It has been suggested that an image consisting of strong vertical elements can convey dignity, solemnity and serenity.

The strength of a vertical visual element in a composition means that some kind of design elements have to be introduced to establish image unity. Usually a vertical line requires a horizontal element to cross it at some point in order to achieve a satisfactory composition. If a vertical line simply divides the frame, two disconnected images will be created – a split screen. The most common use of the vertical line is to link two competing areas of the picture to achieve unity. This could be a carefully positioned tree to connect landscape with sky or a strong vertical line in a piece of furniture or architecture to link the lower half of the frame with the top. This vertical element should have its greater proportion in what is being established as the dominant area or subject of the picture.

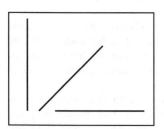

Figure 5.15 An upright line appears balanced, a diagonal line implies movement and a horizontal line is at rest

The leaning line

Diagonal arrangements of lines in a composition produce a greater impression of vitality than either vertical or horizontal lines. A line is most active when it runs from corner to corner. A tree before it is felled is a line that is vertical and stable. From the moment it is cut down it begins its journey to becoming a horizontal line and static. Its most potent and active angle as a line is at 45° where its rush to 'rest' is most keenly anticipated. A line at an angle is perceptually seen as a line that is in motion unless it is so marginally off vertical it could be simply the result of camera set-up. Compositions with a strong diagonal element imply movement or vitality.

Convergence of lines

As we have seen, the distance from lens to subject, lens angle and camera height are a decisive influence on the convergence of lines within a frame. Lines of convergence can be placed to have as their focus the dominant subject in the frame. Strong pictorial lines can be controlled by lens position to lead to and emphasize the main subject (see Figure 5.22).

Line of beauty

The eighteenth-century artist, William Hogarth, identified seven different curved lines and picked out one of these as the most perfect 'line of beauty'. It is similar in shape to the line of a woman's back and has been dubbed the 'S' curve. It occurs frequently in Michelangelo's paintings and is seen in natural form in such things as wind-swept arable crops and the upward swirl of flames (Figure 5.16).

Curves

One of the useful compositional uses of curved lines in an image is to guide the eye to the main point of interest. A straight line takes the eye immediately from point A to point B. A curve can move the eye around the frame in a less direct movement and knit disparate elements together on the way. A curve has the advantage of being a progressive change of direction that allows a softer visual movement around an image, compared with the zigzag pinball movement of straight lines (see Figure 5.18). Also, unlike straight lines, curves do not interact with the edge of frame either in direction or by comparison.

Rivers, roads, the line of a hill or hedge, banister rails, etc., can all be used to rhythmically knit a composition together. Where curves can be duplicated and repeated in different sizes, then not only will a great deal of visual interest be set up, but the spaces between objects enclosed by the boundary lines of the curved shapes have a greater visual interest. The 'ground' to the image will have greater vitality even though it will still act as an anchor to the overall design.

The strength of a composition created by curves can be increased by an all-over pattern across the frame and by the strong contrast of light and shade. Shadows of foliage, decorative wrought iron railings, grilles and blinds, etc., will provide pattern. Even straight-line shadows, such

Line of beauty

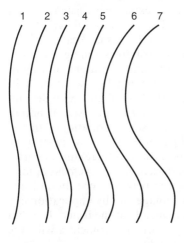

Figure 5.16 Line number 4 was considered by Hogarth to have the most attractive shape

Figure 5.17 Lines of convergence can be placed to have as their focus the dominant subject in the frame. Strong pictorial lines can be controlled by lens position to lead to and emphasize the main subject

as sunlight through Venetian blinds falling on a curved surface, can provide another source of controlled pattern and curve in the frame. Curves can also be implied by repetition of the same type of object and this effect can be emphasized by the use of a long focal length lens.

A curved lead-in line to the main subject of interest has always been one of the most common techniques to get the observer into the frame and then out again. There is often an inclination to try to avoid such a clichéd technique but the perceptual experience is that it is effective, that it holds and guides the attention of the viewer and that alternative 'lead-in' devices can just as quickly become visually devalued and stale.

Using foreground curved shapes to mask off part of the picture to produce a frame within a frame is often employed to break up a series of rectangle compositions. As previously mentioned, the classic tight over-the-shoulder blanking off the side of the frame by a silhouette head and part of the shoulder is a simple way of achieving a new frame outline.

Rhythm and visual beat

Figure 5.18 The curved lines of car headlamps on a city street at night lead the eye into the picture

Rhythm and pattern describe two aspects of a linked series of visual elements. Pattern can be defined as a design or figure repeated across the frame, such as bricks in a wall viewed from a square-on position. A wallpaper design may have an indefinite repetition of a few shapes.

Rhythm, whilst occurring in pattern, can also be present without repetition. Visual rhythm can occur in the relationship between a series of shapes or lines such as a crabbing shot that has foreground objects wiping across the frame. These may be equally spaced such as columns (pattern) or irregularly spaced but still forming a relationship.

Musical rhythm developing over time would appear to be quite different from the experience of perception where it is often assumed that an understanding of an image is grasped instantaneously. But the mind/eye moving over a series of visual accents in an image can respond in a similar way as the mind/ear experiences listening to a series of rhythmic accents. If a connected series of visual accents are present in the image, then it can be said that a visual beat has been established. Sunlight modulated by a row of trees falling on a car travelling along a road will produce a rhythm of pattern and light. The repetitive pitch of a boat will create a regular sweep of light through a porthole onto a cabin wall. Both of these examples are created by movement but static pattern and rhythm exist in nature (the structure of petals in a flower, desert sand formations) and in man-made objects (bridge girders, field patterns, motorway junctions).

The eye readily follows a line or curve in an image and is correspondingly affected by any repetition of direction or movement of lines or shapes it is led on to. It is the transition between repetition of line and shape that sets up the rhythm of the image and by implication can be extended by the eye/mind to continue outside of the frame. Rhythm needs direction and flow and is strongest when it coincides with the natural eye-scan movement from left to right.

Figure 5.19 A curved lead-in line to the main subject of interest has always been one of the most common techniques to get the observer into the frame

Repetition of camera movement can set up a visual rhythm such as crabbing across a series of foreground objects as mentioned above, or

Figure 5.20 A high-angle shot of office desks and workers provides a 'regimented' pattern across the frame

a series of zooms or tracking shots towards a subject that are identically paced. This is often used in dream or fantasy sequences to create an atmosphere of movement without end. Rhythm can express conflict, serenity or confusion and has a strong impact on the front plane composition.

Pattern

Pattern was defined as a design or figure repeated indefinitely. Visually it is strongest if the repetition can occur across the whole of the frame and if the repetition includes a large number of the repeated shapes.

Static pattern in a composition can be uninteresting in the same way that overemphasis on symmetry becomes flat and stale. A shot of a building that has regular windows patterned across the frame will have little impact because the pattern is the centre of interest and, unless a second element is introduced to act as a dissonance or counterpoint to the pattern (e.g., shadows or camera angle, etc.), the composition may not sustain attention.

Moving patterns, however, can create interest and involvement if compositional control of the image is understood. Repetition or pattern may be present in the normal field of view but the observer may be unaware of it. Placing a frame around a portion of the field of view will isolate and emphasize the repetition.

Creating patterns

For example, a shot of a pavement crowded with shoppers with a camera position looking along the pavement using a 25° horizontal angle of view lens will result in a continuous change of subject moving towards and away from the camera. Patterns of people will be created but it will be difficult for the viewer to focus on any one element. Random movement is difficult to observe and to enjoy. There is no centre of interest and no one object to contrast and compare with another. The pattern of the people is changing too rapidly.

To control pattern, frame a similar shot of the shoppers but this time use a long focal length lens of 5° or under to create a pattern of people who stay longer in frame and therefore allow a pattern relationship to be set up. Creating repetition of equally sized shapes by the use of a long focal length lens creates multiple appearances of similar objects which, because of camera distance, stay longer in frame.

This is because – as we discovered in the discussion on the perspective of mass – the image size relationship of subjects in shot will depend upon the camera distance from the objects. If similar sized subjects such as people are walking towards camera or away from camera at a distance (e.g., 50 m) and are framed using the narrow end of the zoom (e.g., 5° or under) the effect will be of little or no change in subject size coupled with a lack of anticipated movement. Because of the distance of the camera from the subject, there is not the anticipated change in subject size usually experienced when people walk to or away from an observer. Movement without changing size is the equivalent of running on the spot and creates the surreal dream-like quality of flight without escape.

Figure 5.21 Repetition of the same shape plus the curved rows provide a strong visual pattern

Making patterns out of people dehumanizes them because it robs them of personality. It makes crowds into abstract statements. This type of composition is frequently used when a voice-over narration is discussing changes in inflation or shopping habits, etc. It is very difficult to find shots to illustrate abstract concepts such as 'inflation' or 'devaluation', topics that often require news footage.

Shots of cars, rooftops, a portion of a mass production process (e.g., bottles moving on a conveyor belt) can be used to create similar abstract patterns. A repetition of the same shape that either moves across the frame in a regular rhythm (e.g., the bottle) or is held within the frame for a longer period than is normally experienced by the use of a long focal length lens compressing space, can provide attractive decorative images. They are created by camera distance, lens angle and the movement of the subject towards or away from the lens.

Interest

Possibly the strongest design element that can be used in a composition to capture attention is for the content to have a strong emotional or psychological connection with the viewer. Either the subject of the shot has a personal association or it features a familiar human experience.

The personal connection can simply be a photo of a location, someone known to the viewer or a loved person. Millions of snapshots are treasured not for any intrinsic photographic values but because of the innate interest of their subject. This does not prevent a photo having a strong subjective interest and also having qualities that would appeal to a 'disinterested' observer with no involvement with the subject. Home videos of domestic or holiday topics can be shot so that they have a much wider appeal beyond their participants or their friends. The usual weakness of home movies is their inability to separate subjective interest from the considerations of structure and design. The content of the video dominates its form.

The most extreme examples of identification are life-threatening situations created by fictional or factual events. It is often puzzling to lay people that professional photographers in war zones or those covering civil catastrophes can still instinctively frame up and find the right angle of view to make 'decorative' images. They can still pay attention to technique, to the mechanics of recording the image, whilst the content would appear to be so overpowering that any normal-feeling person would wish to intervene or help.

The separation of content, whatever its personal implications, and the technique needed to record it is part of the professional character of anyone who aspires to cover highly emotional factual situations. Many people do not have, or wish to have, the detachment necessary to keep filming when people are in extreme distress or danger. But even in less life-threatening situations, the ability not to be involved in order to stand back and, with professional detachment, consider the visual potential of an event, is essential.

The personal significance of the content of a shot will always be the most powerful design element in attracting attention but by its pre-

Figure 5.22 Although the figure in the distance is small, the eye is irresistibly drawn to it by the converging lines

sentation (compositional design) its appeal can be broadened to involve and engage a much wider audience.

Direction

Within the frame there may be a visual element that produces a strong sense of visual movement. A row of poplar trees or a wall, for example, may produce a line that creates a dominant line of movement – a visual direction that is difficult to ignore.

This strong sense of movement can either be built into the composition and provide a leading line to the main subject or it can be balanced against other movement or mass to tone it down or reduce its impact. As we have seen, diagonal lines are the most active within the frame and, in particular, diagonal converging lines pull the eye like a signpost arrow.

These direction indicators pick up the eye and carry it across or around the frame. There must be a resolution to a vigorous movement of directional lines or the composition will be perceived as lacking an essential element. It is similar to a pan that sets up expectation as it moves to a conclusion, only to disappoint if the end image is uninteresting. A strong directional line that leads nowhere in the frame is a frustrated journey.

Colour

Colour as a design element is such a powerful force that it requires a separate discussion (see Chapter 14).

Scale

A great deal of our understanding of the physical nature of the world around us is achieved by comparison of size. We often achieve recognition of an object by its proportions and its normal size relationship with other objects. A 3-m-high shirt button would require a moment to categorize before we had established a new frame of reference. Whereas it would be instantly recognized as a button if it was at the size we normally see it.

A frame around an image seals off most of its frame of reference and can cause problems in recognition unless it is a very familiar object such as the human face or figure. Most people have been visually tricked by a close shot of a model replica when the camera pulls back to reveal it is as a fraction of the size of the original. Some objects need to be set in context in order to visually communicate clearly without any confusion of their identity.

A composition can achieve an impact by introducing an indication of scale or size comparison. It may be simply contrasting one subject with another – a small child in a large space or an ocean liner being pulled by a small tug. Viewers unfamiliar with the subject depicted may need some indication of size by comparison with a known object.

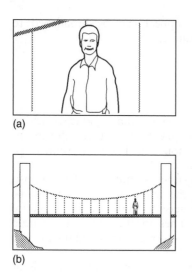

(a)

(b)

Figure 5.23

The human figure is the most easily recognized and most often used in size comparisons. An over-used technique is the familiar zoom out from a presenter (see Figure 5.23(a)) to reveal that he or she is located at the top of an enormous bridge, building or natural feature (see Figure 5.23(b)). This shows scale but requires a great deal of 'dead' visual between the start and the end of the shot, which are the only two images that are being compared.

More attractive compositions can be achieved by using a high angle position looking down, for example, into a valley to see a winding road with a vehicle moving along it or a train puffing through the hills. This type of image appeals to most people's general fascination with model layouts where the spectator can take up a detached position and observe a scene without being part of it.

The proximity of one subject to another allows a frame of reference to be established and associations and comparisons to be made. The same factors are at work over time with adjacent shots allowing a development of new information or continuity in storytelling. Proximity of subject allows judgements of scale and connections. Proximity in time allows continuity and the relationship between visual references which constructs an argument.

Whereas in Figure 5.24(a) the cinema image is viewed in near darkness with no visible object surrounding the screen, the television image is always in proximity with the objects surrounding the TV set (Figure 5.24(b)). The moving image on the screen holds the attention against the surrounding competition of wallpaper, furniture, ornaments and people. The combined two-dimensional designed composition including scale indicators has now to contend, when viewed, with a three-dimensional environment.

Abstraction

(a)

(b)

Figure 5.24

The main theories of the psychology of perception are based on the concept of the perceptual process being an active exploration of form and structure to achieve recognition. Recognition usually involves categorizing and naming the object or process. Perceptual exploration involves assessing the abstract elements of the image such as shape, colour, brightness points, contrast, texture, movement and spatial position.

Recognition by establishing patterns, and grouping by similar shapes, etc., appears to play an important part in the interrogation and exploration of the visual world. Pattern and form can be abstracted from any complex subject and depicted as an image, independent of normal object recognition. An abstract image can therefore be defined as form and colour, independent of subject. It is form without a figurative content and is often created by eliminating or limiting the contrast between figure and ground.

An abstract image can also be achieved by simplification. A shot of undulating sand on the sea shore will have form, texture and contrast but will have an all-over pattern across the frame that binds the composition together.

Reducing or eliminating depth indicators often results in a greater abstract element in a design. Without space or depth in a shot, form

Figure 5.25 The visual appeal of an abstract image often relies on form, texture or colour independent of subject

and design are concentrated in a two-dimensional pattern. This is often seen in shots of reflections and subjects with strong texture.

Although film and television camerawork often aspires to be unequivocally factual and realistic, the images are displayed on a flat screen. This two-dimensional representation often reveals abstract designs in the most mundane subjects. Long focal length lenses or a narrow zone of focus emphasize form and shape; elimination or reduction of depth indicators, interaction between figure and ground, simplification and the over-all repetition of similar shapes all tend towards creating abstract pattern and the basic building blocks of the perceptual process.

Understanding an image

The viewer can only see the image that is selected and presented to them. Of all the thousands of images that could be filmed and recorded on any one subject, the choice of what is presented is whittled down to a few hundred. Those few images are considered to be the most economical way of visually presenting the message to be communicated. It is obviously assumed and hoped that the selected shots will be understood only in terms of the intention of their originators. A verbal instruction of 'Please close the door' would obviously be seen to have been a failed communication if a window was closed instead. How can anyone framing up a shot be certain that the viewer's understanding of the image will be identical to their own?

People's hopes, wishes, fears and personal viewpoint play a major part in their perception. If one person is terrified of spiders, any small scrap of material that is blown across the floor may invoke unreasoned anxiety. The same 'misreading' of visual images occurs especially if they set up associations with opinions strongly held. Our perception or appreciation of an image depends upon our own way of seeing.

One solution to avoid visual misunderstanding or 'misreading' of an image is the use of stereotypes. There is a huge repertoire of stereotype images usually related to the seasons of the year or rites of passage. They are sometimes impossible to resist if a story requires, for example, an indication of Christmas. There are a dozen or more well-used visual clichés that can instantly be used to communicate 'Christmas'. Offsetting the colour balance to get blue exteriors and warm welcoming yellow, interior-lit windows, star filters for Christmas lights, parcels under the tree, instantly establish atmosphere and setting. The problem with such visual clichés is that they are all but drained of their impact. They are simply references to previous well-used images and are therefore instantly recognized and instantly consumed. They lack any visual development or attention-sustaining design.

There are other visual stereotypes such as images of gender, race or religion that may be pressed into service unexamined by the cameraman. Roland Barthes (1973) labels these visual symbols as 'mythic'. Not in the sense of being mythologies, fairy stories or false but having the well-used appearance of being 'natural' or 'common sense'. They are the unexamined prejudgements and assumptions about life nurtured by a specific cultural background that find expression when an image is sought to express an attitude or idea. A newsreel sequence may feature angry or violent people in a street demonstration because the cameraman was briefed to search for shots containing 'action' to illustrate the event. He or she may have ignored thousands of inactive protesters as lacking 'visual' interest.

Shots may express indicators of attitude or feeling that are unconsciously understood by the viewer. A shot behind a row of prison bars looking out will evoke a different response to a shot looking through the bars into a cell. The shot has conditioned or positioned the viewpoint of the viewer to be either as a prisoner or as a visitor to the prison.

Reference by association is common in commercials where images are carefully manufactured to make a connection between a product and a result. For example, a shampoo bottle and glamorous hair are so conjoined in the same shot as to render it impossible not to draw the conclusion that one leads to the other. There is a density of visual themes that imply rather than state overtly their commercial message. The most common visual theme implies that if you are able to buy this product you will be lovable. If you cannot buy it, you will be less lovable.

The viewer, when searching for the best explanation of the available visual information, may add their own interpretation whilst being unaware of the hidden visual message they are absorbing.

Often, a film or television image is not simply a record of an event but becomes an event in itself. The image is then used to symbolize a process or condition. The student standing in front of an approaching tank in Tiananmen Square (Figure 5.26), the street execution of a kneeling enemy prisoner, a young person engulfed in flames running towards the camera, are images that have implications beyond the horrific action portrayed. They continue to be recycled as symbolic images or icons rather than existing as the specific event recorded.

Taking the eye for a walk

Although perceptually we have an awareness of a large field of view, only a small segment can receive our full attention. It is necessary for the eye to continuously make small eye movements called 'saccades' in order to scan an object. It is similar to the eye movement necessary to examine each word of text on a page. The eye scanning around the frame is an important aspect of composition.

In the West, a page of text has a structure to allow the information to be read out in the correct sequence. Starting from the top left of the page to bottom right there is no misunderstanding the path the eye must traverse. There is no similar learnt procedure for scanning an object or image unless a deliberate perceptual route is built-in that channels the eye movement along a preplanned path.

In order to take the eye for a 'walk' around an image there needs to be a start-point and an end-point positioned within the composition. In a shot with deep perspective indicators, a common solution is by way of a series of zigzags using a path, stream, wall, etc., which is connected to the base of the frame. This should steer the eye's attention to the principal subject and then connect up with another visual element to return the eye to the start-point. Getting into the picture requires creating one spot that immediately attracts the eye and then lead it on towards the principal subject. The 'way in' to the composi-

tion must not be too visually dominant or it will act as a competing interest to the main subject.

Emphasizing the main subject involves control of the eye movement across the frame. The eye travels the line of least resistance and in its movement around the frame it is similar to a pin-ball bouncing off different obstacles before being forced by the designer of the composition to end up at the main subject of interest. An interesting composition allows the eye movement moments of repose and this stop/start journey creates visual rhythm. The strongest rhythms occur in patterns. Organization of the image requires the eye to be shown new unsuspected spatial relationships between similar shapes, similar tone, texture or colour.

The positioning of small and large objects, light and shadow edges, colour connections, etc., can all act as visual guides around the image. The essential requirements are that they should lead up to and emphasize the position of the main subject before being led away for the start of a new journey. A well designed composition will provide new visual interests for the second and possibly third circuits. If the main visual route into and out of the composition is the 'melody' of the piece, the secondary design elements can provide variation on top of the main theme.

Strong horizontal lines form a barrier across the frame and require a visual method to 'jump' across to avoid bisecting the frame into sections. A tree or similar upright will allow the eye to move over this division of the image.

The visual exit from the composition need not be positioned at the same point as the start but can be a bright spot, for example, leading to infinity in the distance. What should be guarded against is an exit that leaves the majority of the frame unexplored. The designer of a maze intends the traveller to make a few circuits before discovering the centre and then they are allowed to search for the exit. A well designed image has one entrance for the eye, one principal subject and then several routes to the exit. This can be accomplished with the main elements forming a pyramid, for a strong unified composition, or a circle, which has the virtue, as the classical symbol of unity, of unifying and simplifying the composition. It keeps the eye within the frame. For a more dynamic composition, an irregular shape allows for eye movement that is diverse and asymmetric. Avoid placing the brightest part of the image at the edge of frame.

The other distraction to a well-organized visual tour is allowing the eye to get too close to the edge of the frame and then be led out by speculating on what is beyond the frame (see closed frame above).

Reading left to right

Control of eye movement on a page of text is by way of left-to-right scanning and by structuring the text in lines and paragraphs. The habit of reading left to right is culturally so strong that it is claimed Western readers use the same left-to-right scan when looking at paintings, cinema and theatre. This may be a consideration when staging positions in a set up.

Also important is the eye scan between shots. For example, the circuit rail of a racecourse should be roughly the same position in frame when intercutting on a race. In a western shootout, intercutting on two opposing gunfighters requires the gun barrels to be positioned at the same height in each shot. Like an eye line out of frame, they are pointing at each other.

An audience may anticipate the expected position of interest in an incoming shot but this anticipation can be betrayed for dramatic effect or as a change of direction in the narrative.

Frame and subject size

Filling the frame with the principal subject appears, at first sight, to be an efficient way of eliminating irrelevant detail. A close shot concentrates the attention and avoids the complications of integrating other visual elements into a cohesive composition. The closer you get to the main subject, the easier it is for the viewer to understand the priorities of the shot and the quicker it is for the cameraman to find the optimum framing. The close shot is efficient in communication and often, because it only requires a small area to be designed and lit, economic in production.

There have been many successful productions that stay close almost all the time. A series of close shots builds up tension and intensity, not only because of the claustrophobic impact of the tight images but also because of the absence of any visual information to assist the viewer in locating the action. Mystery and tension are enhanced if the audience is 'lost' and has no frame of reference for the events they are watching. The production style of one television series often involved starting tight on a new scene so that there was suspense and complexity for the audience in deciding where they were and what was happening. Sometimes the audience were released from their confusion by an 'explanation' shot well into the scene, but often there was no visual description of the setting, how many people were involved and their physical relationship to each other.

The composition of a close shot need not be devoid of location information. Because of the magnification of detail, a close shot may be quicker at establishing atmosphere and locality than a more general or vague wide shot. A generalization would be that a close shot intensifies the attention to detail – the viewer cannot easily overlook the visual information that is being presented. A wider shot may be used to show relationships, create atmosphere or express feeling but requires tighter design control of the composition to achieve these objectives. A wider area of view may have more visual elements, lighting, contrast, colour, etc., to integrate for visual unity, whereas a closer shot can be effective with very simple framing.

Fill the frame if possible with interest and avoid large plain areas that are there simply because of the aspect ratio of the screen. If necessary, mask off part of the frame with a feature in the shot to give a more interesting composition and to emphasize the most important element in the frame.

Attracting or switching the centre of interest

Because film/TV is often concerned with movement, compositions have to accommodate changes in the position of the principal subject in the frame. Action can be staged to change who is the principal subject. Switching the viewer's attention to a new principal subject can be achieved by a number of methods. These include the position of subject in the frame, where the significant player is staged in the dominant position. Within a group he/she must be separated from the 'crowd'. One method of separation from a background crowd can be achieved by a low camera height increasing the height of the foreground actor.

Actor movement can control which is the principal subject of the composition. For example, there is a scene in John Ford's 'Stagecoach' (1939), of a number of people in a room. The stagecoach driver is standing and is the dominant subject by height and lighting. He moves into the shadows on the left of frame to leave the dominant position now to the actor seated at the head of the table. This type of actor 'choreography' is a frequent controller of composition without change of shot or camera movement.

Creating a front surface design

For an image to hold our attention, relationships within the frame must be constantly changing. This can be achieved by movement or sound (e.g., dialogue flip-flopping between actors). It can be achieved by skilful compositional elements that lead the eye around the frame finding new patterns or visual contrasts or it can be achieved by having an involving and agreeable front surface pattern.

There is often an attempt to compensate for the loss of the third dimension in a film or television image by introducing a string of depth indicators that draws the eye into the picture. Space and the depiction of depth can provide visual interest but so can pattern. The screen on which the image is reproduced is a flat two-dimensional plane and, as we have seen with the structural skeleton of the shot and in abstract shots, the patterns that lay on the surface of the screen independent of the replication of depth can hold the attention because organization of shape, form and contrast are basic to the act of perception.

A composition can create interest if it achieves the twin objectives of creating depth and also a front surface two-dimensional pattern. This pattern can be created by strong contrast of tone, shape, colour or texture that simplifies the image. An easy way of judging this quality of the composition is through half-closed eyes, which can reveal the main compositional groupings and reduce the awareness of specific visual elements.

Only the content can determine which pattern can be created by balancing out colour, mass, direction, etc., and which aspect of visual design is to be chosen and subjected to the business of pictorial organization. The function of visual design can be shown only by pointing out the meaning it helps to make visible.

Creating mood or atmosphere

As well as action and dialogue, framing and camera movement can contribute to establishing the mood or atmosphere of a scene. Static or a slow panning camera, combined with long horizontal lines, soft lighting, slow moving or static actor staging can result in a quiet, calm, restful mood. This can be disrupted for narrative requirements by faster camera movement, faster cutting pace or more active actor movement. Speed or the excitement of action can be increased by jagged diagonal movement across the frame, whereas a skater or skier often has a smoother change of direction and camera movement needs to echo this fluid action. Instability, mystery or menace can be created by dramatic lighting but also by wide-angle distortion of verticals, rapid movement, canted camera angles and unexpected action from an unanticipated screen direction.

Summary

The aim of a balanced composition is to integrate all the visual factors such as shape, colour and location so that no change seems possible. The image achieves unity as a result of all its essential elements. Visual design means actively using the available design elements in the shot such as grouping and organization, balance, figure and ground, shape, line, curves, pattern, etc., to emphasize and draw the observer's attention to the main subject in the shot.

A shot should feature one centre of interest and the viewer's attention should always be attracted to the most significant portion of the scene. Even in a two or three shot, movement, dialogue, lighting or staging will direct attention to the dominant subject at that moment. Background action or setting should not overwhelm the foreground. Groups of subjects (e.g., a crowd, trees or houses) need a camera position and appropriate focal length lens in order to be organized into a cohesive shape unless the aim of the shot is to depict riots, battles or a catastrophe. Odd number of actors (e.g., three or five, etc.) are easier to group.

In capturing attention, movement and sound take precedence over visual design. A moving object possesses more compositional impact than a stationary object. Regardless of size, a small moving, light, bright object will grab greater attention than a large static object.

In seeking to balance a composition, an object positioned on the edge of the frame will be stronger than in the centre. Movement towards or away from the camera is more active than across the frame. An isolated subject carries more weight than a group, particularly in the top part of the frame compared with the lower part.

A generalization would be that a close shot intensifies the attention to detail – the viewer cannot easily overlook the visual information that is being presented. A wider shot may be used to show relationships, create atmosphere or express feeling but requires tighter design control of the composition to achieve these objectives. A wider area of view may have more visual elements, lighting, contrast, colour, etc., to integrate for visual unity, whereas a closer shot can be effective with very simple framing.

If in doubt, choose a simple composition that is economical in the use of line, form, mass and movement. The test of simplicity is that no item can be removed without destroying the balance of the composition.

6
Frame

Composition and the frame

Composition can be controlled by the position of the lens and a variety of visual design techniques, but there is another 'invisible' force acting upon the design of a film or television image and how it is perceived. The enclosing frame of a picture exerts three powerful influences on a composition.

Firstly, the shape of the viewing screen, its aspect ratio (the proportion of its width to its height) has a significant influence on how a picture is to be composed. This is dealt with in the next chapter. Secondly, the spatial relationship between the main subject and the edge of the picture is critical. Lastly, how the frame contains the image, how it in effect limits and concentrates the observer's attention on the subject of the image. Looking through a small window from inside a house we can only see part of the surrounding neighbourhood. Standing in a greenhouse we have an unconstrained view of the environment but without the guiding focus of the selective boundary of a frame. Framing up a shot is selecting and presenting a portion of the setting/subject for the attention of the audience.

Frame – an invisible focus of power

It is often difficult to assess the influence the border of a picture has on the main subject of the image. An experiment was devised to measure this effect using a number of individual observers.

In a darkened room using a brightly lit border and positioning a white dot at various positions within this frame, perceptual psychologists established that observers will unconsciously imply potential motion to a static object, the white dot, depending on its position within the frame.

They will ascribe movement to a static object that will either be 'pulling' towards the centre or to the corners and/or edge of the

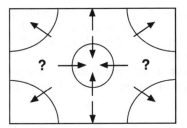

Figure 6.1 A single object will either be 'pulling' towards the centre or to the corners and/or edge of the frame. There are also positions of ambiguity where an observer cannot predict the potential motion of the object

frame, depending on its position relative to the edge of the frame. Based on the experience of a large number of individuals, a field of forces can be plotted (Figure 6.1), which shows the position of rest or balance (centre and mid-point on the diagonal between corner and centre) and positions of ambiguity where the observer cannot predict the potential motion of the object and therefore an element of perceptual unease is created. Whether the object is passively attracted by centre or edge, or whether the object actively moved of its own volition, depends on content.

At the same moment that we look at an object within a frame, we are also aware (often unconsciously) of the spatial relationship between the object and the frame.

This common experience of an awareness of motion of a static visual element with relation to the frame is an intrinsic part of perception. It is not an intellectual judgement tacked on to the content of an image based on previous experience, but an integral part of perception. The edge of the frame and also the shape of the frame therefore have a strong influence on composition.

The pattern of a photographic image is more than the relationship between size, shape, brightness differences and colour contrast of the visual elements, there is also a hidden structural pattern created by the frame. An image contains more than the visible elements that make up the shot and these 'unseen' aspects can exert a powerful influence on the composition. As we saw in the discussion on perspective, an observer can be aware of the position of the vanishing point (within or outside of the frame) even if it is not self evidently indicated.

These frame 'field' of forces exert pressure on the objects contained within the frame and any adjustment to the composition of a group of visual elements will be arranged with reference to these pressures. This strong perceptual awareness of the invisible reference points of the frame can be demonstrated by examining a simple medium close-up shot framed with normal headroom. If the camera is panned up, a point is reached, with a large amount of headroom, where the subject appears to be slipping out of the bottom of the frame. Panning down to create a shot with no headroom produces the feeling that the subject is leaving through the top of the frame (Figure 6.2(a)–(c)).

Framing anything towards the corners gives the impression that the subject matter is slipping away from the dead centre reference point. Placing the subject dead centre of the frame resists or balances out the 'pulling effect' of the corners. By eliminating tension the resulting image lacks visual excitement because there is no visual stress within the frame. The subject is at such a condition of equilibrium that it lacks any visual energy (Figure 6.3(a)–(c)).

A different placement of the subject within the frame's 'field of forces' can therefore induce a perceptual feeling of equilibrium, of motion or of ambiguity.

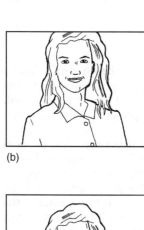

(a)

(b)

(c)

Figure 6.2 There is a strong perceptual awareness of the invisible reference points of the frame. **(a)** If the camera is panned up, a point is reached, with a large amount of headroom, where the subject appears to be slipping out of the bottom of the frame. **(b)** Panning down to create a shot with no headroom produces the feeling that the subject is leaving through the top of the frame. **(c)** There is a point of equilibrium where the subject is balanced against the invisible forces of the frame

Static viewpoint

Human perception is unable to be as static and as continuously focused and attentive on a selected portion of a field of view as a camera. Attention, after a short period of time, will inevitably be

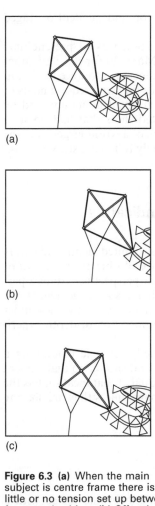

(a)

(b)

(c)

Figure 6.3 (a) When the main subject is centre frame there is little or no tension set up between frame and subject. **(b)** Offsetting the subject to this degree suggests that the frame is ahead of the kite. There is a marked contrast between the space in the left of the frame and the kite. It is ambiguous visual communication as it could imply that either the kite is losing height or that it has unlimited space to climb. **(c)** Placing the subject too close to centre can also be ambiguous as it remains unclear whether the kite is moving to equilibrium or is being pulled towards one of the sides of the frame

captured by movement or noise from subjects outside the selected zone of view. The camera can continue its static unblinking gaze until altered by the cameraman.

A hard cut-off

There is no awareness of what lies outside the selected viewfinder image except by deduction based on content or previous shots. By selective editing, a completely fictitious environment can be suggested to lie outside the hard cut-off point of the frame. Human perception has the ability to focus on one section of its view whilst being aware of visual activity on the edge of the field of view.

One of the early Hollywood conventions designed to hold and concentrate the audience's attention on the subject of the shot was to compose the shot so that it contained the action within the frame and then, by cutting, followed the action in discrete, complete shots. Each shot was self-contained and referred only to what was seen and shut out or excluded anything outside of the frame. This is the closed frame technique and is structured in such a way as to keep the attention only on the information that is presented. If there is any significant reference to a subject outside of the frame, then there is a cut or a camera move to bring the referred subject into frame. This convention is still followed in many different programme formats. For example, in a television demonstration, the demonstrator in MCU may refer to some item that is outside the frame. Either the MCU is immediately loosened to reveal the object or there is a cutaway on another camera to a close-up of the object.

The open frame convention allows action to move in and out of the frame. An example would be a character in a hallway who would be held on screen whilst in dialogue with someone who is moving into, and out of, frame whilst entering and leaving various rooms that are unseen. Their movement while they are out of frame is implied and not cut to as separate shots. The open frame does not disguise the fact that the shot is only a partial viewpoint of a much larger environment. This technique considers that it is not necessary for the audience to see the reality beyond the shot in order to be convinced that it exists (Figure 6.4(a), (b)).

In the mid-nineteenth century the increased speed of film emulsion allowed faster exposure and the ability to capture movement. Photographs of street scenes now became possible and often featured, by chance, people on the edge of frame either moving into or out of the shot. These snapshot 'chance' compositions, as we have mentioned, appealed to painters such as Degas (see Figure 10.3) who used the same convention of objects on the edge of frame to add to the dynamics of the composition (see Chapter 5) and as a pointer to the arbitrary nature of the placing of the frame, which excluded a greater reality outside the frame.

Some film directors, such as the Italian Michelangelo Antonioni, have emphasized the arbitrary nature of the frame as a device that switches on pieces of 'reality' only when required, by holding the shot of a location when any significant action has ended. For example, the shot may continue of an empty room when the actors have exited to

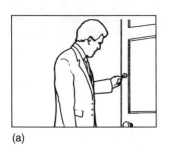

(a)

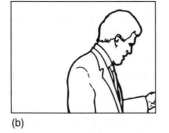

(b)

Figure 6.4 (a) A closed frame contains all the relevant action. **(b)** An open frame requires the audience to assume what they cannot see – that there is a door and keyhole beyond the confines of the frame

underline the continuing existence of the room independent of staged action or the demands of the narrative.

The classic Hollywood narrative convention was to present only what was essential to advance the plot. Many European and other film makers have challenged this slavish adherence to an edited construction of film time and space, restricted to the strict requirements of a story. They moved away from the conventional limits imposed by Hollywood narrative continuity and inserted shots that had possibly no plot requirement but provided indicators of a world larger than the limitations imposed by the constraints of only following story requirements.

Limited depth and perspective indicators

The two-dimensional viewfinder image has limited depth indicators created by overlap of objects, change of size of objects moving to or away from the camera, mass, line and aerial perspective. Human perception, with binocular vision, allows depth and size judgements to be made by head and body movement. The perspective of the viewfinder picture can be entirely different from the impression of depth experienced by an observer beside the camera.

The viewfinder image is a bright selected rectangle containing a portion of the field of view that is personal and specific to that camera position, lens and framing. No other individual at that location has the same visual experience as the viewfinder image unless they are sharing a video output from the camera.

Monochrome

An electronic viewfinder will produce a monochrome image with a much smaller contrast range than that experienced by human sight. This tends to provide a much simpler image than the original, eliminating colour contrasts and the emotional effect of colour and emphasizing tone, mass and the perspective of line.

A stronger sense of pattern is usually displayed by a two-dimensional viewfinder picture than is seen by human perception unless an individual has trained himself to 'see' as a camera does.

The viewfinder image therefore helps in composing a picture because, to some extent, it accentuates certain compositional elements. A well designed image has information included but also has information that has been excluded. The frame acts as a controller of attention by limiting what is to be in shot. The edge of the frame is a frontier checkpoint and the basic advice often given to trainee cameramen is to always check the edge of the frame for unnecessary detail. With a small viewfinder image it is not always easy to see 'border incidents' of items creeping into the frame and others sliding out. When observing a large projected image or colour picture, these fringe visual activities are immediately obvious and distracting and shift the emphasis from the main subject of the shot (see colour plates 4 and 5).

The edge of frame as a reference

Because of the strong influence of the frame edges, they tend to act as an immediate reference point to horizontal and vertical lines in the image. The camera needs to be levelled to produce the horizon or equivalent lines parallel to the bottom of the frame and vertical lines parallel to the side of the frame unless a canted picture is required (a Dutch tilt). If this does not happen, any camera movement will produce greater or lesser distortion of the vertical and horizontal elements.

As there is constant feedback in our biological make-up between the inner ear and eye to achieve balance and remain upright, a canted shot that displaces strong verticals can have a disturbing visual effect. Carol Reed in the 'Third Man' (1949), uses a sequence of canted shots of faces peering out of doorways and windows to create an atmosphere of suspicion and instability. This reflects the central character's uneasiness in his search through Vienna where he suspects that there are mysterious events beyond his knowledge.

In one television series, all the flashback sequences were shot in monochrome and canted to provide a separate identity to the main narrative. The fight sequences in 'Batman' (1989) were canted not only to reflect the style of the original comic book illustrations but also to provide greater dynamics to the shot composition.

Frames within frames

The shape of the frame and the relationship of the subject to the edge of the frame have a considerable impact on the composition of a shot. Historically, in print photography, there have been two preferred aspect ratios – the landscape format, which has a predominantly horizontal shape, and the portrait format, which emphasizes the vertical aspect ratio.

Film and television programmes usually stay with one aspect ratio for the whole production. There have been a few examples of multi-image films that either use a split screen of two, four or more separate images, whilst other productions have altered the shape of the screen according to content.

One simple way of breaking up the repetition of the same projected shape and of adjusting the aspect ratio to suit the content is to create compositions that involve frames within frames. The simplest device is to frame a shot through a doorway or arch that emphasizes the enclosed view and plays down the enclosing frame and wall. Another popular convention is to include in the top of the frame of a wide shot a bit of 'dingle dangle' – a tree branch often supported out of vision by a gallows arm or a similar structure.

By using foreground masking, an irregular 'new' frame can be created that gives variety to the constant repetition of the screen shape. A frame within a frame breaks the monotony and also provides the opportunity for compositional diversity. The familiar over-the-shoulder two shot is, in effect, a frame within a frame image as the back of the foreground head is redundant information and is there to allow greater attention to be focused on the speaker, and the curve of

Figure 6.5 Although the newsreader is well into the frame the background logo competes for interest

the head into the shoulder gives a more visually attractive shape to the side of the frame (see Figure 1.4).

Often the object that is being used to create a secondary frame has some narrative connection with the subject of the shot. For example, the arm of a crane may be used to mask a wide shot of docks or the curve of the span of a bridge will frame a town or cityscape.

A second frame

A frame within a frame emphasizes the principal subject by enclosing it with a secondary frame and often gives added depth to the shot. There are a number of ways of creating a secondary frame including the use of semi-silhouette foreground objects, or windows or mirrors that divide the frame into a smaller rectangle. If this is badly done there is the risk of creating a divided frame with equal and competing areas of interest. Strong vertical and horizontal elements can create two images that are unconnected and provide no visual direction, thus allowing ambiguity in the viewer's mind as to which image is dominant.

The other compositional problem occurs with the relationship between the edge of frame and the frame-within-a-frame shape. If these are similar and the inside shape follows the frame line then there is simply a contraction of the screen size. Divided interest in a frame can be created by the overemphasis of visual elements that are not the principal subject or there may be indecision of what is the principal subject.

The top of the doorway in 'The Big Combo' shot (see front cover) is angled to the frame of the shot by offsetting the camera position from a square-on position and by using a low lens height. This avoids the top and the sides of the entrance running parallel with the outside edge of the frame, which would simply reduce the size of the screen. If the camera position had been chosen to centre on the entrance, the top line would run parallel to the top of frame and produce a less dynamic image. A sloping line across the frame produces a more active composition when it is obviously at a different angle to the frame top. The low camera height and the distance of the actors from the lens creates size difference and depth.

As always when offering compositional guidelines in film or television there are always exceptions that can be found. The end shot of John Ford's 'The Searchers' (1956) is a square-on shot of a doorway from the interior with an enclosing unlit frame so, in effect, the screen contracts down to the doorway through which one can see the familiar figure of John Wayne walking away from camera.

Frame and divided interest

The most common example of a frame within a frame creating a divided interest is the newsreader framed in one half of the shot, 'balanced' by a logo or generic graphic enclosed in a 'window' in the other half. The two images are usually not visually integrated and fight each other for attention. Often, the newsreader appears to be uncomfortably near one edge of the frame being pushed out by the dominant position of the graphic.

It is almost impossible to achieve visual unity with a combination of presenter plus a strong graphic 'window' unless the presenter occupies at least three-quarters of the frame and can overlap the graphics window. A fifty–fifty split in the frame is often seen in news bulletins reflecting journalistic preferences formed by experiences of text page newspaper layouts.

Electronic graphics have a generous surround of 'non-action' area that is required because some domestic television sets are overscanned and the margins of the transmitted picture are not seen. Essential information such as text (name supers, telephone numbers, etc.) is automatically kept out of this border. Pictures derived from cameras have no such automatic control and can and do produce images that overlap the action area boundary. Consequently many factual programmes allow electronic graphic material to push presenters off the screen or squeeze them to the edge of the frame in composite shots.

Summary

At the same moment that we see an object within a frame, we are also aware of the relationship between the object and the frame. These frame 'field of forces' exert pressure on the objects contained within the frame and all adjustment to the composition of a group of visual elements will be arranged with reference to these pressures. Different placement of the subject within the frame's 'field of forces' can therefore induce a feeling of equilibrium, of motion or of ambiguity.

The closed frame technique is structured to keep the attention only on the information that is contained in the shot. The open frame convention allows action to move in and out of the frame and does not disguise the fact that the shot is only a partial viewpoint of a much larger environment.

A stronger sense of pattern is usually displayed by a two dimensional viewfinder picture than is seen by human perception unless an individual has trained himself to 'see' as a camera does. The viewfinder image therefore helps in composing a picture because, to some extent, it accentuates certain compositional elements.

In general, when using frames within frames, the inside frame should be at an angle to avoid a cardboard cutout appearance or contracting the screen size. The inside frame should be in sharp focus and need not completely enclose the main subject of the shot. Partial frames, such as top of frame foliage or the classic over-the-shoulder framing, can be equally effective in breaking up the repetition of the main aspect ratio of the production.

7

The shape of the screen

Aspect ratio

The ratio of the longest side of a rectangle to the shortest side is called the aspect ratio of that rectangle. The aspect ratio of a film or television frame and the relationship of the subject to the edge of frame has a considerable impact on the composition of a shot. Historically, film progressed from the Academy aspect ratio of 1.33:1 (a 4:3 rectangle) to a mixture of CinemaScope and widescreen ratios. TV inherited the 4:3 screen size and then, with the advent of digital production and reception, some countries took the opportunity to convert to a TV widescreen ratio of 1.78:1 (16:9).

There is a striking similarity between the commercial considerations involved in the introduction of film widescreen in the 1950s and the national politics and commercial debate to establish TV widescreen transmissions in the 1990s. It was hoped to increase cinema attendance by changing the shape of the film screen in the mid-twentieth century just as 50 years later it was hoped to sell more television sets by changing its shape. In fact manufacturers were guaranteed to sell more digital widescreen sets if they could convince governments to switch of the existing 4:3 analogue sets and render them obsolete. This chapter discusses how film and TV images arrived at their present displayed aspect ratios and the influences that have changed these shapes over time.

As well as the production aspect ratio there is also the aspect ratio of the screen on which the image is displayed. If there is a mismatch between the aspect ratio of the original and that of the reproduced image, a number of problems arise. Considerations about the different shapes of display screens now and in the future and their effect on how the original composition of an image could be protected, are dealt with in Chapters 8 and 9.

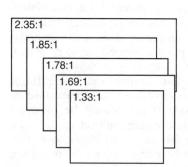

Figure 7.1 Film and TV aspect ratios include: **(a)** 2.35:1 – 35 mm anamorphic (Panavision/CinemaScope); **(b)** 1.85:1 – widescreen film; **(c)** 1.78:1 (16:9) – video widescreen; **(d)** 1.69:1 – super 16 mm; **(e)** 1.33:1 (4:3) – Academy ratio and TV

The shape of the screen and composition

The composition of a film or TV image can only be designed in relation to an enclosing frame. As we discussed in the previous chapter, the enclosing frame has a significant influence on how we perceive a shot. Many images created in the past such as cave paintings, wall painting and frescoes had no frame, but film and TV images are watched on a display screen with a specific shape. That shape has been the subject of commercial, political and technological debate but seldom have the aesthetics of the shape been discussed. The shape of the screen is vitally important to directors and cameramen but their work is often mangled by the technology of delivery to an audience. Sometimes, in this development, the shape of the screen is either seen as a technical consideration or sometimes as a commercial requirement. What is often ignored is the incompatibility of the original creative decisions by the image makers for their images to be all things to all screens.

Framing for a specific aspect ratio is an inherent part of a production's identity. Directors, cinematographers and cameramen should have the assurance that the aspect ratio of the presentation screen matches their original compositions. Both in the cinema and via the television screen, film and TV images are often subject to gross distortion for commercial considerations. There are a variety of film and TV aspect ratios and they are not compatible. Neither can they be made compatible by cropping the projector's aperture, panning and scanning, or shoot and protect production techniques.

In 1952, when newsreel commentator Lowell Thomas introduced Cinerama images to a cinema audience, he suggested that pictures in the past had been restricted in space; that a painting is hemmed in by its frame. Cinerama breaks out the sides of the ordinary screen and presents very nearly the scope of normal vision and hearing. The primary intention of this widescreen innovation was to compete with the television small screen, one of the causes of falling cinema attendance, by offering a 'wrap around' image – a different visual experience. The Cinerama image filled the spectator's field of view (at least towards the front of the cinema), and virtually eliminated the awareness of a horizontal border to the picture. After the brief success of Cinerama, films were produced in a variety of widescreen formats but faced increasing problems in projection and television showings. The edge of the screen came back as a major consideration when composing an image.

Viewfinder as an editing tool

The viewfinder is selective – it excludes as well as includes visual material. The frame of a shot creates an 'enclosure', a fence that separates the image from its environment – a bright rectangle surrounded by blackness. To some extent (ignoring size) a film image is viewed in a darkened cinema in a similar condition as an optical viewfinder on a camera. A video viewfinder image, however, is seen by the cameraman in very different conditions to the television viewer (see Figure 5.24). But both optical and electronic viewfinders display images that deviate in significant ways from our normal experience of perception. A viewfinder image has a hard cut-off, a border that concentrates the compositional elements of the shot. When viewing this small image magnified and projected on a large screen, certain compositional elements lose their impact. How the image will be displayed – cinema or television screen – affects compositional decisions as well as the aspect ratio of the image frame.

Could it have been different?

There is nothing inevitable about technological development or innovation in film or television. Contemporary film aspect ratios and changing television aspect ratios are the result of vested interests, competing commercial requirements and economic competition between countries. In tracing the history of how the current situation was created what is often missing are accounts of decisions that could have been taken and the reasons why they were not taken.

There is a story of a three-hour hospital management meeting that discussed details of the structure and organization of a hospital without ever mentioning the patient. The development of widescreen in television is very similar. For nearly 20 years there have been endless technical discussion groups and committees about new forms of television but little or no mention of the needs of the viewer. The viewer is probably very happy with their 4:3 analogue set and have no wish to buy new and expensive equipment. It is the content they are interested in, not the hardware. In the words of a prominent television executive:

Widescreen has proven to be an important element in attracting the public to digital services, as it is a very visible differentiating factor for simulcast services that might otherwise be regarded as merely 'more of the same'. The 16:9 format is seen as a particularly important feature of the digitally simulcast traditional analogue terrestrial services. It provides a highly visible new element in a world dominated by multiplicity of channels. It also provides a 'fresh look' to go with the new services.

A 'fresh look' to re-brand an old product is, in this case, to change the shape of the screen. In unravelling the history of any decision making it is easier to identify the decisions that were made, rather than the ideas that failed to be taken up or were simply not reported. It is the views and opinions that were never adopted that are the most difficult to trace but they are the ones that could have shaped an alternative present. The current mixture of aspects ratios is neither inevitable nor a logical progression to near perfection. It is simply the end result of a series of commercial pressures.

The invention of a world format standard

Throughout the economic and political arguments over a proposed international video format, one standard format has remained relatively unchanged for over 100 years. 35 mm film has remained a universal standard in the cinema and television and, before sound was introduced in the late 1920s, any 35 mm print could be shown and understood in any cinema throughout the world. How a 35 mm film frame became the standard appears to rely on the work of one man who was in fact looking, in the late 1890s, for a convenient film strip for Edison's Kinetoscope (peepshow).

In 1889 (Edison and Dickson may have created an earlier date for their inventions in order to support their patents), W.K.L. Dickson, Edison's assistant, an engineer, was searching for a film strip that *provided an image of sufficient quality at minimal cost* (Belton, 1992). Dickson was an amateur photographer and he had to decide between the traditional vertical portrait format and the horizontal format of landscape used in painting and photography at that time. He settled on a negative image, 1 inch wide and $\frac{3}{4}$ inch high. He arrived at this frame because Eastman mass-produced film strips of 70 mm and 90 mm gauge. Dickson slit the 70 mm strip into two 35 mm widths and then had to decide on the frame size. Some still cameras at this time produced circular images. Dickson rejected this shape and, after perforations were punched in the film, he had an image width of 1 inch. To match the 1-inch horizontal frame he could have chosen a frame height of 1 inch, which would have resulted in a square frame. Instead he decided on a $\frac{3}{4}$-inch frame height to maximize the number of frames in the 50-foot strips of film he was using. This negative frame size provided sufficient quality of image for the peepshow.

The golden rectangle was greatly admired by mathematicians and engineers such as Dickson (but not necessarily by artists – see misunderstandings about the golden rectangle below) and the 1.33:1 dimensions of a 1 inch $\times$ $\frac{3}{4}$-inch frame size he chose was close to the 1.618:1 of the golden rectangle. The 4:3 shape was also a compromise shape between the portrait and landscape formats used in still photography. With slight modifications, Dickson's design lasted for over 60 years in the cinema and up to the present day in television film production.

The early days of film production were enmeshed in contested patents and legal challenges to infringements of patents. One method of circumventing Edison's patent was to film using a non-standard aspect ratio. This involved not only widescreen film apertures but also the ability to project in widescreen. Alternative widescreen aspect ratios died out by the 1910s, probably because cinemas could not economically handle different aspect ratio formats.

Widescreen appeared again with Abel Gance's three-screen production of 'Napoleon' (1927) and the development by Henri Chrétien of his 'anamorphoser' lens, which not only allowed widescreen but also 'tall' screen as well (2.66:1 widescreen and 1:2.66 tall screen). In the quest to attract audiences, larger cinemas were built, which in turn required larger screens. Some of these cinemas could seat 3000–6000 people, but most of this extended audience was viewing a smaller image. There was a demand for a larger negative size but there was no agreement between studios on a standard width and they experimented with film gauges of 50 mm, 65 mm and 70 mm, although an aspect ratio of 2:1 was commonly favoured.

Widescreen film gauge may have eventually been agreed during the late 1920s if the experiment had not coincided with the advent of sound in 1926–1927, which required expensive re-equipping of film studios and cinemas.

Sound forced a reduction in the standard 1.33:1 aspect ratio into a nearly square shape of 1.15:1 to accommodate the 2 mm sound track.

Because the cost of re-equipping with sound and a new shape screen, many cinemas carried on projecting the new 'squarer' shape on their old 4:3 screens. Heads and feet were cropped in the mismatch of the two aspect ratios. The Academy of Motion Pictures in 1932 agreed to a modified 4:3 shape to accommodate the sound track but the smaller frame took up 36 per cent less negative. Although cinemas could use their old screen and slightly magnify the projected image, it did result in a slightly lower quality image. Cameras were fitted with the new 1.37:1 aspect ratio masks. It is still customary for cameramen to talk about Academy Ratio of 1.33:1 when they really mean 1.37:1. It probably occurs in this book as well!

Widescreen returns

Cinema-going in the USA fell from an average weekly attendance of 90 million in 1948, to an average of 60 million in 1950 and down to 18 million by 1972. The collapse of the cinema-going habit was the result of a number of social changes. In the post-war years the American population became more affluent and developed the taste, time and money for more active recreation. The studios had always relied on mass urban audiences. People now had the money and the ambition to move out to the suburbs and, although drive-in cinemas were a cheap and convenient way to reconnect with this relocated audience, film entertainment was a passive activity provided for the audience whereas many of them wanted recreation in their leisure time that allowed them to participate.

Studios saw television as its principal competitor. They believed that with a greater emphasis centred on the suburban home, television kept people away from the cinemas. They decided to fight back by offering a widescreen image and surround-sound experience that attempted to completely involve the audience in the film.

During the twentieth century, large screen displays had occurred in expositions, amusement parks and exhibitions. Cinerama was developed by Fred Waller away from the film industry and shot on three ganged cameras each covering 48° of the field of view, making up a composite image of 146° horizontal by 55° vertical. This closely approached human vision of 165° × 60°.

Because of Cinerama's enormous curved screen, stereo sound and an aspect ratio of 2.77:1, many of the audience were less aware, if aware at all, of the edge of the horizontal frame, unlike their normal visual experience of the standard Academy ratio movie. Most of the Cinerama audience was seated so that the screen filled their field of view. Human vision uses a series of small eye motions called saccadic eye movement to scan 5–35° of their field of view. The Cinerama screen, covering 146°, meant the audience's visual attention was scattered across the screen. This duplicated the experience in reality of scanning across a panoramic view. Unlike the Academy ratio movie, the audience's attention (unless you were sitting in the front seats), was not focused on a single framed image. Cinerama, and later CinemaScope, attempted to reduce or eliminate the audience's awareness of the horizontal screen border in the cinema.

The advertising for Cinerama suggested that the audience was drawn into the film and had the physical experience of whatever motion was depicted. The emphasis of the film was on movement, not story. The audience did not watch the screen, they participated in a roller coaster ride. It was not something they *saw* but something they *did*. Avoiding any strong plot or stars, the film was an extended travelogue with sequences of Niagara Falls, a gondolier ride in Venice, etc. Waller suggested it was the large curved screen duplicating peripheral vision that enhanced the visual experience.

Cinerama had a number of limitations compared with the standard 'flat' screen with a 4:3 aspect ratio. 'Flat' was used to differentiate between the curved cinema screen of Cinerama and the flat screen of standard aspect ratio. The joins between the three screens were difficult to hide and required special compositional arrangements when shooting. The seams, once disguised in shooting, also precluded tracking, panning or tilting. Flat lighting had to be used to balance out the enormous width of screen and the three separate images, and the film cameras were fitted with 28 mm lenses, which made normal camerawork technique of close-ups, etc., impossible. In essence, Cinerama was a fairground entertainment and not part of the Hollywood standard movie of star and story. The technology was the hero and appeared to be only suitable for travelogues and spectacle. And yet it had an enormous impact on the limited audience that saw it and the major studios recognized its crowd-pulling appeal. Cinerama opened at the Broadway Theatre, New York on 30 September 1952 and played, on its opening run, for 122 weeks.

1953 was the crucial year for the studios looking for a similar widescreen format as Cinerama but without its technical imperfections. Twentieth-Century Fox made it a top priority and agreed with Henry Chrétien to use his Hypergona lens. He was surprised they needed to make any agreement with him as it was out of patent in 1951 and the design was in the public domain. But Twentieth-Century Fox was in a hurry to get a film into production and could not wait for new (and subsequently better) lenses to be designed and built. CinemaScope started with an aspect ratio of 2.66:1 (later 2.55:1) projected onto a slightly curved screen with four-track magnetic sound. It was advertised as three-dimensional to distinguish it from the older 4:3 'flat' screen movies, but its illusion of depth was only achieved by a larger screen. True three-dimensional (use bi-coloured spectacles) only had a commercial life of one year. Twentieth-Century Fox research engineers redesigned the 35 mm frame to have smaller sprocket holes to carry two, two-track magnetic strips either edge of the film, positioned outside the sprocket holes, which allowed a slightly larger negative area for the picture.

Twentieth-Century Fox attempted to make this the standard widescreen format and pressurized other studios and cinema owners to convert to this gauge. Every major studio wanted a widescreen format to duplicate the Cinerama 'experience'. Eventually, after initial rivalry and haggling, United Artists, MGM, Columbia, Warners and Disney signed up to make films in CinemaScope. Paramount held out and launched VistaVision, an eight sprocket hole, two frame negative image rotated 90° but reduced to a 35 mm projected print in a variety of aspect ratios varying from 2:1, 1.85:1 to 1.33:1. Paramount had a

(a)

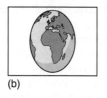

(b)

Figure 7.2 (a) The full 2:1 ratio frame; **(b)** the compressed 4:3 frame

secondary format argument and claimed that height was as important as width of screen.

Before they were allowed to show CinemaScope, Twentieth-Century Fox required cinemas to re-equip with new projectors, a new screen (their patented Magic Mirror screen for a brighter image), and a complex magnetic track stereo sound system. Most cinema owners ignored the sound requirements and although Twentieth-Century Fox provided various prints to accommodate monaural, optical stereo systems, they finally capitulated and in 1956 they reverted to standard sprocket holes and an aspect ratio of 2.35:1. The release print had a combined magnetic and optical sound track.

CinemaScope was developed in ten months. New Bausch & Lomb CinemaScope lenses in 1954 allowed the anamorphic attachment to be combined with the objective lens to make focusing easier and constant.

Other widescreen formats followed, including CinemaScope 55 shooting on 56.625 mm negative but projected using 35 mm prints. Although it was sharper on the large screens the audience was not generally aware of the difference. CinemaScope as a format finished at Fox in 1967.

In order to reduce anamorphic camera distortion, Panavision was created using a pair of prisms that could be moved in relation to each other to alter the anamorphic horizontal expansion factor. Cinema projectionists could adjust to accommodate any film with compression squeeze ratios from × 1.1 to × 2.

Todd AO arrived in the mid- to late 1950s and used 65 mm negative to film and 70 mm prints (to accommodate sound tracks). This process allowed four lenses to be used – 128, 64, 48, 37° so that standard storytelling technique could be employed through a range of shot size and camera movement. Other widescreen processes such as MGM Camera 65, Super Panavision 70 mm, Super Technirama 70 meant that many cinemas re-equipped to project 70 mm film. 70 mm film became synonymous with image quality even when, to save production costs, some producers used 35 mm to shoot and then print up to 70 mm for release.

Widescreen film aspect ratios still remain a mixture of sizes but the most common are Academy Flat (1.85:1) and Anamorphic Scope (2.35:1). 1.66:1 and 2.20:1 (70 mm) ratios are also used (see Figure 7.1). Composition is often planned, when shooting, so that the release print can be accommodated on different aspect ratio display screens without seriously compromising information or the integrity of the image (see Chapters 8 and 9).

Design of the TV aspect ratio

The factors that influence the aspect ratio of television, such as resolution, line structure and bandwidth, share certain similarities to film in the debate about negative frame size, release print and the size of projected image.

Most video images are eventually displayed on a television screen. The quality of the screen, how it has been aligned and adjusted, any reflections or ambient light on the surface of the screen, the size of the screen and the distance at which it is viewed will all affect the quality of the image as seen by the viewer. Some compensation can be built into the video signal to mitigate receiver limitations but other factors affecting viewing conditions are outside the control of the programme maker.

Unlike film, where the projected image consists of light reflected from a screen, a television tube emits light. The maximum white it can emit is dependent on its design and how the display has been adjusted. Black is displayed when there is an absence of any signal but, even when the set is switched off, there is never a true black. The glass front surface of the tube, acting like a mirror, will reflect any images or light falling on the screen, degrading 'black'. These two aspects of the display, its maximum high intensity white and how much ambient light is reflected from its screen, set the contrast range that the display will reproduce independent of its received signal.

The size of the display screen and its viewing distance will be one factor in how much detail is discernible in a televised image. Because of the regulation of television transmissions, the design of the system (e.g., number of lines, interlace, etc.) and the permitted bandwidth will affect the detail (sharpness) of the broadcast picture. Bandwidth will determine how much fine detail can be transmitted.

In those countries with a 50 Hz power supply using PAL 625 analogue colour system, the active number of lines (visible on screen) in a 4:3 picture is 575. However, a subject televised that alternated between black and white, 575 times in the vertical direction would not necessarily coincide with the line structure and therefore this detail would not be resolved. The limit of resolution that can be achieved is deduced by applying the Kell factor, which for the above example is typically 0.7. This results in a practical resolution of 400 lines/picture height. The horizontal resolution will be 4/3 of 400, equalling 533. The number of cycles of information/line equals 533/2, resulting in 266.5, taking place in 52 µS (time taken per line).This results in a bandwidth requirement of 266.5/52 µS – approximately 5.2 MHz for 625 4:3 picture transmission.

5.2 MHz bandwidth will be required for each channel broadcast using PAL 625, 4:3 picture origination. Other systems will have different bandwidth requirements, such as 1250 HDTV PAL, which has twice the resolution and needs 30 MHz. Digital transmission allows some bandwidth reduction using compression.

The basis of these electronic parameters were designed in the 1920s and the early 1930s. A number of different methods of creating an electronic picture could have been developed but, like Dickinson deciding on the aspect ratio of the first 35 mm film frame, research engineers such as Philo T. Farnsworth and Vladimir Zworykin in the USA and Blumlein & McGee in England, devised a television signal that varied in detail but was similar in principle.

On 2 November 1936 the British Broadcasting Corporation started the first television service alternating between the 240 line Baird system and the 405 line Marconi/EMI system. In February 1937 the Baird transmissions were discontinued. Circular faced cathode ray tubes were used as television display screens and it was felt the maximum area of the tube face could be used if the aspect ratio of the television image was 5:4. On 3 April 1950, the BBC changed the screen shape to a 4:3 image, which coincided with the Academy film ratio. It was ironic that this shared film and television standard aspect ratio would only last three years before CinemaScope was launched in 1953 with an aspect ratio of 2.66:1. It would be nearly 50 years before television changed its screen shape to 16:9 widescreen.

HDTV

The first developmental work on a high definition television system began in 1968 at the technical research laboratories of Nippon Hoso Kyokai (NHK) in Tokyo. Dr Takashi Fujio at the NHK research laboratories carried out research on viewers' preference for screen size and aspect ratio and his findings largely formed the justification for the NHK HDTV parameters. The research suggests that the majority of viewers preferred a wider aspect ratio than 4:3, plus a larger screen with a corresponding increase in resolution, brightness and colour rendition. His conclusion was that maximum involvement by the viewer was achieved with a 5:3 picture aspect ratio viewed at 3–4 picture height distance. Normal viewing distance (in Japan) was 2–2.5 m, which suggested an ideal screen size of between 1 m × 60 cm and 1.5 m × 90 cm. With bigger average room dimensions in the USA and Europe, even larger screen sizes may be desirable. Sitting closer to a smaller screen did not involve the viewer in the action in the same way. High quality stereo sound increased viewer involvement.

By 1980, when the NHK system of a 60 Hz field rate and 1125 lines picture was publicly demonstrated, all the necessary production and domestic equipment was available. There was widespread support for a single worldwide standard for HDTV service. The International Radio Consultative Committee (CCIR) supported a 60 Hz-field rate but this was incompatible with the PAL/SECAM field rate of 50 Hz and the NTSC 59.94 Hz. The NHK choice of 1125 lines was chosen after the calculation that the midpoint between 525 and 625 lines is 575 lines. Twice that number corresponds to 1150 lines, but this even number of lines could not produce the alternate line interlacing thought to be essential in any scanning standard. The nearest odd number having a common factor with 525 and 625 was the NHK choice: 1125 lines. The common factor 25 would make line-rate transcoding NHK HDTV, NTSC and PAL/SECAM systems comparatively simple.

On 3 June 1989, NHK inaugurated a regular HDTV programme transmission by satellite for about an hour each day. In the USA, the 1125/60 format was proposed by the Society of Motion Picture and Television Engineers (SMPTE) for adoption as an American National Standard. After many objections, the standard was rejected because it would be difficult to convert to the NTSC system. The same objections were made in PAL countries. A more significant reason was the concern that a world standard originated by NHK would lead to Japanese manufacturers dominating world equipment supplies and it would require a completely separate HDTV production and reception service. At an international standards meeting in Dubrovnik, Yugoslavia, in May 1986 the conference voted to delay a decision until 1990.

Throughout the following years the commercial considerations were intertwined with the technological implications of two frame rates.

Also, it was foreseen that the existing analogue services would be replaced by digital transmission. All parties wanted to protect their own broadcasting industry and their domestic TV services. There were two competing concepts of the future of television. The USA wanted to phase in HDTV alongside its existing NTSC system. It wanted the same compatibility that had been achieved with the introduction of colour. The viewer could choose at what time they paid for HDTV. It would be available to all.

The Europeans, after developing a 50 Hz HDTV system, decided to jettison the use of the larger bandwidths necessary for HDTV and, instead, introduce a multi-channel, digital, widescreen service. The viewer would have more choice of channels, a widescreen, but there would be no high definition system.

The need for a universal video format

Broadcasting is a massive industry worldwide. As well as the manufacture and sales of production and domestic television equipment, video programme exchange and using video in film post-production play a significant part in world trade. 35 mm and 16 mm film can be shown in nearly every country in the world. The three major analogue/digital TV systems require conversion before the exchange of programmes. Dual-format post-production (525/625) is commonplace for international distribution but, when agreement broke down to provide an international standard HDTV, there was still the search for a video format of sufficient quality that would be invisible when transferring film to video or to any format required.

With the transition from analogue to digital and the introduction of new television formats, as well as duplicating and designing very complex technical systems to accommodate all of the required standards, the post-production portion of programme generation would inevitably increase.

There was a need for a single originating video format that could be easily converted to all other formats with the minimum of degradation. A 1080 line, progressive scan picture with a frame rate of 60 Hz (1080P/24) is the most likely format to be adopted as a world production standard. This will not be transmitted but will be the 'master' originating format.

16:9 television widescreen

After 30 years of worldwide research, international debate, arguments and proposals for high definition television, improved definition television (IDTV) systems, conventional systems modified to offer improved vertical and/or horizontal definition known as advanced television (ATV) or enhanced definition television (EDTV) systems, the one common characteristic that survived in the changeover from an analogue to a digital television service in Europe is the widescreen aspect ratio of 16:9. Why was this single (non-technical) factor retained?

Since the early 1970s when NHK (the Japan Broadcasting Corporation) first began research into a high definition television system, there has been a prolonged and often heated debate about what constitutes the ideal aspect ratio for television. These arguments often repeated the same concerns and advantages expressed in the earlier film industry controversies when widescreen aspect ratios were introduced.

Although there were numerous technical committees and meetings on the technology of the 'new' television system, the shape of the screen was usually assumed to need no discussion. Although research carried out by Dr Takashi at NDK established that most viewers preferred a 5:3 (15:9) shape, endorsed in March 1984 by the Advanced Television Systems Committee (ATSC) in the USA, very few people challenged the orthodoxy of the 16:9 shape – except the 230 members of The American Society of Cinematographers. In 1993, an *ad hoc* committee of the society studied the various HDTV proposals from a creative perspective (a rare event in the 30-year history of TV transition). They felt that either recomposing or letterboxing 35 mm anamorphic (2.35:1) or unsqueezed 70 mm format (2.2:1) film would require unacceptable artistic compromises. ASC president Victor Kemper commented: 'There is a rich artistic heritage of some 40 years of widescreen Hollywood films, which would be compromised with a 16:9 or 1.78:1 aspect ratio.' ASC felt that 2:1 was an acceptable compromise between artistic purity and commercial realism.

Despite their collective prestige, they had little influence in Washington, DC, against the economic lobbying power of manufacturers who, after ten years of research and development had a vested interest in maintaining the HDTV status quo. To them, the 16:9 aspect ratio was an irrevocable fact.

The supporters of 16:9 were in the majority and their reasons for changing the television screen shape to this aspect ratio usually centred on five basic points:

1. the shape is more 'natural' because human vision sees more horizontally than vertically;
2. 16:9 is a reasonable compromise between competing aspect ratios and can accommodate film widescreen productions easier. It is therefore more efficient to have a universal screen shape for film and TV;
3. any problems that arise with the changeover to widescreen TV are 'interim' problems that will eventually be resolved when 16:9 reception is universally adopted;
4. the 16:9 rectangle is close to the golden ratio, which has been the preferred shape of artists for centuries. The divine proportion has been traditionally accepted as the perfect shape;
5. the fierce debate and unwillingness to agree to a universal TV format indicates the fifth pressure to change. There was a huge economic incentive to re-brand and make obsolete a worldwide product.

16:9 aspect ratio is closer to human vision

Television widescreen enthusiasts usually suggest that the wider format is more closely akin to the human perceptual experience. As we have discussed, the eye focuses on a very small segment of the total field of view, such that the smallest detail of interest in the scene subtends an angle of about one minute ($1/60°$) of arc, which is the limit of angular discrimination for normal vision. The eye jerks quickly from one point of interest to another in what are termed saccade patterns. The eye must constantly move in order to perceive an object of any size. To enhance the experience of increased depth or 'realism' with a two-dimensional image, Cinerama demonstrated that a very large curved screen is required in order to provide the experience of peripheral vision. With peripheral vision there is an awareness of peripheral movement but no real information is collected. It is unlikely that a domestic television screen large enough to provide the Cinerama or CinemaScope 'wraparound' visual experience would be economically viable or desired. *Average television viewing involves watching a screen that is a very small part of the field of view. Whatever the shape of the screen, it cannot duplicate the experience of peripheral vision.* Human perception relies on short saccadic eye movements. Television production units and viewers may prefer the wider screen television but it has little or nothing to do with human visual perception or an enhanced experience of increased depth.

A reasonable compromise between competing aspect ratios

One of the considerations for changing the television screen shape was the need to accommodate the showing of widescreen films. During the last 40 years, virtually all movies made for the cinema were widescreen. Pan and scan and letterboxing are discussed in Chapters 8 and 9, respectively – it was the need to address the problem of simulcasting different aspect ratios on television that led to a compromise aspect ratio of 16:9 being proposed. In addition, television programme makers wanted to originate their productions in one aspect ratio (16:9) that, after compositional precautions, would be suitable for existing 4:3 viewers. Dr Kerns Powers made the initial recommendation for a 16:9 aspect ratio within the Society of Motion Picture and Television Engineers (SMPTE).

An engineer who suggested that the ASC were too late with their recommendations for a 2:1 ratio and that 16:9 falls nearly exactly in the middle between 1.66:1 and the 1.85:1 aspect ratio met with the rejoinder:

The logic of picking something right in the middle between 1.66 and 1.85 may make sense from a mathematical standpoint, and carry international goodwill, but ... in the real world ... It's like saying that if you want to build kitchen appliances and sell them in the US and UK, you should build them to run on 165 volts, because that's halfway between 110 and 220.

(Sgt Joe Beats, a pen name)

But Dr Kerns Powers points to additional features of the 16:9 aspect ratio:

Other than the universal 'shoot-and-protect' feature, there are additional potential advantages of this choice. The rounding up to 16:9 permits some interesting polyscreen displays in consumer TV sets equipped with 16:9 picture tubes, but displaying 4:3 images. A possibility for film production would be to capture images on 3-perf 35 mm film at a full-frame aspect ratio of 1.78, using the above shoot-and-protect method, thereby saving some cost in raw film stock during shooting and editing. 3-perf film has been discussed in combination with 30 frame-per-second shooting as a method of balancing the 25 per cent increase in cost of the film stock from the higher frame rate. Finally, the 16:9 aspect ratio would be appropriate to a new proposed Scope format with 1.5:1 anamorphic lenses, leading to possibly higher brightness and lower-grain presentation. Scope's on-film aspect ratio would be retained.

The divine proportion

The golden section, golden ratio or divine proportion is called by a number of different names but all refer to the number achieved when dividing a line so that the ratio of the whole line (a) to the largest section of the line (b) is equal to the ratio of the larger piece to the smaller piece (c).

Figure 7.3

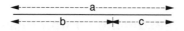

The divine proportion is when the value of (a) divided by (b) equals 1.61803 and the value of (b) divided by (c) equals 1.61803. If a rectangle is constructed that has the ratio of the longest side to the shortest side of 1.61803:1, it is called a golden rectangle.

The proportion to achieve this condition is 1.61803. A rectangle can be constructed that follows this ratio with its sides 14.5623:9. A rectangle with such properties is dubbed the golden rectangle.

This proportion has fascinated mathematicians for many centuries. From it can be constructed a nest of rectangles, all with the same ratios, spirals, and pentagons and pentagrams. The conclusion by some people is that a ratio that has so many symmetrical relationships must have a universal significance.

How the golden rectangle was used in antiquity

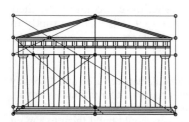

Figure 7.4 The front face of the Parthenon, Athens, with the golden section ratios proposed by numerical mystics. Although it is quite likely that the Greeks used the 'divine' proportion it is very difficult to provide accurate measurements to substantiate some of the golden section claims

Many people following this numerical mysticism have sought to reveal this proportion in structures such as the pyramids and the Parthenon in Athens. The difficulty of measuring a building, such as the Parthenon, which has been eroded or has fallen into ruin with no clear indication of what the precise original lengths were, undermines the accuracy of this type of 'proof'. The ancient Greeks did use the ratio as a building module not because they thought it had outstanding aesthetic attraction – the most pleasing shape known to man, as some advocate – but because it was a useful theory of design. The concept of it as a pleasing or beautiful shape only originated in the late 1800s and does not seem to have any written texts (ancient Greek, Egyptian or Babylonian) supporting this claim.

Another popular example by a golden ratio enthusiast is the work of Leonardo da Vinci, particularly the drawing of the head of an old man. By superimposing rectangles over this profile it is relatively simple to achieve 'proof' of the existence of golden ratios by varying the thickness of the line and choosing on which points of the drawing to centre the rectangles. Most descriptions of Leonardo's life and work give no indication that he used the golden rectangle.

Gustav Fechner in the 1860s claimed that the preferred choice of most people was the golden rectangle. His conclusion was arrived at by offering participants ten different rectangle shapes. When 48 rectangles were used in a similar experiment in the twentieth century, many people could see little or no difference with ratios close to the golden rectangle.

Another popular myth about the golden rectangle concerns the proportions of the human body. This suggests that the ratio of a person's height to the height of their navel conforms to the divine proportion. The height of a person's navel is an imprecise measurement that allows the maths to work if numerical mysticism requires it to.

Engineers still have a fascination with the mathematical flexibility of the ratio. It has been suggested that it influenced W.K.L. Dickson in his choice of the 4:3 film aspect ratio that he designed in the 1890s, and the golden rectangle is still advanced in support of the 16:9 widescreen, even though 1.777:1 is not the 1.61803:1 of the golden ratio and is not the preferred 'most pleasing shape' of the average viewer.

Widescreen – the shape of a banknote

The findings discovered by the research carried out by Dr Takashi Fujio at the NHK on viewer's preference for screen size and aspect ratio have never been properly implemented in the USA or Europe. His findings did, however, give a quasi-scientific justification for a completely new television service. They provided a pretext for the massive re-equipping for production and reception required for the separate HDTV service set up in Japan. If a manufacturer is to persuade the consumer that his old TV set is redundant, the new replacement model has to be significantly different from 'yesterday's' model. CinemaScope 55, shooting on 56.625 negative but projected using 35 mm prints, was sharper on the larger cinema screens but the audiences were largely unaware of the difference and the format was withdrawn.

The changeover to the 16:9 format in European television has been extensively used to market the new digital services. In Europe, NHK research into HDTV has gradually been usurped by 16:9 digital broadcasting. The quest for high definition has gradually been eroded by market forces to end up with a 16:9 digital system, which is a muddle of different aspect ratios that provide lower definition (often less lines than are available) distortion of the image (viewer choice of aspect ratio to fill the screen) and, because of the greed for maximum channels, sometimes excessive digital compression that causes blocking of the digital image. How have we ended up with a worse system than the 4:3 analogue system it sought to replace?

The disturbing element in this aspect ratio debate is that frequently the technical quality and economic viability is argued in detail whereas the knock-on effects of cropping and compositional distortions are considered a side issue. The justification of widescreen in the first place was that it was closer to human vision, it was a reasonable compromise between worldwide competing formats, it was close to the 'most pleasing shape' preferred by most people, and it was able to engage the audience. Most of these arguments are tenuous, if not untrue.

We are moving to a universal 16:9 shape (but still without a universal format for the exchange of programmes) not because of aesthetic, technological or even compelling physiological reasons but because of the commercial pressure to make the existing TV sets forcibly redundant by switching off the analogue delivery system. The redesign of screen shape is to provide a marketing brand to sell digital television to a public who are not interested in the hardware that provides them with their favourite programme but only in the intrinsic interest of the programmes themselves. A 16:9 widescreen screen has been commercially spun into a 'must have' consumer product with a complete disregard of the huge back library of 4:3 productions and with a muddle of distorted images stretching beyond a supposedly 'interim' period until all programmes are produce in widescreen. The question the viewer should ask is, for whose benefit is this forcible transition (there is no choice) being undertaken, and at what cost to the huge back library of 4:3 TV productions on the shelves of TV companies?

The 16:9 format is the hardware – programmes are the software. It is what is done with equipment that is important, not the equipment itself, but it is the hardware that is constantly being promoted. With Cinerama, it was the format that took precedence over story or star, the content followed on from the widescreen 'experience'.

Widescreen television is a technical toy to be played with. There are buttons for the viewer to push to distort or expand the image to fit the new shape. From a manufacturer's point of view, the new product must look different (e.g., at least 16:9 – 14:9 is too similar to 4:3). Manufacturers (and engineers) claim they simply deliver the message – someone else is responsible for the content, but their motive is to re-brand an old product whilst ensuring the existing product is made legally obsolete.

The promotion of widescreen stereo television as home cinema is a misleading label. A curved large cinema screen cannot be duplicated as a viable domestic TV screen. Most people live in small rooms. TV is quite a different communication system, despite sharing many similar characteristics with the cinema.

Of all the justifications for changing the shape of the TV screen the need to expand markets appears to be the most compelling. If governments can be persuaded to switch off the old analogue services, there will be a huge boom in the sale of digital widescreen TV. Until that day, the decision to simulcast programmes in both 4:3 and 16:9 in Europe does allow the continuation of a single production format. We will discuss in 'Widescreen composition and TV' (Chapter 9) if a single format can be all things to all screens.

Summary of film and television formats mentioned

During the development of film widescreen and HDTV, a number of formats were developed and performance levels classified. These include:

- *standard systems*: the NTSC, PAL and SECAM systems prior to proposals to develop advanced systems;
- *improved definition television (IDTV) systems*: standard systems modified to offer improved vertical and/or horizontal definition. These are also known as advanced television (ATV) or enhanced definition television (EDTV) systems. 'Advanced systems' often refers to all systems other than standard ones, or all systems other than standard and 'true' HDTV;
- *high definition television (HDTV) systems*: systems having vertical and horizontal resolutions approximately twice those of conventional systems;
- *simulcast systems*: systems transmitting conventional NTSC, PAL or SECAM on existing channels and HDTV of the same programme on one or more additional channels;
- *production systems*: systems intended for use in the production of programmes, but not necessarily in their distribution;
- *distribution systems*: terrestrial broadcast, cable, satellite, videocassette and videodisc methods of bringing programmes to the viewing audience.

8
Widescreen composition and film

Finding ways to compose for the new shape

As we discussed in the previous chapter, the widescreen format was promoted as a new visual experience. Following on from Cinerama, Twentieth Century Fox introduced CinemaScope, and head of production Darryl Zanuck repeatedly reminded his directors that they should take full advantage of the screen width by staging action all the way across the frame – in his words, 'keep the people spread out'. He wanted the audience to experience the full width of the new screen shape. Initially it was the technology that was being promoted rather than story or stars.

There had been a fashion in Academy ratio black and white films to stage in depth with tight groups in the foreground and background. The lack of colour film sensitivity, and initially the longer lenses available for CinemaScope, did not allow the same depth-of-field for this type of staging and so alternative compositions – the 'washing line' staging demanded by Zanuck – were a practical solution as well as a commercial imperative. Anamorphic shorter focal length lenses (standard in black and white production) produced distortion, dizzying swoops in perspective when panned and curved horizon lines. Later, Panavision allowed a wider choice of lenses and colour film sensitivity improved.

There was a continuous discussion on what changes were required in the standard 4:3 visual framing conventions that had developed in cinema since its beginnings. Academy ratio and staging in depth encouraged the spectator to look into the frame; widescreen and staging across the frame required the spectator to scan across the frame. When depth was added to width in widescreen films, the director or cinematographer had to devise ways of directing the attention across the frame and into the frame. The American film director Howard Hawks complained that the audience had too much to look at.

In Academy ratio composition blocking, when people were split at either end of the frame, either they were restaged or the camera repositioned to 'lose' the space between them. Cinema widescreen compositions relied less on the previous fashion for tight, diagonal, dynamic groupings in favour of seeing the participants in a setting. But using the full widescreen width as required by the studio bosses could have an unintended meaning. In a widescreen frame, a two shot with actors on either side of the frame left a large space in the centre of the frame. An audience may understand this image to signify that the two people were estranged or 'distant' with each other compared with a similar shot in Academy ratio.

Lining up the actors across the frame was quickly abandoned in favour of masking off portions of the frame with unimportant bland areas in order to emphasize the main subject. This effectively created a frame within a frame. Other compositions simply grouped the participants in the centre of the frame and allowed the edges to look after themselves – a premature 'protect and save' design (see below). There were directors who balanced an off-centre artiste with a small area of colour or highlight on the opposite side of the frame. This type of widescreen composition was destroyed if the whole frame was not seen (e.g., when broadcast on 4:3 television).

The initial concern was that the decrease in frame height meant that shots had to be looser and therefore had less dramatic tension. Another problem was that if artistes were staged at either side of the screen, the intervening setting became more prominent.

Many film directors exploited the compositional potential of the new shape. They made big bold compositional widescreen designs knowing that they would be seen in the cinema as they were framed. Their adventurous widescreen compositions were later massacred on TV with pan and scan or simply being shown in 4:3 with the sides chopped off.

Widescreen advantages

There were several compositional advantages of widescreen. Although very big close-ups on a giant screen were slightly ludicrous, directors could stage dialogue scenes between two or three characters within the same frame in close shot without intercutting. Because of the screen width, closer shots of actors would still leave space for location of background action (if it could be held in focus). Widescreen, in the words of the director Henry King, 'allows cause and effect to be shown in the same shot'.

With the technical problems solved, the solutions to guiding attention were found and widescreen composition quickly reverted to similar stagings used in Academy format. The fear of 'too much to look at' was eventually seen as an advantage and compositions were created that had a rich visual complexity. The other end of visual design is seen in David Lean's 'Lawrence of Arabia' (1962) where, in a very wide shot, two camel riders gallop towards each other from opposite sides of the screen. The staging of the action contrasts the space of the desert with the smallness of the characters. This is widescreen spectacle as envisaged when the screen shape was changed but achieved with an

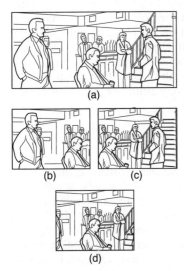

(a)

(b)   (c)

(d)

Figure 8.1 (a) This three shot composition uses the full width of the widescreen but it could not be adequately converted for 4:3 TV showing. If there was an attempt to produce two shots **(b)** and **(c)** in order to cover the dialogue exchange between the two outside characters, the middle character would jump across frame on the cut. If a centre portion of the shot was used **(d)** then both dialogue actors would be out of shot

almost empty frame instead of cramming it with action. The same sense of space is created by John Sturges in 'Bad Day at Black Rock' (1955) in the title sequence featuring a train travelling in an empty landscape. These widescreen compositions reinforce the old advice that sometimes 'less means more'.

Widescreen composition, once the technology allowed, returned to Academy format conventions with complex camera movement, staging to provide lines of force across or into the background and eye line glances to counterweigh the composition. Lighting, focus zone, actor position and setting directed the spectator's attention to the dominant subject/s of the shot.

Selling off the redundant format

Film, and later TV, always had problems with the mismatch between recorded aspect ratio and the aspect ratio of display. In the 1950s it had been the non-standard widescreen formats that caused problems in cinema screenings. Even in April 1953, the first year of widescreen, in order for Paramount to get a 'widescreen' film into the cinema, 'Shane' (1953), which had been shot Academy ratio, was recommended by Paramount to be projected in a 1.66:1 ratio. Cropping the original frame provided a bargain basement version of widescreen.

Academy ratio became associated with TV, whilst widescreen ratio was linked to film. The back film libraries of the studios were now considered obsolete and could be sold off to TV. But not only 'flat' (screen) aspect ratio productions. In September 1961, Twentieth Century Fox's 'How to Marry a Millionaire' became the first widescreen film to be shown on television in the USA. It was also the first film to be panned and scanned with a very primitive pan/scan device.

Pan and scan

Any widescreen aspect ratio other than Academy format created problems when shown on a 4:3 television screen. It could be shown with large black bands at the top and bottom of the TV screen, but broadcasters considered this was unacceptable to the viewer. If the full height of a widescreen frame filled the TV screen, then only a portion of the width could be seen. At the worst, 43 per cent of the film area is lost in pan and scan transfers of 2.35:1 format. Of 1.85:1 format, 28 per cent is lost in pan and scan transfers.

As many early widescreen films intentionally filled the full width of the frame, at the very least compositions could be wrecked and at the very worst, important subjects could be out of the frame when shown on TV (see Figure 8.1). In an early widescreen film, 'The High and the Mighty' (1954) shown on television, John Wayne's nose talks to Robert Stack's ear across a TV frame filled with an aircraft cockpit.

These early widescreen film compositions made no concession to the film being viewed on television. When transmitted on a 4:3 TV screen attempts were made to 'pan' the image to keep significant action within the transmission frame. The 'pan and scan' conversion of widescreen to 4:3 aspect ratio often introduced unmotivated pans following

Figure 8.2 Nose talks to ear on television

dialogue from one side of the widescreen to the other. Portions of the widescreen composition were plundered from the original shot to form new shots and this devalued the original camerawork and editing.

Pan and scan either took a portion of the frame that was considered the most important (usually dialogue led) or panned from subject to subject to follow dialogue or cut from one portion of the screen to another portion of the screen (again following dialogue) introducing a cutting rate that never occurred when the film was originally produced.

These decisions were usually made by a technician employed by the broadcasting organizations working to a simple rule of keeping whoever was speaking in a 4:3 frame, or to follow the central character. This elimination of up to 43 per cent of the frame significantly altered the look, pace and tempo of the film. In 1985 Woody Allen managed to secure a contractual agreement with United Artists giving him control of the video versions of his films. He introduced letterboxing on the video cassette versions of his work. Twentieth Fox developed an optical printer that extracted a 4:3 portion of a CinemaScope frame to provide a print for television. Whatever system was used, up to 43 per cent of the original frame was lost and the aesthetics of the film completely altered.

Cinematographers alarmed

Cinematographers and directors were naturally alarmed at the way their widescreen compositions were butchered by the pan and scan process. The reframing and recutting of the film for TV transmission was completely out of their control. Many film makers began to take precautions against the worst excesses of this arbitrary and casual recomposing and recutting of their productions.

They had to consider when shooting a film, that if shown on TV (as films often were) they were, in effect, creating a production for two incompatible aspect ratios. The simple solution would be to group any significant information in the centre of frame. This made for ugly widescreen compositions and in effect negated the whole reason for having a wider format.

During the late 1960s and 1970s, they devised other and more subtle ways of providing compositions suitable for the two formats. One solution was to keep the dominant subject/s in an area of the frame that could be cleanly extracted for 4:3 viewing, but to use the remaining 50 per cent of the widescreen frame for supporting visual motifs to amplify or reinforce the main plot structure. These helped to enrich the visual images but could be deleted for a simpler television shot structure.

The disposable two-shot was another popular fudge to bridge the two formats. In widescreen the two-shot was standard framing of a foreground figure with their back to camera. When this was panned and scanned for television, the foreground figure's back of head could easily be lost, turning the widescreen shot into a standard MCU. The reverse shot of this set-up was similarly turned into a MCU.

In a similar way, singles of actors were framed either extreme right or left for intercut dialogue scenes. When the 4:3 frame was extracted

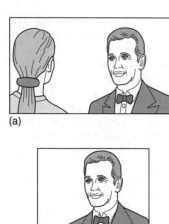

(a)

(b)

Figure 8.3 The disposable two shot allowed pan/scan cropping when converting a widescreen film **(a)** for TV transmission to produce a clean MCU **(b)**. The reverse two shot would produce a complementary MCU

most of the empty widescreen space was lost and standard intercut dialogue shots remained.

Boom in shot

A secondary problem with TV transmissions of widescreen films was that many films achieved a 1.66:1 or 1.85:1 aspect ratio by cropping or masking the top and bottom of a standard 35 mm frame. These films were shot in full frame with the intention of a widescreen aperture plate being used in the projector. The top and bottom of the 35 mm frame could include booms, lamps, shooting off the top of sets, etc., because they were in a part of the frame that would never be seen by a cinema audience. When shown on TV, the whole of the frame was transmitted and this unrequired 'garbage' was seen by the TV viewer. More of Faye Dunaway's nudity in the opening sequence of 'Bonnie and Clyde' (1967) was seen by TV viewers than by cinema audiences.

The growth of multiplexes

Apart from television format incompatibility, two problems often occur in widescreen cinema projection. The first is a simple lack of communication when labelling film cans. Often no detailed advice about the right aspect ratio is mentioned apart from 'scope', and if the print shows Academy frames (as most American prints do) it is very difficult for the projectionist to guess which aspect ratio mask and which lens will be required. Contrary to this, the sound systems are very clearly defined! Regardless of the aperture plate used in the camera, the prints should show the one aspect ratio established by the director and the DoP.

Often only one projectionist operates all projectors. In the proliferation of Multiplexes in Europe, a projector may have only one anamorphic lens and a spherical lens plus variable masks. Selecting lens and mask automatically sets the screen curtains. If the projector can only handle Cinemascope/1.85:1 formats the top and bottom of films shot in 1.375:1 or 1.66:1 are projected outside of the screen! The number of cinemas that are able to screen all formats is decreasing.

Common topline and super 35

To protect essential information in one format for viewing in another format causes a number of problems, no more so than in the protection of headroom. Safeguarding the top of the frame to avoid heads being cropped resulted in the development of the common topline on super 35 mm. The full aperture area is exposed but each format (2.35:1, 1.85:1, 1.66:1 and 1.33:1) share a common topline. However the print is projected, the headroom is safeguarded, even if the sides of the wider frames are cropped for a narrower width viewing format.

This does involve the lower part of the frame, which is not part of the widescreen frame, being seen when the whole frame is transmitted in 4:3. Cables, tracks, microphones are often just below the widescreen frame but these will all be seen in the bottom part of the 1.33:1 TV frame. The use of zoom lenses can also cause problems because the middle of the 2.35:1 frame is not only offset horizontally because of the super 35 format but is also higher than the middle of the regular frame. When zooming, the centre of the lens needs to coincide with the centre of the aspect ratio otherwise the camera will need to be continuously reframed to compensate.

Summary

Directors and cameramen attempted to use the full width of widescreen but were finally forced to find ways of shooting for two aspect ratios – CinemaScope and TV.

Television converted widescreen film for its 4:3 aspect ratio by the crude use of pan and scan.

9

Widescreen composition and TV

Introduction

After more than 20 years of argument about what should be the technical standards for a universal higher definition television system (see Chapter 7), the only consensus arrived at was to change the shape of the screen. The new aspect ratio was to be 16:9. In most countries, apart from a gradual transition from analogue to digital production/reception, this new screen shape was the only change that survived the international aspiration towards an HDTV service.

The adoption of a 16:9 television screen was a compromise that enabled programme makers to avoid producing programmes in two aspect ratios during the transitional period, provided precautions were taken in the composition of shots during production. That is, each shot was a compromise between the two aspect ratios (see 'Protect and save', below). Just as film makers had faced many compositional problems in trying to accommodate two or more incompatible viewing formats on the same negative, so television programme makers, 30 or 40 years later, were faced with similar irreconcilable framings.

Secondly, it allowed improved transmission of feature films although still requiring either the much disliked (by the film industry) panning and scanning or, alternatively, transmitting the whole frame with black bands at the top and bottom of the new 16:9 screen.

Letterboxing

Cinema widescreen film production continues in aspect ratios of 2.35:1, 1.85:1, 1.66:1 and others. There is also a huge library of film and television material shot in the ratio of 1.33:1 (4:3). If the whole of a frame of a format wider than 16:9 is transmitted on television then it will fill only a portion of the 16:9 screen. The remaining part of the screen will be filled with black bands top and bottom. The wider the aspect ratio, the broader the bands. This is called letterboxing. If uncropped 4:3 aspect ratio productions are shown on a 16:9 screen they will be accompanied by black vertical bands left and right of the screen (side curtains).

The use of only a portion of their display screen was resisted by viewers in some countries, for example, some UK viewers complained to the BBC that they paid a full licence fee and therefore they wanted a full screen image! Other countries, those who were accustomed to viewing foreign programmes with subtitles inserted in this bottom black band letterbox area, were unworried by watching the whole of a widescreen feature film with no cropping. Perhaps broadcasters should attempt to educate their viewers with the truth that by filling their TV screens with a film image they are not getting more for their money but less. When viewing on 4:3 screens, they are denying themselves up to 40 per cent of the film they are watching (see Figure 8.1).

Similar complaints were voiced when colour TV was introduced and a monochrome film was transmitted. The viewer then argued: 'I bought a colour TV set and I demand that all programmes I receive should be in colour.' This led to the synthetic colourizing of classic black and white films such as 'Casablanca' (1942), Laurel and Hardy, and the Astaire/Rogers films in order to make them more 'acceptable' to a section of the viewing public.

Aspect ratio conversion

As we have discussed, some widescreen film makers, when they saw their compositions massacred on TV, adopted a composition policy of keeping their main groupings and action in the centre of frame. This defeated the advantages of the widescreen shape but it safeguarded their product for a bigger market. Television programme makers have had to adopt the same policy to service display screens that have different aspect ratios.

Electronically, a picture could be cropped or expanded to fit any shape, but this would lead to loss of information, loss of resolution and possibly picture distortion when images are stretched to fit a different shape to their production aspect ratio. It would also destroy the compositional skills of the originators of the programmes.

Some type of aspect ratio conversion has to be employed either before the programme is transmitted or at the receiver. Several countries utilize a compromise aspect ratio of 14:9 to bridge the gap between 16:9 production demands and 4:3 receivers. The ratio converter chops out portions of the left and right of the frame for 4:3 viewers who watch with a small black border top and bottom of the frame.

16:9 set-top aspect ratio conversion is also under the control of the viewer who can select full frame with black side curtains left and right of the image when watching a 4:3 transmission or partial expansion of the 4:3 frame to a 14:9 shape when information is equally lost at top and bottom of frame. Full expansion of the 4:3 image to fill the 16:9 frame (zooming in) with information lost balanced between top and bottom or distributed according to picture content. Picture content, of

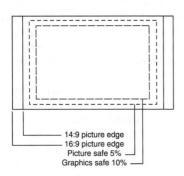

14:9 picture edge
16:9 picture edge
Picture safe 5%
Graphics safe 10%

Figure 9.1 The viewfinder is set to display the full 16:9 picture with a graticule superimposed showing the border of a 14:9 frame and a 4:3 frame

(a)

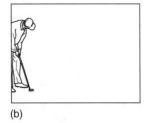

(b)

Figure 9.2 If the 'protect and save' viewfinder indicators are ignored when framing, for example, a golf shot in 16:9 aspect ratio **(a)**, viewers watching a 4:3 picture will have a poorly composed picture **(b)** and no indication, when the ball exits right on their viewed picture, if the ball has entered the hole. With this framing, it is likely that even if the programme is transmitted in 14:9 aspect ratio, many viewers (with over-scanned TV receivers) will not be able to see the hole on the right of the frame present in the original 16:9 framing

course, changes with each shot. Some set-top aspect ratio converters also provide for non-linear distortion of the horizontal part of the 4:3 frame to fit a 16:9 TV set.

Transmitting a mixture of aspect ratio formats will always need conversion unless the unlikely step is taken to scrap all 4:3 programme material when everyone has converted to 16:9 reception. Black and white movies continue to be popular 40 years after the introduction of colour television. The decision to change the TV aspect ratio was not simply a technological change, it has and will have continuous programme making and programme watching implications.

Protect and save

Cameramen shooting in 16:9 follow a 'shoot and protect' framing policy. The viewfinder is set to display the full 16:9 picture with a graticule superimposed showing the border of a 14:9 frame and a 4:3 frame (Figure 9.1). Significant subject matter is kept within the 14:9 border or, if there is a likelihood of the production being transmitted in 4:3, within the smaller 4:3 frame. The area between 16:9 and 14:9 must be still usable for future full digital transmissions and therefore must be kept clear of unwanted subject matter. This is similar to the problems experienced in feature film productions that were shot in 4:3 but were intended to be projected in the cinema with a hard matte in widescreen. 'Shoot and protect' attempts to avoid the hazards of multi-aspect viewing by centring most of the essential information and avoiding any unwanted elements at the extreme edge of the horizontal frame that may be seen in the future.

Shooting for two formats

Shoot and protect negates the claimed advantages of the widescreen shape because for the transitional period the full widescreen potential cannot be used. The film and television widescreen format has the potential for dynamic and arresting compositions; the problem is that the width of the format both in film and TV is rarely exploited. More often than not, the director or cameraman has to safeguard the composition for showing in other format sizes.

Some broadcasters who have adopted a 14:9 transmission aspect ratio have not fully converted all their cameras to 16:9 shooting. Camera operators using 4:3 cameras need to increase the headroom on a shot because the top and bottom of the frame will be cropped when it passes through an aspect ratio converter. This often leads to poor framing because the only guide the operator has is usually an inaccurate piece of gaffer tape indicating a notional top of a 14:9 frame. Not for the first time, in many cameramen's experience, has 'state-of-the-art' technology been made workable with gaffer tape. For some years, one of the first questions a cameraman will ask is 'what aspect ratio is the programme going to be transmitted in?'.

Composing for 16:9

If anything, television is more of a 'talking heads' medium than cinema but the advent of the larger, wider aspect TV screen has tended to emphasize location and setting. There are compositional advantages and disadvantages in using different aspect ratios. Widescreen is good at showing relationships between people and location. Sports coverage benefits from the extra width in following live events. Composing closer shots of faces is usually easier in the 4:3 aspect ratio but, as in film, during the transition to widescreen framing during the 1950s, new framing conventions are being developed and old 4:3 compositional conventions that do not work are abandoned. The shared priority in working in any aspect ratio is knowing under what conditions the audience will view the image.

One of the main compositional conventions with 4:3 television framing is the search for ways of tightening up the overall composition. This is partly due to fashion but also because viewing a TV picture occupies a much smaller zone of the human field of view compared with cinema viewing. Wide shots on television with small detail are not easily perceived on an average size receiver. Tight compositions eliminating all but the essential information have traditionally been preferred.

A conventional TV single can cause problems in framing in widescreen and bits of people tend to intrude into the edge of frame. This is sometimes called a 'dirty single'. Headroom has tended to be smaller than 4:3 framing and there are some problems in editing, particularly if the cut is motivated by action on the edge of a 16:9 frame, which may not be visible to 14:9 or 4:3 screen viewers.

The problem with the video compositional transition to widescreen is the inhibition to use the full potential of the 16:9 shape because the composition has to be all things to all viewers. It must fit the 14:9 shape but also satisfy the 4:3 viewer. It is difficult to know when the full potential of the widescreen shape can be utilized because, even if the majority of countries switch off analogue transmissions at some time in the first decades of the century, there will probably be billions of TV sets worldwide that will still be 4:3 analogue.

Widescreen television composition faces some of the same problems that film solved 40 years ago. Many film and television scripts require the speaker and the listener to be in the same frame. Two people talking created the mixture of close-ups, medium close-ups and over-the-shoulder two shots that form the basic shot pattern of many scenes. Shots tighter than MCU can be difficult to frame for 16:9 and the tendency is to continually tighten to lose the 'space' around the ears. Low angles appear more dynamic than similar 4:3 aspect ratio shots but hand-held camerawork in 16:9 can be very obtrusive and distracting.

When people are being interviewed, there is an optimum distance between them where they both feel at ease. The single shot on 16:9 has the problem of avoiding being too tight and producing a 'looking through a letterbox' look whilst avoiding being too loose and getting the interviewer in shot in the 'looking space' of the interviewee. The compromise is an over-the-shoulder two shot but care must be taken in the reverse to get good continuity in body posture, etc. There needs to be greater physical separation between presenters, interviewers, etc., to avoid edges of arms, shoulders creeping into the edge of the frame. This has a knock-on effect on the front-on two shot where the participants now appear to have too much space between them.

The advantage claimed for 16:9 (especially HDTV) is that the increased size of screen and the improved definition in wide shots is so good that fewer close-ups are required. This can create its own problems in editing. Wide shots need to be sufficiently different in their distribution of similar objects to avoid jump cuts in editing. Typical bad cuts can happen with seascape horizons (yacht racing, etc.) where the yachts jump in and out of frame if the horizon is in the same position in successive shots. The same 'jump' can happen with some types of landscape. A good cut needs a change in shot size or significant change in content to be invisible. Decisions about edit points on slow entrances and exits that hover on the edge of frame can be very difficult when shot 16:9 if the majority of viewers are watching a 14:9 frame on a 4:3 screen.

There is the advantage of 16:9 allowing a wider shot with less sky or ground, and square-on shots of buildings can replace the angled shot necessary in a 4:3 frame to include all the structure. Close-ups of strong vertical subjects (e.g., fingering on clarinets and saxophones) are a problem but keyboard shots are easier, and 'edgy' objects on the edge of frame do not seem to be so distracting in the wide format.

Film at least had one advantage over TV widescreen. At some time in the film's history it was usually shown in full frame width in a cinema. Widescreen TV at the moment, in many countries, is in effect 14:9 – nearly widescreen. It does not satisfy the 16:9 viewer, and it doesn't help the 4:3 viewer who is now getting a smaller image on his set.

Fidgety zooms

Widescreen working has brought with it a new camera-operating pitfall. Whilst broadcasting an opera, two singers were framed in midshot and transmitted to analogue viewers in 14:9 and to digital viewers in 16:9. They swayed away from each other towards their respective edge of frames with a gap opening between them. It became an awkward, clumsy composition that quickly needed adjustment.

The cameraman watching his/her 16:9 viewfinder with a 14:9 'safe area' obviously let them get close to the edge of the 14:9 frame. In a 16:9 viewfinder picture it probably began to make quite a good composition with the two-shot spread across the frame. In 14:9 it began to get very uncomfortable. A simple operating solution, when the action begins to burst out of the frame, is to loosen the shot. It is almost nearly always unobtrusive because the action naturally forces the shot wider. It is good 'invisible' technique, which is the bedrock of camerawork. Watching in 16:9 however, correcting the shot for the 14:9 viewer would result in a fidgety zoom-out as the two subjects were swaying into a more balanced composition. In 16:9, there was no obvious visual reason to slightly widen the shot. It would become one of those nasty fidgety zoom corrections that are inevitable in live TV, forced on the cameramen when covering unrehearsed action.

So the worst of both worlds. The 14:9 viewer gets an edgy, unbalanced shot followed by the 16:9 viewer suddenly having his balanced widescreen shot loosened to unbalance the shot again. In most countries this transitional period is due to last for a minimum of ten years but mixed aspect ratio problems will roll on across the broadcasting world for very much longer and probably will never be resolved.

Transitional period

The worldwide change-over period from mass viewing on a 4:3 analogue set to mass viewing on a 16:9 digital monitor, and therefore mass programme production for 16:9 television, will take many years. The transition period will require a compromise composition but the compositional problems do not end there. The back-library of 4:3 programmes and films is enormous and valuable and will continue to be transmitted across a wide range of channels in the future. The complete image can be viewed on a 16:9 screen if black bars are displayed either side of the frame. They can be viewed by filling the full width of the 16:9 display at the cost of cutting part of the top and bottom of the frame or, at the viewer's discretion, they can be viewed by a non-linear expansion of picture width, progressively distorting the edges of the frame to fill the screen 4:3 aspect ratio.

The same size camera viewfinders used for 4:3 aspect ratio are often switched to a 16:9 display. This in effect gives a smaller picture area if the 14:9 'shoot and protect' centre of frame framing is used and makes focus and following distant action more difficult. Also, the majority of video cameramen are probably the only viewers still watching colour TV pictures in monochrome. Colour is not only essential to pick up individuals in sports events such as football, where opposing team shirts may look identical in monochrome, but in all forms of programme production colour plays a dominant role in composition.

From a cameraman's point of view, the biggest difficulty during the transition period is attempting to find a compositional compromise between the two aspect ratios. If a 16:9 image is transmitted in a letterbox format then all shots can be framed with respect to the 16:9 border. However, most broadcasters still provide an analogue 4:3/14:9 service. There is very little satisfactory compromise that can be made in an attempt to compose for both formats at the same time.

Composition problems will continue while 16:9 and 4:3 simultaneous productions are being shot during the analogue/digital change-over. They neither take full advantage of the width of 16:9 nor do they fit comfortably with the old 4:3 shape. Possibly ten years of dual format compromise production will then join the back library and be transmitted from then on. The only safe solution is the 'protect and save' advice of putting essential information in the centre of frame, but that is a sad limitation on the compositional potential of the widescreen shape.

The viewer takes control

Often the widescreen signal is embedded with active format descriptor (AFD) – widescreen signalling to the set, which automatically selects the appropriate display format for the incoming programme. Many

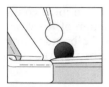

(a) 4:3
Original framing

(b) 4:3
Picture on 16:9 receiver

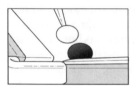

(c) 4:3
Stretched to fill 16:9 receiver
screen

(d) 4:3
Centre of frame zoomed to
fill 16:9 receiver

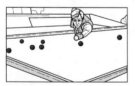

(e) 4:3
Centre of frame zoomed to
fill 16:9 receiver

Figure 9.3 It is a paradox that in some countries, viewers actively dislike the black band side curtains **(b)** when watching a 4:3 picture on a 16:9 receiver and appear to prefer either the distortion introduced when stretching the 4:3 picture to fit the 16:9 screen **(c)** or to crop the top and bottom of the transmitted image **(d)**. Unless the viewer constantly monitors and adjust this last option (zooming), subsequent shots may suffer loss of essential information **(e)**

16:9 digital receivers also provide the viewer with control of how the picture is to be displayed. They can select full frame with black side curtains left and right of the image when watching a 4:3 transmission or select a partial expansion of the 4:3 frame to a 14:9 shape when information is equally lost at top and bottom of frame. They can choose full expansion of the 4:3 image to fill the 16:9 frame (zooming in) with information lost balanced between top and bottom or distributed according to picture content. Picture content, of course, changes with each shot, therefore the viewer would need to monitor and adjust for every shot. Some receiver aspect ratio converters also provide for non-linear distortion of the horizontal part of the 4:3 frame to fit a 16:9 TV set.

Some 16:9 TV receivers have a progressive distortion (anamorphic) facility to stretch a 4:3 transmitted image. This progressive rate of expansion across the screen results in the snooker example (Figure 9.3) of the ball's shape changing as it travels across the frame. It is ironic that decades of research and development expended on producing perfect electronic images that are free from geometric distortion can be negated by the touch of a button on a channel changer. Weather presenters change shape from fat to thin as they walk across the frame, or shoot out their arm to double its apparent length when this aspect ratio conversion option is selected.

Inserting 4:3 material into a 16:9 production

In many types of programme there is often the need to use archive material. For example, a sports programme profiling a well known sportsman may be shot in 16:9 when interviewing the main subject but will insert 4:3 material of past sporting success. The 4:3 material can be inserted via an aspect ratio converter into a 16:9 frame but will have large black 'side curtains'. These will pass unnoticed by a 4:3 viewer watching a 14:9 version of the programme but a 16:9 viewer will have constant obtrusive vertical black bars jumping in and out of the frame whenever the archive material is used.

To make the 4:3 material less intrusive to the widescreen viewer the producer/director may, in post-production, expand the 4:3 material to fit a 14:9 frame losing variable proportions of top or bottom of the 4:3 image. Depending on content, this may smooth out the transition between the formats whilst still inserting narrow vertical bars in the 16:9 viewer's display whenever the archive footage is used. The difficulty comes when, for example, the head, feet and football are hard framed in the 4:3 material allowing no flexibility in cropping top or bottom. Either the head is cut off or the football goes out of frame. This is often solved by expanding the 4:3 image horizontally to fit the 14:9 frame but, of course, this causes distortion to the image and a thin footballer instantly gains weight and becomes fatter and wider. Although this distortion may seem unacceptable it is in fact seen in programmes most weeks.

Film has had similar problems of incorporating different aspect ratios in the same production. In the widescreen film 'The Guns of Navarone' (1961) 4:3 aspect ratio film is intercut with widescreen. François Truffaut's 'Jules and Jim' (1962) uses Academy ratio first war footage expanded to fill the widescreen aspect ratio. This obviously distorts the early film footage.

If a production is originally shot in 4:3 and is then converted to a 16:9 version by using a selected area of the frame, further loss of image can occur when the 16:9 version is then transmitted in a 4:3 broadcast. Credits and graphics often suffer the most from aspect ratio conversion. An early victim was the opening titles of 'Picnic' (1955) starring William Holden. His credit was transmitted on US television as William Ho.

Compilation programmes

One hundred years of film footage provide the raw material for television history programmes that reflect social history and the lives of ordinary people as reflected in film and TV archives. There is no distortion of this primary source, other than what is present in the script treatment, if the images are presented in their original aspect ratio. However, with the growth of 16:9 TV, this authentic material is subject to distortion and cropping to fit the newer aspect ratio. It is, in effect, a distortion of historical material that would be unacceptable to historians if the primary source was written archives. Compilation programmes that review popular culture in the past by showing clips of popular 4:3 television shows also crop and chop the originals to fit the newer shape. They are not doing what they purport to be doing – showing the original programme. They are showing a portion of the original programme.

One of the fallacies voiced when 16:9 screen format was adopted was that, although there would be incompatibilities, these would soon pass after a transitional period. This is based on the assumption that when all new programmes are produced in 16:9 there would be no problems when viewed on 16:9 screens. This limited view completely ignores the huge back library of 4:3 programmes. These programmes are not only very popular and therefore a commercial asset, but there is no sign of a decline in the demand for such titles (e.g., Tom and Jerry cartoons, classic feature films). It is as if a library with a standard shelf size decides to reduce its shelf height and thereafter requires all new books to fit this module. Anything written and printed before this changeover is deemed obsolete. Old book sizes that won't fit are casually cropped or squashed to fit the new shelf height.

What was also ignored in the decision to change to 16:9 was the huge international trade in television and film programming that would involve shooting in one ratio, converting to another and possibly shown in a third aspect ratio with each conversion losing part of the image.

Distortion and definition

Twentieth Century Fox engineer, Lorin Grignon, provided a report on the Cinerama format when it was first introduced and suggested that it had inherent picture distortion. Continually in television studios, invision monitors have cropped or distorted images. Distorted pictures in mixed-format programmes are transmitted as standard, which 20 years ago would have been rejected. A magazine advertisement urging the consumer to buy a widescreen television to increase their enjoyment of television football matches, displays a TV set with a footballer whose head is almost out of the top of the frame whilst kicking a football that is almost out of the bottom of the frame. For the advert, they have simply inserted a 4:3 picture into a 16:9 set and obviously missed the irony of urging people to buy a TV set that displays less of their favourite sport than their existing receiver.

Widescreen equals spectacle

The assumption that widescreen equates with spectacle is a throwback to the Hollywood attempts in the 1950s to meet the growing competition of television with 'spectacular' productions that TV could not provide. Since that period, there have been many productions that have demonstrated how effective widescreen is when shooting interiors. The 'visual fluff' at the edge of a 2.35:1 widescreen image, as one technical commentator described it, 'was unnecessary, and could always be cropped when transmitted on TV'. The implication of this thinking by vested interests, eager to persuade the public to change the shape of their television sets, is that widescreen composition is simply 4:3 with a little bit of 'visual fluff' tacked on to each end of the frame.

The disturbing element in this aspect ratio debate is that frequently the technical quality and economic viability is argued in detail whereas the knock-on effects of cropping and compositional distortions are considered a side issue. The justification of widescreen in the first place was its ability to engage the audience. The practicalities of achieving a compatible widescreen/Academy size television system appear to have swept past that basic point.

A Hollywood studio boss, Adolph Zukor, claimed that Twentieth Century Fox's emphasis on technology in the 1950s, when they introduced CinemaScope, had blinded them to their chief responsibility, which was to make good films. Of course, Zukor at that time was chairman of rival company Paramount who had not signed up to CinemaScope.

Screen size

There is a further consideration in the aspect ratio debate that concerns size of screen. Someone sitting in a front-row cinema seat may have as much as 58° of their field of view taken up by the screen image where the viewing distance is 0.9 times the picture height. This can be reduced to as little as 9.5° when the same screen is viewed from the back row of the cinema at a viewing distance of 6.0 times the picture height. A television viewer watching a 51-cm diagonal tube (21″) at a viewing distance of 6.3 times the picture height will have only 9.2° of their field of view taken up by the TV picture. Human vision is aware of about 200° in the horizontal plane (although only fully concentrating on a small proportion of this) and therefore the proportion of the visual area of a 51-cm screen in the home occupies only approximately 4.6 per cent of the maximum field of view of the viewer.

TV or cinema pictures with rapid movement produce no visual fatigue if viewed at a distance equal to about four times picture height, although the resolution of the viewed image should be good enough to allow a viewing distance of three times the picture height. According to NHK research, most people prefer a 5:3 aspect ratio television screen with increased definition although, when viewing landscapes and sport, many people favoured a 2:1 ratio.

1.5″ viewfinders

One of the most significant differences between normal perceptual experience and the experience of viewing an image in a viewfinder, is size. The 1.5″ viewfinder image on a standard portable video camera is very small and therefore a condensed version of what can be perceived. The eye can quickly scan a great diversity of detail in the viewfinder image that would not be possible in the original scale. The subject is scaled down and perceptually dealt with in a different manner than the original.

HDTV has a greatly enhanced definition and a greatly increased screen size. Finding focus and the limits of focus on a 1.5″ monochrome viewfinder will become more and more critical and demanding. Monochrome TV camera viewfinders are two generations behind the technology of other areas of television engineering.

Endnote, or in a different aspect ratio, NDNOT

The correct aspect ratio in film and television production is virtually ignored except by the director and cameraman who laboured over the original image. The final display of this image is in the hands of commerce whose visual dead eye only takes into consideration stars and action except, of course, when the screen shape is promoted to sell more cinema tickets or to urge consumers to buy new TV receivers.

It will never happen, but the intellectual property control of film makers concerning the correct aspect ratio for their production should be guaranteed from camera to audience display. The audience should see the image uncropped, or squeezed or aspect ratio converted exactly as the programme maker intended. Aspect ratios are not compatible if the chosen frame shape is fully creatively exploited. No programme maker should be asked/instructed to provide images that will fit different formats. To frame for several formats at once will inevitably degrade the production values and result in an inferior product. Panning and scanning destroys the craftsmanship expended on a feature film. Broadcasters should resist audience clamour for a cropped image simply to fill their TV screen. 'Casablanca' (1942) in colour, is a different and inferior film to 'Casablanca' in its original black and white. '2001: A Space Odyssey' (1968), when viewed on a panned and scanned TV screen is shortchanging the audience even if they want to be duped. They are not enriched by a screen full of image. They are cheated of the complete experience of the film.

Summary

In many countries, the 16:9 screen shape will be the only element left of the new worldwide HDTV standard proposed in the 1980s and 1990s.

In order to cater for programme production for two, or possibly three aspect ratio display systems, (16:9, 14:9, 4:3), a policy of 'protect and save' has been adopted. This requires essential subject or information to be contained within a 14:9 or a 4:3 aspect ratio.

There are aspect ratio conversion problems when incorporating 4:3 material into a widescreen programme.

10
Past influences

Intuition

Many cameramen insist that composition is intuitive and assume that framing decisions are based on personal and subjective opinion. Even a cursory examination of an evening's output of television will demonstrate the near uniformity of standard conventions in composition. The exceptions to what is considered 'good' composition are either provided by inexperienced cameramen who have yet to become aware of professional techniques (e.g., 'video diaries') or those productions where there has been a conscious decision to be 'different'. This usually entails misframing conventional shots in the mistaken belief that something new and original has been created. In effect, it is simply mispronouncing standard visual language.

These conventions are learnt and do not arise spontaneously as intuitive promptings. Their origins are to be found in changes in painting styles over the last 500 years, in the influence of still photography and in changes in the style and the technology of film and television production.

No one working in the media can escape the influence of past solutions to visual problems. The evidence is contained in the products of more than a century of film making and half a century of television production. These are consciously or unconsciously absorbed from the moment we begin to watch moving images. Whereas most people never concern themselves with the nature of these influences, anyone who wishes to make a career in visual communication should be aware of the changes and influences on current conventions in composition and examine the assumptions that may underpin their own 'intuitive' practices.

Early influences

Greek and Renaissance ideals

The concept of proportion and ratio in composition played an important part in Greek/Roman art and architecture and reappears in some

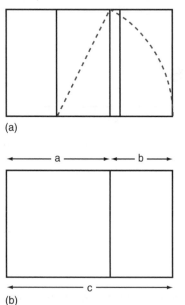

(a)

(b)

Figure 10.1 To create a 'Golden Rectangle', use the diagonal of one half of a square **(a)** as a radius to extend the dimensions of the square. The 'Golden Rectangle' has the proportions a:b = c:a and was used by the Greeks in architectural design and by Renaissance painters and architects

contemporary discussion in the 'format' war (see Chapter 7, 'The shape of the screen').

Compositional balance using this ratio revolves around positioning the main visual elements on the subdivisions obtained by dividing the golden section according to a prescribed formula (Figure 10.1).

The Rule of Thirds

The academic emphasis on proportion and ratio was probably the precursor to a popular compositional convention called the Rule of Thirds. This 'rule' proposes that a useful starting point for any compositional grouping is to place the main subject of interest on any one of the four intersections made by two equally spaced horizontal and vertical lines (Figure 10.2(a) and (b)).

The ratio of dividing the frame into areas of one-third and two-thirds is close to the approximation of a golden section division. These ratios occur so often in Western art, architecture and design that they became almost a visual convention. The proportions are learnt and anticipated in a way that is similar to the expectation of a listener to the resolution of musical harmony. Because of this unconscious anticipation, composition based on academic principles can seem stale and static to those people who have experienced the avalanche of visual imagery generated by contemporary technology. A repetitive simple tune can rapidly lose its appeal if continuously heard. Compositions that provide no visual surprises are quickly 'consumed' and require no second appraisal.

Another convention of Renaissance composition, especially with religious subjects, is to position the main subject in the centre of the frame and then to balance this with equal weight subjects on either side (see Figure 13.1).

The equal duplication of figures on either side of the main subject gives the centre figure importance but splits the composition into two halves and can produce two equally competing subjects of interest. This style of precise formal balance on either side of the frame contrasts with later fashions in composition which sought, by more dynamic visual design, to create a strong sense of movement by leading the eye, by line and structure, around the frame.

The influence of photography

After the invention of the photographic image in the 1830s, the initial novelty of accurate, realistic portraiture gave way to attempts at photographic 'art'. Photographers grouped their subjects according to the academic conventions of the day and were inclined to favour themes and subjects similar to academic painting. The long exposure required by the early photographic process also required the subjects to remain stiff and immobile to avoid blurring. The evolution of faster film allowed snapshot street scenes to be captured. The composition now consisted of enclosing a frame around a continuing event and this, compared with academic painting, resulted in unbalanced and scattered compositional groupings.

People were captured on the move, entering and leaving the frame, which resulted in quite different images from the carefully posed

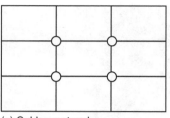

(a) Golden rectangle

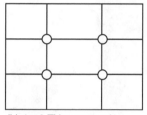

(b) 4 x 3 TV aspect ratio

Figure 10.2 The 'Rule of Thirds' proposes that a useful starting point for any compositional grouping is to place the main subject of interest on any one of the four intersections made by two equally spaced horizontal and vertical lines. Dividing the frame into areas of one-third and two-thirds is a method of constructing a golden rectangle (1.618:1) and these intersections were often used to position key elements of the composition

groups of the long exposure film. The accidental quality of these snapshot compositions was considered by many to be more realistic and life-like than the immobile studio set-ups. Painters were attracted by the sense of movement that could be suggested by allowing subjects to hover on the edge of the frame (Figure 10.3).

When the frame cuts a figure there is the implication that the frame position is arbitrary, that the scene is endless and a portion of the event just happened to be cut by the frame at that point by chance. The accidental character of the boundary was indeed arbitrary in many snapshots but, as a conscious compositional device, it had been used centuries before in Donattelo reliefs and in paintings by Mantegna and it is to be found, as a considered design element, in Japanese painting (Figure 10.4).

In an outside broadcast event the viewer may be aware that they are being shown selected 'portions' of the event and that the frame can be instantly adjusted by zooming in, to provide more detailed information or by zooming out, to include more of the televised event.

Photography developed a compositional style of the instantaneous framing of an everyday event. The most effective 'freeze frame' images of arrested motion use the tension created by subjects moving apart from each other, and the relationship of subjects (often on the edge of frame) in opposition to their environment. The considered 'spontaneity' of advertising imagery is an artifice carefully crafted to make use of naturally occurring events and presented in an attempt at innocent simplicity and naturalness. The sophisticated technique used to create a seemingly accidental, non-designed image is a long way removed from the typical 'holiday' snapshotter who haphazardly puts a frame around an event and rarely achieves a print with the impact of the controlled image made by an experienced photographer. The quality of 'random chance' in a composition therefore contains many formal devices that an experienced photographer will employ and exploit.

In copying from photographs in the mid-nineteenth century, artists attempted to correct this lack of order, the unnaturalness of the snapshot and the lack of pictorial logic, according to academic compositional principles. The distortion of perspective that sometimes gives the snapshot its special power and the accidents of composition were ironed out when painters translated photographs into paintings. Some painters, however, recognized that the 'non-style' of snapshot composition had a vitality lacking in conventional groupings and gave it artistic respectability by using in many of their paintings the characteristics of the arbitrary frame and perspective of short exposure photography (see Figure 10.3).

More recent influences

If photographic imagery provided an alternative to an over-intellectual approach to composition, many late nineteenth-century and early twentieth-century painters also challenged the received conventions of academic subject and design. Part of their traditional role of providing a visual record of faces and places was also being eroded by the growth of photography.

Figure 10.3 *Place de la Concord* (Vicomete Ludvic Lepic and his daughters) (1875), Degas

The predominant style of painting in the mid-nineteenth century favoured realistic illusionism. Photography, in providing an accurate imitation of external realities, reinforced this existing fashion and to some extent supplanted the social role of the artist as the only supplier of visual copies of nature, people or places.

In the 1840s photographic portraiture challenged the traditional painted portrait. This was followed in the 1850s, as the emerging technology allowed, by a fashion for landscape photography. Increasing film sensitivity during the next three decades permitted shutter speeds of up to 1/1000th second to be used and enabled fast-moving objects to be frozen. Artists discovered that their customary methods of depicting objects in motion were false even though they appeared to correspond to normal perception.

The increased shutter speeds of the 1860s and 1870s allowed snap-shot compositions of normal everyday street activity, subjects that had rarely been thought suitable for painting. This type of urban realism not only displayed a new type of composition, utilizing the accidental and random design of people and traffic, frozen in motion, but also provided new viewpoints of these events, such as the high angle shot from the top of a building looking down on to a street. When, in the late 1880s, Kodak announced 'You press the button – we do the rest', a flood of new 'image makers' were unleashed, unfettered by academic art training or academic precepts.

Realism was considered by some to be the new enemy of art and it was thought to have been nurtured by the growth of photography. Those artists who considered photographs to be no more than 'reflections in a looking glass', had to consider what personal aesthetic qualities they brought to their own paintings. In many cases they moved

Figure 10.4 *The Haneda Ferry and Benten Shrine* (1858), Hiroshige. This composition pre-dates the widespread use of wide-angle foreground framing in film and television

away from an attempt at the literal imitation of nature to more impressionistic images and later, to colour and form as the prime subject of their work. If the camera alone was to be the final arbiter in questions concerning visual truths then artists would move to new themes and subjects and explore the underlying structure of the psychology of perception and the ambiguity of imagery. They examined the differences between what one saw and what one knew about a subject.

Apart from the early photographic attempts to mimic academic painting subjects and groupings, the influence in the nineteenth century appeared to flow from photographs to painting. When painting found new themes and forms away from realistic illusionism in the twentieth century, photographers followed their lead and also attempted to place more emphasis on form and structure – on the abstraction of design from nature.

The use of simple shapes devoid of detail, patterns produced by everyday objects, the reduction of tone, colour producing sharp contrasts, 'distressed' texture and fragments of printed ephemera are popular photographic images influenced by the changing styles in painting in the first decades of the twentieth century.

There developed a two-way influence between painting and photography with some artists rejecting the Renaissance perspective of a single viewpoint and ultimately eliminating figurative subjects from their frame. Many became interested in creating compositions of colour, line and tone abstracted from three-dimensional objects.

These investigations into the nature of two-dimensional pattern on a surface influenced photographers who used monochrome to simplify the image and to create semi-abstract designs of line, light and shade. Many contemporary photographic images used in advertising are influenced by the experiments carried out in painting 70 or 80 years ago.

A painter has control of all the design elements in his painting and works towards a particular effect. A photographer, recognizing the freshness of the design, can find a parallel image and, by careful selection, recreate the more abstract graphic image of fine art. The cycle of 'new' art image followed by repetition and recreation within photography (particularly in advertising) all occurred during the twentieth century. The process reached a peak in the 1960s when painting incorporated advertising imagery. This reworking of the original commercial graphic conventions was immediately reclaimed by advertising and emerged as a new photographic style.

Photographic style

There was anxiety in the mid-1860s of the growing photographic style in painting. There was fierce resistance from the academic exhibitions to hanging paintings that appeared to be based on photographs and there was a heated debate about the nature of photographic style.

As we have discussed, one aspect of monochrome compositions is the tendency to emphasize line and tone. Also, people were unused to some types of photographic perspective that, although often identical to retina perspective, remained ignored or unacknowledged because of size constancy (see Chapter 3, 'Size constancy'). Photographic perspective, conditioned by size of reproduction, lens position, distance from subject and focal length, appeared to many people to be unnatural and distorted compared with perspective used in painting. Usually it was 'unpainterly' subjects that emphasized what were considered perspective distortions.

Photography allowed the most accurate reproduction of the most minute detail, which incited great interest in the general public even though, as one artist claimed, there is no great visual truth in counting how many slates there are on an image of a roof.

Although the eye unconsciously changes focus depending on the distance of the subject of interest, the degree of 'out of focus' of subjects at other distances goes unrecognized. Depending on the aperture used, a camera's depth-of-focus produces an image that may blur the foreground and background of a subject. This photographic zone of focus effect created a new visual representation of depth.

Alternative viewpoints, such as a high angle from a building looking down on to a street, appeared to be a photographic innovation unseen in painting. The ability, with high shutter speeds and extreme magnification, to reveal visual truths unavailable to normal human perception were amongst other photographic innovations that excited interest. Even blurred motion and photographic defects such as halation provided inspiration for artists such as Corot to experiment with new painting conventions.

The innovation of film technique

The development of film technique began in 1895/1910 and centred around finding methods of changing shot without distracting the audience. As we discussed in Chapter 1, a number of 'invisible' techniques were discovered and became the standard conventions of film making and later television.

Distinctive compositions that only made sense in the context of the film narrative (such as point-of-view shots) occurred pre-1914 when high and low angles began to be used. This style of composition, although not unique to film, was infrequently used in the still photography of the day.

As we discussed in Chapter 4, 'The lens and perspective', another convention that had an important influence on the composition of the shot was the 'Vitagraph Angle'. The lens was positioned at eye height, then later chest height, and this produced foreground heads of figures higher in the frame than background figures. At times the camera was positioned at waist height, which resulted in a more dynamic relationship between foreground and background. These departures from head-high lens position also eliminated the large amount of dead space above the actors' heads seen in many films of the period.

Development of TV camera technique

Standard television multi-camera conventions grew out of film technique and the same objectives of disguising technique in order to suspend disbelief in the viewer were adopted. The problem for actuality television was not to recreate 'real time' as in discontinuous film shooting but to meld together multi-camera shooting of an actuality event so that, for example, change of camera angle or cutting between different shot sizes was not obtrusive and distracting to the viewer. The aim once again was towards an 'invisible technique'.

Summary

The origins of contemporary camerawork composition are to be found in changes in painting styles over the last 500 years, in the influence of still photography and in changes in the style and the technology of film and television production. The influence of past solutions to visual problems conditions much of current practice.

Photography in the nineteenth century developed a compositional style of the instantaneous framing of an everyday event. The most effective 'freeze frame' images of motion arrested use the tension between subjects moving apart, and subjects and their relationship to their surroundings. When the frame cuts a figure there is the implication that the frame position is arbitrary, that the scene is endless and a portion of the event just happened to be cut by the frame at that point by chance.

The innovations in film at the beginning of the twentieth century and television in the 1950s are still valid and much of the pioneering work in the first decades of the twentieth century remains intact in current camera technique.

11

News and documentary

Fact and fiction

A television drama about a military engagement was criticized by an
army spokesman as being 'too realistic'. The camerawork style was
indistinguishable from news coverage and the army spokesman complained that the audience could easily be confused into thinking they
were watching 'a real event'. 'The Blair Witch Project', another piece
of fiction, was complimented on its realistic camerawork treatment.
The low tech image quality, the nervous unrehearsed hand-held
camerawork combined to persuade the audience that they were
watching an authentic event.

'Realistic' in this usage was achieved by imitating the characteristics
of news coverage. 'The camera surprised by events' has a number of
visual mannerisms such as rapid reframing, an unsteady frame, 'hose-
piping' the camera in rapid panning movements in search of the significant event, etc. This 'breaking news' appearance can be reinforced
by low tech image quality and poor colour rendition (see 'Composition
styles' in Chapter 12).

Apart from this type of visual mannerisms, what separates fact and
fiction camerawork? From the early days of film making, camerawork
conventions have been used to convince and persuade the intended
audience of the 'reality' of the story depicted. The criticism of 'realistic' camerawork appears to rest on the false assumption that there is
one set of 'fiction' visual conventions and another set of 'news' visual
conventions. Although there are differences in work practices when
shooting news such as, for example, less or no control of staging
subject matter, in general both types of camerawork use a variant of
invisible technique. What usually confuses some people in identifying
what is 'real' is that fiction film making has often borrowed certain
visual 'tics' of news gathering. Orson Welles, in his spoof version of a
'March of Time' newsreel at the start of 'Citizen Kane' employed
scratched film, jump cuts and ungraded film to 'authenticate' a newsreel appearance.

The fashionable view of what is considered realistic camerawork has undergone many changes. It was ironic that just as Steadicam was evolved to give smooth 360° movement anywhere, the fashion developed for unsteady camerawork as a signature of realism. Invisible technique that is fluid, smooth, unobtrusive camerawork is equated with fiction and the highly manufactured commercial commodity produced within the traditional conventions of Hollywood. Degrading the image and a hand-tooled 'wobbly' shot was seen as returning to the basics of realism and objectivity.

Realism and fantasy

As was discussed in Chapter 2, 'Alternative technique', the argument about objective and subjective camera effects were present at the birth of film. The Lumière brothers and Mèliès provided a template for the two opposing views. The choice was between film making as an attempt at realism – providing the audience with believable people caught up in believable events – or, like Mèliès, a fantasy setting of a fabulous activity. Film narration has to use a number of basic visual conventions in order to ensure that the audience can follow the story.

The first moving images presented to an audience were Lumière factory workers leaving their place of work, a train arriving at a station, etc. These prosaic factual events were soon overtaken by the audience's appetite for mystery, action, pace and excitement and the expanding film industry in the first quarter of the twentieth century soon learnt how to construct shot sequences that engaged the audience's attention. These visual conventions of unobtrusive editing and camera movement are still present in most types of programming, including news.

But news also has an obligation to separate fact from opinion, to be objective in its reporting and, by selection, to emphasize that which is significant to its potential audience. These considerations therefore needed to be borne in mind when composing shots for news as well as the standard camera technique associated with visual storytelling. There is a trade-off between the need to visually hold the attention of the audience and the need to be objective when covering news. Pace, action and visual excitement have always been used in film to tell a story but, in a news story, these standard techniques cannot be employed to capture the audience's attention if they are reconstructions. Subjectivity is increased by restaging the event to serve the needs of television (e.g., re-enacting significant action that occurred before the camera arrived), selecting only 'action' events to record unless qualified by a reporter, and the use of standard 'invisible' technique editing to produce a partial account of an event. Although there is an attempt to avoid these 'entertainment' aspects of storytelling in news reportage, they are often unavoidable because of the nature of the news item or the demands of attracting viewers.

Film as illusion

Whether fact or fiction, all film making is in some way creating an illusion. Part of the role of the director or cameraman is find the appropriate technique to create a convincing illusion. There are a number of ways of achieving this, such as by immersing the audience in a story with convincing detail and choosing techniques that do not disturb their concentration on content or by convincing the audience they are watching an accurate account of reality – news coverage in the raw. They may be aware of unsteady camerawork or disjointed continuity, etc., but that visual style simply reinforces their belief in the authenticity of the event.

An objective representation of 'reality' in a news, documentary or current affairs production uses the same perennial camerawork techniques as the subjective personal impression or the creation of atmosphere in fictional films. A football match appears to be a factual event whereas music coverage may appear more impressionistic. In both types of coverage there is selection and the use of visual conventions. Football uses a mixture of close-ups and wide shots, variation of lens height, camera position, cutaways to managers, fans, slow motion replays, etc., to inject pace, tension and drama to hold the attention of the audience. Music coverage will use similar techniques in interpreting the music, but with different rates of pans and zooms motivated by the mood and rhythm of the music. If it is a pop video, there are no limits to the visual effects the Director may feel are relevant. All camerawork is in one way or another an interpretation of an event. The degree of subjective personal impression fashioning the account will depend on which type of programme it is created for.

Objectivity

Although news aims to be objective and free from the entertainment values of standard television storytelling (e.g., suspense, excitement, etc.) it must also aim to engage the audience's attention and keep them watching. The trade-off between the need to visually hold the attention of the audience and the need to be objective when covering news centres on structure and shot composition.

There are a number of standard shots used in feature work such as a canted camera, rapid camera movement, racking focus between speakers, etc., which appear mannered and subjective when used in new coverage. Any composition that appears subjective and impressionistic is usually avoided.

As the popularity of cinema films has shown, an audience enjoys a strong story that involves them in suspense and moves them through the action by wanting to know 'what happens next?'. This is often incompatible with the need for news to be objective and factual. The production techniques used for shooting and cutting fiction and factual material are almost the same. These visual storytelling techniques have been learned by the audiences from a lifetime of watching fictional accounts of life. The twin aims of communication and engaging the attention of the audience apply to news as they do to entertainment programmes.

Record versus comment

Whilst news camerawork aims to be simply a record of an event, inevitably it becomes a comment on an event. It is comment or opinion because choices always have to be made whenever a shot is recorded. Apart from the obvious decision on the content of the shot, whether it be politician, building or crowd, there are also the subtle influences on the viewers' perception of the event produced by camera position, lighting, lens angle, lens height and camera movement. The camera is not an objective optical instrument such as a microscope. In setting up a shot, there is considerable scope for influencing the appearance and therefore the impact of the image. There is always the temptation to find the 'best' composition, even when shooting, for example, the effects of poverty and deprivation in city slums.

A news cameraman arriving to cover a street riot will be unable, at first, to understand fully the complexity of the situation. For personal safety, he/she can choose to film from behind the police lines or they can, if they are sufficiently courageous, get in amongst the protesters who are facing the police. The camera position they choose will, to some extent, colour the response of the viewer. From behind police lines the image is of missiles and petrol bombs aimed in the direction of the camera. Subjectively the viewer is under attack. The viewpoint in amongst the protesters is of a phalanx of police shields, guns and batons bearing down on the camera. The viewer is subjectively under violent attack from the forces of law and order. Usually there is no third choice, such as access to the roof of a building providing a high camera position looking down on the street avoiding any partisan identification. Even if available, this is an inflexible position that is quickly unusable once the point of conflict moves on. The criticism sometimes heard about the bias of this type of camera coverage simply fails to take into account the impossibility, in a fast-moving, confused situation, of finding a neutral, detached camera viewpoint. Almost every shot will suggest culpability.

With the development of digital manipulation in video post-production, no shot can be taken as an incontrovertible record of an event. The audience's trust in news coverage is based more on standard news conventions – the appearance of an item – than an absolute faith in the information provided.

(a)

(b)

Figure 11.1 **(a)** Riot police advancing towards the camera; the viewer in position of the protesters; **(b)** from the police viewpoint facing a cage of demonstrators

Operational awareness

It is easy to believe that all one requires to be a good news cameraman is an understanding of technology, technique and an appreciation of news programmes' customary styles. But news camerawork requires a fourth essential ingredient, the ability to professionally respond to sudden violent, unforeseen, spontaneous events and provide shots that can be edited to provide an informative news item. Keeping a cool head and providing competent coverage is the opposite to the often seen amateur video accounts of dramatic events where the camera is hose-piped all over the scene in a panic response to action that surprised the operator. News stories are often shot in real time with no opportunity (or requirement) to influence what is happening. The news cameraman must immediately respond to the occurrence in front of the lens and make split-second decisions about composition, what to frame and where to capture the significant shots. Essentially, news camerawork is looking for things moving or in the process of change. A shot of a closed door and curtained windows of a house where a siege is taking place can only be held on screen for a very short time and requires the supporting coverage of the flurry of activity that is taking place in the surrounding area.

Realistic camerawork

Realism in film is that attitude that is opposed to 'expressionism'. Realism emphasizes the subject as opposed to the director's *view* of the subject. Expressionism or any form of fiction narrative can make any juxtaposition of images achieve either an expression of the film maker or to move, affect and provoke an effect in the audience. There is no limit to how fantastic a film narrative can be. There are no agreed restraints on technique or form, although there are social concerns about the effects of pornographic and violent subject matter.

'Realism', on the other hand, is attempting to be objective – to remove the conditioning influence of its creator. There are competing definitions of what it means to be 'objective' and factual film makers are expected not to fabricate an event. Does this mean avoiding any influence on the subject of the film? Is the presence of the camera an influence? Would the material be different if the camera was not present?

There are always two influences at work on any sequence of shots. Firstly, there are the requirements of the film and television form – the mechanics of the media. In some way, the audience has to see and hear what is being presented. Secondly, the personal subjectivity of the film maker – his or her creative ambitions and viewpoint are difficult to eradicate. The fingerprint of their aims and intentions will somehow be present.

It is not possible to remove all traces of the creative decision making in film. For example, the 'found' form of a piece of driftwood on the beach is selected when it is picked up and taken to be displayed. Aesthetic values have been exercised. A choice has been made. Some productions avoid making these decisions and leave the camera running and the framing to chance. The images cannot be free of all subjective decision making because simply recording and placing the camera in a position conditions the appearance of the shot. A surveillance camera has a number of prearranged factors affecting the way the shot looks. How 'realistic' is the security camera system in a superstore?

There is in fact a new lust for authenticity – no interpretation, just a flat statement of reality. Standard programme production, particularly on crime, has been able to achieve increasing standards of glossiness that is in contrast to actuality footage.

Surveillance cameras provide the jolt of raw footage that is unmediated – a direct access to the real without modification. There are compilation programmes featuring cameras in police car chases, city centre fixed cameras of street crime, etc. This 'reality' TV also includes secret filming and the self-documentation of video diaries. The very roughness of surveillance images guarantees total authenticity. The appeal of this video reality TV is that it is perceived as real – it is not re-creation. New technology can go where TV cameras have never been before.

Secret filming allows evidence to be collected that is obtainable by no other method – it is an unglamorous version of crime. Its raw appearance feels closer to reality. How something was shot becomes more important than the reason it was shot. The stylized conventions of secret filming and the imitation of raw footage such as 'grained up' images, converting colour images to black and white, shaky camera-work and the appearance of voyeurism is a developed programme 'style'.

Technology as an aid to 'realism'

The invention of film and the projection of life-sized figures was proclaimed by the Lumière brothers as 'life on the run' – a greater realism than could be achieved with still photography. Movement and screen size enhanced the illusion. Later sound, and then colour and stereo sound, expanded the experience. Cinerama claimed 'it creates all the illusion of reality...you see things the way you do in real life not only in front of you as in conventional motion pictures, but also out of the corners of your eyes...you hear with the same startling realism'.

As we mentioned in Chapter 7, 'The shape of the screen', the giant screen size and stereo were used mainly as novelty attractions. They were seen as an experience in themselves rather than at the service of realistic storytelling. The development of stereo sound, colour and widescreen were identified with spectacle.

Documentary programmes

The definition of what is a documentary depends on where people position themselves in this debate. The word 'documentary' was coined by a group of British film makers in the 1930s who were aiming to change the audience's perception about other people's lives. Over time, the word has changed in meaning and, to most audiences, 'documentary' implies visual factual evidence that is a truthful record of an event or activity.

The early British documentary makers often followed John Grierson's famous definition of documentary as being 'the creative treatment of actuality'. But the concept that truth can be creatively interpreted allows considerable latitude in how visual factual evidence is produced. In the 1930s and 1940s, bulky 35-mm film equipment made substantial reconstruction and restaging almost inevitable. In his documentary 'Drifters', Grierson built a trawler deckhouse on land and then got genuine fishermen to recreate their normal seagoing activities. It is claimed that Robert Flaherty, following the activities of Nanook, an Eskimo, wanted a very much larger igloo built to accommodate interior shots. The traditional igloo had obviously an optimum functional design size because the roof of a larger constructed igloo collapsed.

Another British documentary film maker, Paul Rotha, identified a distinction between news and documentary by suggesting that news cameramen 'make no effort to approach their subjects from a creative or dramatic point of view other than those of plain description', whereas documentary cameramen must be 'poets of the camera'. This early auteur theory (film as the exclusive creation of *one* person), suggests that documentary is the artistic vision of one man.

In the 1950s, French anthropologists' use of the film camera as a 'scientific' recording instrument led to the development of the portable 16-mm camera with synch sound. There was a growing awareness of the influence the observer has on the subject. A famous example, before the documentary movement began, was of the study of working conditions at Western Electric's Hawthorne plant in Illinois in 1927, which discovered that output increased on the production line not only when, for example, lighting conditions were improved but also when they were made worse. The fact of being studied, rather than the experimental factors being manipulated, had caused the workers to react.

Observation, with or without a camera, affects the subject being observed. Once people become aware of being watched, their behaviour is altered. There can be no disinterested bystander with a camera who does not in some way affect the behaviour of their attention. In the 1960s, the American documentary film makers loosely grouped under the title of Direct Cinema were confident that they could remain detached from their subject. Liberated by the go-anywhere film equipment they suggested they were simply an uninvolved bystander at the 'filmed event'. Their claim of non-intervention with their subject was hard to substantiate. Any documentary maker has to select a subject, a camera viewpoint and then edit the material. These are all areas where personal preconceptions, knowledge and attitude can influence choice in addition to the effect of the filming process on the participants.

At the same time, across the Atlantic, the French Cinema-Vérité documentary movement were doubtful if the subjective attitudes of a film maker could remain detached from his/her work. Jean Luc-Goddard suggested that the quest for uncontaminated reportage throws away the two most important assets of a film maker – intelligence and sensitivity.

Some French film makers deliberately put themselves in their documentaries because they believed their influence was always present. It is like a cameraman filming in a fairground Hall of Mirrors. At some stage, whichever way you point the camera, you are bound to get yourself into shot. Sometimes you will be sharply recognized and sometimes you film a distorted image of yourself. It is impossible to film/video a sequence without the originator's fingerprints appearing somewhere on a shot. The man/woman behind the camera can never keep him/herself out of shot.

Many people attempt to show things 'as they really are', but film/video as straightforward documentary truthful evidence is always suspect because:

• the film or tape is a representation and is not equivalent to the actual event filmed. Converting three-dimensions into a flat image converts an event into a replication of that event. The two are not interchangeable;

- the camera is not an impartial scientific instrument that provides a truthful record of the subject. Lens, film tape stock and camera position all colour the truthfulness of the record;
- the camera operator and then editor exert conscious and subconscious influences. They put themselves between the subject and the viewer and cannot be eliminated from the frame.

Professionalism

The packaging of 'facts' in an attempt to attract and keep a mass audience occurs in news, current affairs and documentaries, but the 'package' of technique is usually so well disguised or so familiar that it is not intrusive. The disquiet felt by some people is when a highly dramatic and sometimes life-threatening event is recorded by a news crew with no one from the television organization attempting to intervene or assist those in distress. It exposes the implications of adopting the role of professional 'looker-on', indifferent or detached from subject matter, and also the extent to which the illusion-making technique that has sustained countless fictional entertainments can be employed in the presentation of 'real' events.

There is the example of an ENG crew who videotaped a woman struggling for her life in an icy river after surviving a plane crash. This ENG crew even captured the moment when a bystander leapt into the water and rescued her. Or, in the most extreme example, the cameraman who stood his ground and zoomed out to contain the 'action' of a Vietnamese child running towards the camera, screaming and immersed in flame.

The convention in television is that the broadcast organization delegates responsibility for content to a few individuals, removing the majority of employees from any public accountability for the effect of their work. It is considered that market forces will take care of any lapse in taste. Give the public what it wants, it is suggested, and they will either watch and endorse the choice or switch to another channel. There is also, in many countries, the safety net of government-appointed regulatory bodies that require the companies to comply with certain codes of political balance, avoidance of offensive material, etc. The broadcast system would therefore appear to have sufficient safeguards to eliminate any moral dilemma that a crew may have in not assisting those in distress.

Professional 'looking-on' would appear to be a mandate for non-involvement with people 'out there' in front of the camera – a suspension of personal responsibility to act and the surrendering to the employing organization the task of evaluating the morality of any particular situation. A dispensation is claimed for the professional 'news collector' so that he/she may stand outside the event and objectively report. Whatever is happening, the news cameraman has, in one sense, a professional vested interest to see that it continues until he/she has got the essential material. Crews will struggle through blizzards and will be the first to arrive at snowed-in villages but they will bring no food or other essential supplies. They will search for possible suffering, hardship, death or even cheerful 'community spirit' stories and then leave with a 'factual' report. If the inhabitants are fortunate enough to have their electricity reconnected they can watch a replay of the triumphant arrival of the crew on the evening news.

The broadcast employee is cushioned and actively encouraged to make no moral judgements about his professional activity. Machine-like, he is programmed to be a neutral transmitter of messages and he either takes the money or resigns. The accolade 'professional' is in fact often used in television to describe, amongst other qualities, the ability to meet a deadline within budget, to satisfy standards and the values of fellow practitioners but, above all, to preserve some degree of objectivity and detachment. This is also interpreted as the ability to give the best possible presentation of subject matter that engages the interest of the audience whilst avoiding commitment or bias. But this professional detachment cannot be compared with that of, say, a doctor, who although he may avoid identifying with the suffering of his patient is nevertheless required to avoid administering poison or harming his patient.

It is unlikely that the crew who clambered over the wreckage of a train to get the close-up of the driver's face just before his leg was amputated to free him would have gone there to stare unless they had a camera between themselves and the event. This special dispensation for the professional 'looker-on' allows such material as the expression on the train driver's face before he loses his leg and is endorsed by the news editor as of 'human interest', or of news value. Exploitation of grief and suffering is certainly not unique to television. Public executions were very popular (and still are in some countries) until abolished. Possibly the same frisson is still available in the comfort of our own homes when we look into the eyes of a drowning woman as she desperately scrabbles for safety in icy water and legitimize it by calling it news. It is this extra quality of vivid immediacy of news film that is particularly sought for and endorsed as having great 'human interest'. Watching a person die or suffer extreme emotion is sanctioned by appealing to 'news values'. But if the audience makes a trip to the scene of the disaster instead of watching it on television in order to catch a glimpse (in the distance) of the same victim, it brings down the full self-righteous wrath of journalism and denouncements of 'ghoulish rubber necking' and 'sick voyeurism'.

There is in broadcasting a belief that a mass audience is attracted and held by production techniques that relay an experience of an event rather than analysis. Instant access to the 'real' is in demand, it is suggested, as long as it is highly packaged within the conventions derived from fiction films. This results in the search for impact to grab the audience and hyping the 'real' has not only borrowed all the standard entertainment conventions but has invented a few of its own.

A round-up programme of the day's sport becomes not the selected 'highlights' of a football match but an entertainment package of slow motion replays, personalities, comment and the collapse of real time to produce an interpretation of an event that is entirely different from the experience of a spectator at that event. The search for good 'factual' television, equalling popular television, equalling large audience, often runs the risk, in using the narrative conventions of fiction films, of obliterating the truthful representation of the event.

Engaging the attention of the audience

The 'fly on the wall' technique claims to have the least effect on the
participants, but one policeman, commenting on a police documentary series, complained that TV fictional crime series have 50 minutes
to solve their crimes in order to fit a TV schedule. Real police work
is boring, repetitive, with hours, days and weeks of routine before a
result (or sometimes no result), and yet the edited version of the
police documentary runs 50 minutes of 'highlights' – it has more
action than the non-fictional equivalent. The producer of the documentary justified the trimming out and heightening up of action on
the basis that it would bore the viewer if repetitive, extended police
routine was presented in its entirety. He elected to give a flavour of
police procedures. This interpreting an event, giving a 'flavour', is
not a mirror held up to actuality, as is sometimes claimed for this
approach, but a creation in television terms of an event. It involves
considerable decision and selection of material and, when those decisions are biased in favour of mass entertainment techniques such as
pace, action, tension and impact, then reality becomes packaged in
formula film conventions. This soon deteriorates into the recycling of
clichés and stereotypes; the fictionalizing of reality to fit the conventions of a thousand movies. In fact the highest endorsement some
people can give to the vividness of an event they have experienced is
that 'it was just like a movie'.

It is suggested that television has turned its audience into 'image
junkies' where endless newsreels of horror and spectacle are consumed
at an alarming rate. Each new shock horror image de-sensitizing feeling and raising the ante for audience response. Possibly the danger of
hyping the 'real' is not in the confusion experienced by the viewer who
begins to expect the same production and entertainment values in the
storming of a terrorist-held embassy as they experience with a Bond
film, but in the ambition of programme makers, seeking large audiences, who appear to have deliberately blurred the programme distinction between fact and fiction.

American writer John Knightly in his book *The First Casualty*
describes how GIs in Vietnam acted out the 'John Wayne' walk of
Hollywood war movies when they saw CBS newsreel cameras arrive.
They were filmed doing this and no doubt viewers, when they saw this
footage, were convinced that this was a 'real' event. With life imitating
'art' there may be a new category for an Oscar – best dramatic
performance in a news bulletin.

Summary

Although there are differences in work practices when shooting news
such as, for example, less or no control of staging subject matter, in
general both news and fiction camerawork use a variant of invisible
technique.

All camerawork is in one way or another an interpretation of an
event. The degree of subjective personal impression fashioning the
account will depend on which type of programme it is created for.

In news camerawork, compositions that appear mannered or subjective (e.g., a canted camera) are avoided but composition still influences impartiality.

It is often impossible in a fast-moving, confused news story to find a neutral detached camera viewpoint.

News camerawork requires the ability to professionally respond to sudden violent, unforeseen, spontaneous events and provide shots that can be edited to provide an informative news item.

Observation, with or without a camera, affects the subject being observed. Once people become aware of being watched, their behaviour is altered. There can be no disinterested bystander with a camera who does not in some way affect the behaviour of the subject/s of their attention.

12
Composition styles

Visual styles

There are a range of film styles as distinct, for example, as Laurence Olivier's 'Henry V' and Billy Wilder's 'Double Indemnity', which were both made in the same year (1944). Olivier achieved a formalism based on sets designed with the colour and perspective of mediaeval illustrations, whilst Wilder's visual style is often based on film noir's low-key lighting and night shooting on wet, rain-streaked roads. Camerawork styles and visual imagery are not always influenced by contemporary fashion. The above two films, made in different countries, had two very distinct visual styles. To detail fully the variety of styles that have originated in the history of film and television would require a separate book. Below are just a few examples of different approaches to compositional styles.

The dominant influence on the look of the film is usually the director, although often the director of photography or production designer have a significant input. Styles of camerawork technique range from the standard storytelling coverage designed as an uncomplicated, undemanding entertainment that keeps faith with the expectations of most of its potential audience, to productions that completely reject conventional visual codes and favour an indirect and oblique presentation. This 'alternative technique' has been discussed in Chapter 2.

Style and technique

Visual style may rely on the repetition of visual motifs such as long focal length lenses condensing space, as for example, in John Altman's film 'Short Cuts' (1993), in order to provide an impression of American suburban claustrophobia. The same film uses another visual motif with long zooms, but change in image size is motivated and disguised by the action such as Earl Piggot's (John Waite) entrance to the cafe where his wife Doreen (Lily Tomalin) works, or the steady zoom movement towards a telephone that repeatedly rings. These stylistic flourishes are achieved within the standard conventions of invisible technique.

In 'Tokyo Story' (1953), Yasujiro Ozu consistently uses a low camera height, equivalent to the eye height of someone seated on the floor, shooting a medium shot of two, three or four people. There is one small camera movement in the two hours fifteen minutes of the film. Although it has a very distinctive style, that style is again achieved mainly within the invisible technique conventions. These two films have a very different visual appearance created by the director's choice of lens angle, camera movement, camera height and camera distance when shooting the majority of scenes.

Not all productions consistently follow one style of shooting. A television cookery programme may introduce into a very prosaic presentation a few swerving camera movements to suggest the breathless excitement of unrehearsed news coverage. Of course, everything about filming the cookery demonstration is under the complete control of the producer/director, but the camera style implies that 'reality' is being recorded without production control. 'Life' is being captured on the run.

Style becomes content

Style sometimes overwhelms a weak narrative and becomes the dominant interest of the film. Exaggerated style elements such as the continuous use of a wide-angle distorting lens make the world less natural and will distance the viewer from the narrative. The audience will become less involved with the protagonists but may enjoy the stylistic flourishes.

Style building blocks

The style of a film or television programme can be influenced by any of the skills and crafts of the people that are involved in its production, such as the script treatment, artiste's performance, editing, soundtrack, music, etc. They all play a part in shaping the style of the production. This chapter will concentrate on the camerawork contribution.

There are a number of standard styles and camerawork conventions inherited from the past. The history of film and TV is one of innovation and change enhancing a body of standard technique. In general, the look of a film or TV production is created by the treatment of space, light, camera movement, choice of lens, colour or shot structure. The changes and variations in these visual building blocks are influenced by:

- *technological development* – screen shape, lightweight cameras, new film stock, Steadicam, etc.;
- *lighting styles and fashion* – e.g., realistic or expressionistic;
- *choice of lens and camera placement* – naturalistic or stylized compositions;
- *camera movement* – invisible or obtrusive, pace of movement;

- *the staging of the artistes* – juxtaposition of foreground and background people or things – small depth or wide depth;
- *choice of studio or location shooting*;
- *monochrome and colour application*;
- *shot structure and editing* – camera movement to explain narrative or cutting to follow action.

Technological development

The changes and innovation in cameras, camera mountings, film stock, lighting equipment, sound, post-production and electronic processing have had an enormous impact on what is possible in production. Sometimes it appears as if technical change stimulates new styles (e.g., portable video cameras, Steadicam, etc.). Sometimes a problem finds a solution in a technical breakthrough (e.g., the exchange of TV productions in different electronic standards solved by digital conversion). Film and TV are only possible through technology. Technology and technique intertwine. How you do something in camerawork is dependent on what equipment you are using. It is not simply a question of being told which button to press in order to get a professional result.

In television camerawork, for example, an understanding of camera technology plus the ability to exploit and take into consideration the attributes of the camera and the lens characteristics are the basis of practical programme production. Although television and film production can only be created with technology, there seems to be a growing trend to ignore the mechanics and simply trust auto-technique features. In an age of de-skilling, euphemistically called multiskilling, most video equipment is now wrapped up with auto-features in the hope of being user-friendly to technophobic customers, but cameramen usually understand what is happening when they are operating equipment rather than the uninformed passively pressing a button and hoping the equipment 'will do the rest'.

One of the enduring characteristics of film and television broadcasting is that it is in a continuous state of change. New equipment, new techniques, new outlets are introduced almost annually. Each change in technology requires evaluation in order to understand how it can be exploited in production. Keeping up with change is a crucial requirement otherwise old skills will be as redundant as old equipment.

As we discussed in the chapters on widescreen, some types of new technology are taken up whereas others are ignored. It may be misleading to believe that the methods of production are simply 'given', but often new technology stimulates new styles just as the quest for new technique stimulates technological innovation. The lightweight portable video camera enabled 'hot head' camera booms to be developed that allowed much more fluid movement compared with manned cameras (see Chapter 16, 'Movement'), just as in the late 1950s/early 1960s the introduction of ring-steer pedestals in television studios enabled more complex camerawork and greater mobility in smaller sets that coincided with the new fashion for realistic 'kitchen sink' dramas staged in small sets.

Lighting styles

See Chapter 13, section on lighting technique.

Choice of lens and camera placement

Film director Sidney Lumet claimed that the (focal) length of the lens is the director's most fundamental camera choice. As we discussed in Chapter 4, 'The lens and perspective', choosing the camera distance from the main subject and the focal length of the lens to be used not only decides the size of the shot, but also controls the depiction of depth and the 'internal' space of the shot. These two aspects of style – size of shot and the depiction of depth – have had many different treatments in the history of film.

Lens angle and focal length

Firstly, when discussing film and television camerawork, it is better to use lens angle rather than the focal length of a lens. Lens angle or angle of view is related to the focal length of the lens and the format size of the pick-up sensor, whether it be CCD or a frame of film. As we discussed in Chapter 7, for some time there was a universal film frame that was either 35 mm or 16 mm. Widescreen processes and innovations such as super 16 mm added to the number of frame sizes when calculating angle of view.

Television cameras have had as many different pick-up frame sizes as film, and from an early time in TV history it became customary not to quote focal length to indicate the size of shot obtainable from a lens, but its angle of view. When discussing the depiction of depth and perspective, either in film or television, identifying the angle of view of a specific lens will provide a better guidance of the lens/camera distance effect.

For example, a lens less than 35 mm focal length (35°) on a 35 mm film camera may be considered a wide-angle lens. The same focal length lens on a 2/3″ video camera would have a lens angle of approximately 14°. It would need a 14 mm lens to match the 35 mm lens on a 35 mm camera. A medium lens angle on all cameras would range from 35° to 25°. A narrow angle of view (a long focal length lens) would range from 17° to less than 3°. There is no scientific basis for the boundaries of these categories – simply custom and practice. To avoid confusion, state the angle of view in degrees rather than the dimension of the focal length of a lens.

In the early days of film making, 25°–17° approximate (50 mm–75 mm) lenses were routinely employed, although longer lenses were sometimes used. As was mentioned in Chapter 4, American silent film production at the beginning of the twentieth century used a convention of a 25° lens at eye level and actor movement was restricted to being no closer to the lens than 12 ft. With an actor standing 12 ft from the lens, the bottom of the frame cuts him at knee height. By 1910, the Vitagraph company allowed the actors to play up to 9 ft from the lens and the camera was lowered to chest height. This convention produced a distinct visual depiction of depth.

Not only lens angle and camera distance but depth-of-field also gives indications of space. The development of the close-up on a longer lens set at an aperture that threw the background out of focus became a staple style convention.

As film technology evolved with faster film speeds and more efficient lighting, it was possible, if desired, to have a much greater depth-of-field and, when staging in depth, to have all the artistes in sharp focus. Deep focus shots were a feature of Greg Toland's work on 'Citizen Kane', released in the spring of 1941. He used the hard light of arc lamps that had been used for Technicolour in the mid-1930s, the new faster film stock and coated lenses which allowed an $f$no that could hold foreground close-ups and background figures in focus. Many of the deep focus shots, however, were achieved by back projection, optical tricks or special effects.

Staging in depth became a feature of the 1940s and 1950s up to the expansion of colour and the use of anamorphic lenses for widescreen. The standard CinemaScope lens provided for a 46° angle (50 mm), but equivalent to 16.5° (30 mm) in normal 35 mm format. Colour film was less sensitive than the faster black and white stock and deep focus was restricted to exteriors because of the high lighting levels required for larger $f$nos in the studio. As mentioned in Chapter 8, early widescreen films were composed with artistes staged across the frame rather than in depth. A common aperture setting in the early years of widescreen was f2.8. With focus on artistes at 10 ft, depth-of-field extended from 8 ft to 12 ft. Any foreground MCU would have been out of focus.

As colour film increased in speed, a full range of lenses could be used ranging from 3° to 60°. In the 1980s and 1990s longer lenses were used as the fashion for following action on tight shots became popular. A major influence of this style was the Japanese director Akira Kurasawa who, in his monochrome 1950s films, used long focal length lenses on battle scenes.

In the 1960s and 1970s, many countries converted their TV services to colour. The standard four lens turret on a monochrome camera, which had a range of lenses of typically 9°, 16°, 24° and 35°, was replaced with a zoom lens. In the following decades the zoom range improved from 10:1 up to 50:1 and decreased minimum object distance (MOD) to hold sharp focus. This was particularly vital in studio productions and, with some zooms, the MOD was decreased from 3 m down to 0.5 m. Using a wide-angle lens with the camera close to the action produced accelerated action and movement. It was also popular for depicting a surreal, distorted view of everyday 'reality'.

Depth-of-field

Depth-of-field is the term used to describe the range of acceptable focus in a shot. It is a function of camera aperture and the distance of the main subject from the camera. A small depth-of-field created by wide open aperture and a narrow lens angle, for example, is a useful compositional device for separating foreground subject from background. Because of its lack of background detail, if this style is used continuously it gives very little information to the audience about setting or location. Withholding information about the 'geography' of the action creates mystery and is more expressionistic than a large depth-of field that provides more information and appears to be more 'realistic'. If the director wishes to provide a shot to explain the loca-

Plate 1 A colour wheel showing the complementaries of the main colours

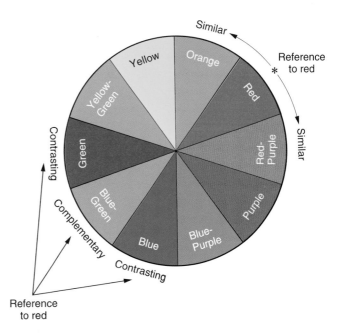

Plates 2 and 3 A small saturated colour such as red against green has a greater impact than when it is placed against a lower illuminance colour such as blue

Plate 4 Using a monochrome viewfinder the subject of the shot – a red flower against green foliage, almost disappears and the shot would be tightened in an effort to emphasize the flower

Plate 5 The same shot displayed in colour provides sufficient separation between flower and background. The defocused orange aubretia creeping into the right of frame, unseen in a monochrome viewfinder, becomes more noticeable and could have been eliminated by camera repositioning or tightening on the red flower if the montbretia could have been seen in the viewfinder

Plate 6 This vegetable pack shot framed up in monochrome is disorganized and messy because the colour component of the shot is unable to be utilized

Plate 7 A tighter shot that relies on colour for its composition could be framed if the colour values were available in a colour viewfinder

Plate 8 Rembrandt's self portrait – as the Apostle St Paul. Courtesy of RIJKS Museum, 2002.

tion of the action, he/she would most likely use a medium lens angle (25°–40°) as a scene-setter.

The depth-of-field of a shot will control the staging of the performers. A large depth-of-field will allow staging in depth unless it is possible to rack focus between foreground and background. This is usually achieved, for example, by being sharply in focus on a foreground performer who turns to a background artiste. The focus is racked back to this character on the turn of the head. Racking focus can be used in a number of ways in a shot but, to be effective, it requires a narrow depth-of-field to provide a significant change in focus and motivating action to trigger the focus shift. Throwing the focus to different parts of the frame changes compositional emphasis without reframing.

The sensitivity of the film stock has varied over the years. After 1940 panchromatic film stock was more sensitive than previous orthocromatic film and allowed a black and white fashion for staging in depth. The wider the film gauge the less depth-of-field and the introduction of widescreen and less sensitive colour stock produced a small depth-of-field that required shallow staging to hold focus. This lasted until colour negative film improved in speed.

In television, the same decrease in depth-of-field occurred with the introduction of colour until colour cameras improved their sensitivity. The depth-of-field in studio productions is conditioned by lighting levels. A smaller depth-of-field is often created for dramatic effect but large depth-of-field is often a convention of entertainment shows with large glossy sets. Many television productions feature unrehearsed and spontaneous events. Rapid shot change requires rapid focus and if the cameraman cannot predict the direction of movement a larger depth-of-field helps in following focus. On a narrow-angle lens this is only of marginal help.

Camera movement

A changing viewpoint is one of the unique features of film and television. It allows the spectator to travel through space and take up a new vantage point. A camera movement into a scene takes the audience into the film 'space'. The use of camera movement to create a film style has taken many forms, from the 10-minute single takes of Hitchcock where the camera moved through sets that were peeled away like an onion to allow access, to the fluid lens of contemporary Steadicam technique. Camera movement is another crucial element of image making and is dealt with in Chapter 16.

Staging the artistes

The Dustin Hoffman character in 'Tootsie' (1982) was reproached by his agent for causing trouble on a commercial shoot. 'But I was dressed as a tomato in that commercial', he protested, 'Tomatoes don't sit down'. How and when performers move, sit, stand or handle props is often a contentious topic on a film or TV set. There is often actor movement required to justify a camera move and there is movement that the actors feel is necessary for their performance. Staging a performer/presenter, that is, where they stand or move whether in a factual or a fiction production is a crucial part of the look or style of the shot.

There have been a number of different fashions in staging styles from the spread-across-the-frame shots of silent movies to the elaborate foreground and background choreography of staging in depth. Staging and its relationship to composition is discussed in more detail in Chapter 15.

Studio or location shooting

Although it would appear that location backgrounds would be cheaper than constructed scenery in a studio, it has often been the case in the past that a studio complex, like factories, needs a through-put of productions to cover the cost of premises and permanent staff. Television studio complexes for many years handled drama and soaps almost on a production belt system, with overnight 'set and light' to facilitate rapid turnaround of the facilities. Small crews manning portable video cameras allowed drama productions to move out of the studios onto the streets. This often coincided with a production desire to be more 'realistic'. In the past, the Hollywood studio production often favoured a very stylized appearance that maximized the glamorous presentation of its stars. The full-time technicians employed by the studios were very skilled at this form of presentation (see Lighting and composition, Chapter 13). Even those films with considerable exterior scenes would be shot entirely in a studio in order to control costs and be close to the watchful eye of management.

A change in storytelling and type of story appeared in the 1950s when feature films took to the streets with productions such as 'Panic in the Streets' (1950). Of course, silent comedies had been out on the streets 30 years before, whether it was Laurel and Hardy moving a piano up a very long flight of stairs or the Keystone Cops causing traffic havoc in comedy chases. The gritty realism of 'Panic in the Streets' could only be captured at real locations, often with actuality lighting. No set could ever have the patina of use of an actual bar. Costume drama often faces the same problem when it tries to reproduce 'poverty' clothing. It is possible to dirty down cloth to make it grimy and stained but it is impossible to reproduce the threadbare and worn appearance of clothing that has had a lifetime of wear.

Shot structure and editing

Editing has such a significant effect on a production that it requires a separate chapter. See Chapter 17.

Stylistic flourishes

There are a number of stylistic 'flourishes' that occur across the history of film and television. Often they enjoy a brief popularity before falling into disuse. Then suddenly, in a retro revival, they have a brief renaissance. Amongst the more common effects are:

- *flare* – the deliberate introduction of degradation across the frame caused by sun or hard light source. The cinematographer on 'Easy Rider' said the studio previously would not let them use flare and always wanted well exposed films because of drive-in audiences;
- *filters* – there is a wide range of filter effects from diffusion to high contrast;
- *smoke* – acts as a three-dimensional filter allowing light to be shown, e.g., a beam of sunlight, etc.;
- *canted camera* – the Dutch tilt or canted camera has had various revivals over time. Carol Reed was a great exponent of the canted camera in 'Odd Man Out' (1946) and 'The Third Man' (1949). Also in canted low angles;
- *pulsed zooms* – the zoom is rapidly zoomed in and out many times, sometimes on the beat of the music in a music video. As an effect it was superseded by the flexibility of digital effects, although sharp jittery zoom pulls are often used in alternative, punk style – see below;
- *freeze frame* – one of the most famous freeze frames was at the end of François Truffaut's 'Les Quatre Cents Coups' (1959) but as a stylistic flourish it has been used in many films;
- *whip pan* – the whip pan has a long tradition and is still seen in contemporary films;
- *vignettes* – opening and closing circle vignettes were a feature of silent films and are usually employed as a stylistic reference to their period of film making;
- *wipes, etc.* – wiping to a new scene or image is mainly used in television, although film travelogues at one time made frequent use of the wipe.

There are a number of other visual conventions such as montage, etc., which are dealt with below in specific styles.

Multi-camera live television conventions

Film is a record of an event edited and assembled after the event occurs. Live television is a presentation of an event as it occurs. The unique quality of an electronic camera is its ability to produce a picture that can be instantly transmitted. This entails a production technique that involves a number of people perfecting their individual contribution in a production group simultaneously as the event is transmitted. To coordinate such a group activity, it is essential to plan and have some measure of rehearsal before transmission or to rely on standard production conventions that are understood by everyone involved.

Standard television multi-camera conventions grew out of film technique and the same objective of disguising technique in order to suspend disbelief in the viewer was adopted. The problem for actuality television was not to recreate 'real time' as in discontinuous film shooting but to combine a number of camera viewpoints of an actuality event so that, for example, change of camera angle or cutting between different shot sizes was not obtrusive and distracting to the viewer. The aim once again was towards an 'invisible technique'.

Figure 12.1 Multi-camera studio production

Television camerawork tradition includes multi-camera shooting, rapid production techniques and continuous, impromptu framing adjustments. It may seem paradoxical to suggest that speed and flexibility may be just as rigid a convention as any dogmatic rule but, because of the need for a 'conveyor belt' production technique in programme making, productions continually rely on quick workable technique and reject or avoid innovation that may be time-consuming or unfamiliar. Speed of application is a convention and a necessity but frequently leads to shot compositions that have some 'rough edges' that have never been fully resolved, owing to the shortage of rehearsal/ recording time.

The roots of this multi-camera tradition began with the constraints of live television. Live television had all the advantages of immediacy – as it happened so you saw it. Sport, quiz, discussion or drama were sliced up and presented by continuous camera coverage. Production techniques were pioneered, shaped and perfected to accommodate any event that could be staged in or out of a television studio. Lacking the ability to edit, every event dictated its own timescale. If a writhing footballer in a live match took two minutes to 'act out' that every bone in his body was broken, then every second of his agony was faithfully transmitted. Whilst a more legitimate actor in a multi-camera drama might benefit from a continuity of performance similar to his experience in the theatre, the cameraman's activity often reflected the tempo of the production varying from frantic haste to beat the cue light, to a leisurely pull out from the ringing phone to allow actors from the previous set to scuttle in under the lens, seat themselves and look, as they came into shot, as if they had been waiting for that particular phone call for hours. The premier advantage of television compared with film was that it reached an enormous number of people instantaneously. It was also cheaper.

Five, 30-minute 'soap' episodes could, within five studio days, be rehearsed and recorded at a fraction of the cost of a similar length feature film. There was no point in comparing film with television, they were different animals. Soap drama is topical and consumed like a daily newspaper whereas a feature film has a much longer commercial life to recover its financial and creative investment.

Multi-camera television drama is anchored to the clock. If an actor takes ten paces to cross the set, then in some way that time duration will have to be accommodated by the camera coverage or extensive post-production editing will be required. Time and space are the controlling factors for production staging and shooting. A number of shots have to be delivered from a variety of compromise positions. Time to get to the shot, time to deliver the shot and time to reposition for the next shot are fixed by the timescale of the continuous event in front of the cameras. Because of the pressure of time and space many shots in live, or recorded as live, television were a poor compromise between what could be achieved and what was possible to achieve.

The introduction of the portable video camera/recorder allowed the same flexibility of application as a film unit with even greater opportunities in image manipulation in post-production. Drama continued to be shot on video, especially in the hugely popular genre of the twice/thrice-weekly 'soap' series. Discontinuous recording and single-shot takes could have avoided the compromise of multi-camera drama shooting but the full advantage of this is constrained by cost, experience and convention.

Cost is the most restrictive factor in the transition from quickly producing large chunks of usable television direct from a studio to a method of production that involves both an extended studio production period and an extensive post-production period. Television has an insatiable appetite for new programmes and, with a history of rapid production techniques, it was unlikely that any innovation that increased costs would achieve immediate acceptance. Television studios were designed and equipped to produce a finished product – a 'live' transmission. Although many programmes are discontinuously recorded, the mechanics of production are conditioned by a capital investment in a technique that has been superseded. Lightweight location drama other than soaps has side-stepped this tradition and developed its own innovations, its expansion powered not only by the impetus of financial savings but by the results it has achieved.

Obviously there is a part of television that is live or rooted in live technique. Some actuality events such as sport or public events have their own sacrosanct timescale and capitalize on television's ability to transmit instantaneous pictures. There are also those programmes that are simply communicating information and require an unobtrusive technique free from interpretation. Obtrusive technique is usually grabbed by productions seeking 'spontaneity' – pop, quiz and entertainment productions that flash the viewer with visual cacophony in an attempt to communicate in perpetual motion that 'it's all happening here and now'.

The video look

The criticism that electronically generated pictures are unsubtle and scrappy has a basis of truth. Too many shots occur that are expedient rather than essential – mass produced and instantly forgettable. Built into the television system is a back-log of technique that has evolved to meet a condition that is no longer a prime consideration – namely that all productions have to be transmitted live.

Multi-camera records real time. This often results in superfluous movement being left in, otherwise the production process would gravitate to single shot/single take and lose its economic advantage of speed. Single camera/single shot has an entirely different feel to it. Time and space can be manipulated in many different ways to provide a flow of images that defy location and time continuity.

The effect on video camerawork of smaller budgets and a tradition of 'cheap and quick' technique compared with film is that frequently shot structure is expedient rather than optimum. This often results in staging action for two or more cameras to save time on separate set-ups. Shots are often continued past the point where a cut would occur in a film, which results in fidgety reframing by the use of zoom or track to accommodate additional artistes entering or leaving shot. This adjustment of frame (although often expertly disguised) is a common occurrence in video camerawork, probably because the director is constantly monitoring the shot and is prepared to trade-off a less than satisfactory framing against the cost and time of another set-up.

Multi-camera shooting appears to encourage a convention of complicated stagings that require small 'zooms' and 'tidy-up' camera movement to keep a reasonable frame. This can be instantly achieved in a television studio because of smooth floors and cameras mounted on pedestals, unlike feature film production where more deliberation and time is needed if a change of camera movement is required. Television production often favours the two person or three person shot with people edging into small areas of frame. Multi-camera shooting provides a director with an instantly available wide range of shots. This in practice can deteriorate into a choice of shots covering a number of average and sometimes indifferent groupings and staging.

Standard shot sizes

As multi-camera television camerawork dealt with uninterrupted action in a timescale created by the nature of the event covered, 'real' time had to be continuously covered in a mixture of shot sizes and/or camera development. Shot size became standardized around abbreviated shot descriptions such as MCU (medium close-up), CU (close-up), MS (medium shot), LS (long shot) and o/s 2s (over-the-shoulder two shot), etc., in order that matched shot size could be achieved to allow invisible cuts between cameras. Cameramen had to provide cutting points either pre-rehearsed or by monitoring what the rest of the camera crew were providing. Same size shots of the same subject would not cut together, neither

(a) BCU (big close up)
Whole face fills the screen. Top
of frame cuts forehead.

(b) CU (close up)
Bottom of frame cuts where knot
of tie would be

(c) MCU (medium close up)
Bottom of frame cuts where top
of breast pocket of a jacket
would be

(d) MS (medium shot)
Bottom of frame cuts at waist

Figure 12.2 Standard shot sizes

would widely different amounts of head room. Idiosyncratic personal composition by a cameraman would remain unnoticed if they were responsible for the whole of the visual production but would immediately be apparent if intercut with standard camera technique provided by the rest of the crew. Camera technique remained invisible provided it conformed to certain criteria. These conventions are inherited by everyone working within live or multi-camera recordings unless there is a production requirement for shot change to be obtrusive and obvious.

The introduction of the zoom and television picture composition

Before the introduction of colour television in the late 1960s, most television productions were shot using prime lenses. Although zooms were extensively used on outside broadcasts, many studio productions used cameras that were fitted with a rotating turret equipped with four lenses of different focal length. The precise lens angle depended on tube size and camera manufacturer but the four standard focal lengths chosen had lens angles of approximately 35°, 24°, 16° and 8°.

Because of the standardization of lens angle, camera scripts and studio floor plans were produced giving the lens angle and camera position for each shot. Although shots were modified during rehearsal, the initial choice of lens influenced the look of the production and established a discipline of matched size and perspective of intercut shots. Over time, each prime lens was recognized to have a well-defined role in multi-camera studio production.

The 24° was considered the 'natural' perspective lens and allowed camera movement and was often used on 'two' shots or 'three' shots. The 16° and the 8° were close-up lenses and, although an occasional camera movement was attempted on the 16°, it was likely to result in an unsteady frame because of tracking over an uneven studio floor and the difficulty of holding frame with a fluid head using a narrow angle. Camera movement with an 8° lens intensified this problem and was seldom if ever used for tracking.

Small depth-of-field also inhibited camera movement on these lenses as the cameraman had to physically move the camera himself, adjust the framing and follow focus. This required three hands if constant focus pulls were required on the narrow lens.

The 35° lens was considered 'wide angle' and allowed complex shot development without the twin problems of focus and the considerable amount of camera movement required to achieve significant change of viewpoint if a smaller lens angle was employed.

This arrangement of a set of four lenses created a tight discipline in production and aided the twin objectives of matched shot size and perspective matching. Two cameras being intercut on two people talking would, as a matter of good technique, use the same lens angle and camera position/height relative to the participants. The introduction of colour cameras, which were universally fitted with a zoom because of the need for precise alignment of the lens to the four and later three tubes required for colour, caused a significant change in picture composition and in camera movement.

In the first years of television colour production, there was a determined effort to continue with the four-lens convention by using a zoom shot box that had been pre-set to the four standard lens angles. Tracking the camera was usually favoured in preference to zooming, although pop music programmes quickly utilized the visual impact of zooming.

As the range of zoom angles increased, a greater variety of shot sizes were possible from any specific camera position. This allowed the perspective of some types of conventional shots to change considerably. Zoom lenses with a 55° wide angle became common and allowed a shot development that was more dynamic because of the greater exaggeration of artist to background movement. At the narrow end of the zoom, lens angles of 5° allowed close-ups of artistes at the back of the set with the corresponding reduction in the perspective of the depth of the shot.

The most noticeable change in the style of television camerawork came with the use of the zoom to accommodate movement, to trim the shot depending on the action. Whereas in the past, with monochrome cameras, the staging of the artistes may have been repositioned during the blocking of the show to accommodate a fixed lens angle, a flexible lens angle allowed the shot to be recomposed by zooming in or out. Gradually lens angle and camera position were not pre-plotted but relied on the flexibility of the zoom as a variable lens angle to find acceptable framing. This was sometimes to the detriment of matched shots. Intercut shots could be matched on subject size, if not on perspective, by a rapid adjustment of the zoom. The prejudice against zooming even in drama was relaxed until a point was reached where zooming predominated in television production. There is a strong compositional distinction between zooming and tracking which is dealt with in Chapter 16.

Portable cameras

With the widespread use of portable video camera/recorders, the method of discontinuous single shot shooting shared exactly the same technique problems of film. Shooting with editing in mind became an essential part of that technique. Composition, size of shot, camera movement, camera position and lens angle had to be carefully selected in order to facilitate a final 'seamless' string of edited images.

The extensive use of video portable cameras, especially in news and actuality programmes, was also responsible for a change in compositional style. The ability to position rapidly a lightweight video camera broke down the conventions established with turret cameras. A style evolved, particularly in programmes aimed at young people, where the camera was constantly kept on the move. Although some compositional conventions were retained, the prime intention was to inject excitement and pace by nervous, erratic camera movement.

In its extreme form, it was similar to the subjective style of the camera as an actor with other participants in the production treating it as a person. In this style, if someone spoke out of frame, the camera would swerve to find them. It moved around discussions and in and out of groups with very little attempt (or inclination) to disguise the movement. This was a studied attempt to avoid conventional production technique in an endeavour to create a different visual appearance to that seen in mainstream television.

Customary technique

In television, the nature of many programmes (e.g., sport, discussion, etc.), does not allow precise information about shots either to be rehearsed or confirmed. An experienced television cameraman will know the range and type of shots that will be required in each type of programme. A knowledge of programme-making formats must be added to an understanding of technique and how technology influences technique. Any competent cameraman, for example, will automatically apply the appropriate production methods to a news broadcast, and then be able to switch on the following day to the appropriate production methods of a pop concert. Often different techniques are not compatible.

A production team will expect each member of the unit to be familiar with the customary techniques of the programme format in production. Nobody, for example, will have the time to explain the rules of a sport that is being transmitted live. They will assume that the cameraman knows the standard TV response to different phases of the event.

Multi-camera production technique relies on the assumption that every member of the production crew is equipped with a knowledge of the conventions of the specific programme format and has a thorough mastery of the basic skills in their particular craft. Information about shots will be supplied during rehearsal and/or during transmission/recording, but it will be assumed by the Director that the camera crew will respond with customary technique to the specific programme requirements (example – matched shots for interviews).

Genre

Within film as well as TV production there are recognizably separate genres that have their own codes or visual conventions. For example, sports programming covers a team or individual competition that leads to a result. Documentaries have covered sports events in an impressionistic and symbolic style without bothering about results or who was competing. It is unlikely that sports fans would accept a camera coverage that ignored who won and simply concentrated on the 'poetry of motion' of the sports competitors.

To a large extent, genre or the type of programming dictates which of the standard visual treatments will be used. These conventions alter over time as, for example, in sports coverage with the overlay of computer graphics to examine participants' performance, but the crossover of one genre's visual style into another type of production is sufficiently uncommon to be noteworthy. For example, a western will be shot in a different style to a musical. They will both share a common visual grammar but will usually have the distinct convents of their genre. These separate sets of conventions are sometimes inter-changed to inject a fresh presentation to an oft-repeated theme. Errol Morris in his documentary 'The Thin Blue Line' (1988) mixed crime feature film technique with the documentary genre to provide a truth-ful account of the innocence of a wrongly accused murderer. David Lynch's 'Blue Velvet' (1986) mixed film noir conventions with horror conventions.

Within the mass media, most films and TV productions will display stylistic replications and slight revisions rather than a complete rejec-tion of standard conventions. Successful innovation when it occurs, is often rapidly copied and becomes part of the everyday visual grammar such as the freeze frame at the end of François Truffaut's 'Les Quatre Cents Coups' (1959), Sam Pekinpah's slow-motion gunfight deaths, sepia tinting of films set in the past, etc.

Conventional documentary style

A standard documentary structure, popular for many years, involves an unseen presenter (often the producer/director) interviewing the principle subject/s in the film. From the interview (the questions are edited out), appropriate visuals are recorded to match the interviewee comments, which then becomes the voice-over. A professional actor is often used to deliver an impersonal narration on scientific or academic subjects. The choice of the quality of the voice is often based on the aim to avoid an overt personality or 'identity' in the voice-over whilst still keeping a lively delivery.

The camera can follow the documentary subject without production intervention, but often the individual is asked to follow some typical activity in order for the camera to catch the event, and to match up with comments made in previous interviews.

Television documentary attempts to deal with the truth of a partic-ular situation but it also has to engage and hold the attention of a mass audience. John Grierson defined documentary as 'the creative treat-ment of actuality'. How much 'creativity' is mixed in with the attempt at an objective account of the subject has been at the heart of debate for many years.

'Vérité' as a style

The mini DV camera format has allowed the 'vérité' style to prolifer-ate. This type of documentary attempts to be a fly-on-the-wall by simply observing events without influence. It over-relies on chance and the coincidence of being at the right place at the right time to capture an event that will reveal (subjectively judged by the film maker at the editing stage), the nature of the subject. With this style, the main objective of being in the right place at the right time becomes the major creative task. There is often an emphasis on a highly charged atmosphere to inject drama into the story. It may use minimum script-ing and research other than to get 'inside' where the action is estimated to be. The style often incorporates more traditional techniques of commentary, interviews, graphics and reconstruction, using hand-held camerawork and available light technique.

Wildlife

Documentaries featuring the habitat and lives of animals are a perennially popular form of documentary. They often involve long and painstaking observation and filming to get the required footage, added to some very ingenious special effects set-ups. A programme about the Himalayan Black Bear also featured a sequence of the bear hunting for honey on a tree trunk that was filmed in a zoo. The director said it would have been impossible to film it in the wild and it was needed because it made the sequence stronger. It is commonplace in wildlife programmes to mix and match wild and captured animals.

Docusoap

The spontaneous style of ordinary people observed strives for 'realism' and neutral reportage but gives no clue to what has been reconstructed. The viewer is sucked into a totally believable account. Many professional film makers protest that the viewer understands their subterfuge and fabrication and they are forgiven for the sake of entertainment, involvement and pace. But do viewers understand the subtleties of programme making? The viewer needs to question what they are shown but, as 'invisible' techniques are designed to hide the joins, how can the viewer remind themselves at each moment that they are watching a construct of reality? A documentary crew followed a woman who repeatedly failed her driving test. One sequence involved the woman waking her husband in the middle of the night with her worries. Did the viewer question if the crew had spent each night in the bedroom waiting on the off-chance that this was going to happen or did they immediately think 'this is a fake – a reconstruction?'.

Music videos

In 1975, Bruce Gowers directed a seven-minute musical video 'Bohemian Rhapsody' featuring the pop group Queen. It started a trend of using videos to promote pop singles. It was the flexibility of the small portable video camera that led to the development of several contemporary styles of camerawork These styles did not arrive overnight but had a long pedigree that sometimes embraced German expressionist films such as 'Nosferatu' (1922), 'The Cabinet of Dr Calagari' (1919), the short surrealist films 'Un Chien Andalou' (1928) and 'L'Age d'Or' (1930) of Luis Buñuel, the alternative 'jump cut' styles of Jean Luc Goddard, Richard Lester and the Beatles 1960s films, commercials and many other visual sources. This portmanteau of stylistic flourishes is often dubbed the 'MTV' style after the TV channel that transmitted many pop videos.

The main characteristics of the MTV style are:

- it ignores continuity of time and place;
- traditional 'visual' storytelling is replaced by an emphasis on place, feeling or mood, usually with abrupt discontinuity in time and place;

- music form and beat replace traditional continuity as the structuring device;
- pace becomes the source of energy that drives the audience's interest forward, not a 'what happens next?' storyline;
- the music video often involves fragments of performance but not particularly staged in one venue. These clips are juxtaposed with non-performance images similar to CD cover images;
- location and images often allude to the worlds of science fiction, horror, dream states or parodies of TV and film genres, TV formats, comic books and computer games;
- there is also the use of the knowing jokes about popular culture. This involves a mixture of admiration and derision for the second-rate or popular icons and allows the audience to be let in on the joke and invites the audience to join the performer in the conspiracy of ridicule. This is similar to the punk credo of 'we know we can't play or sing – but then why are you paying money to see us!'.

MTV style

Music videos are similar to commercials in that there are many images combined in a very short time. Many visual decisions are made in post-production with a greater use of digital manipulation compared with other programme formats. A characteristic of the MTV style is continuous camera movement and very fast cutting – almost single frame – to inject pace. These flash frame sequences are contrasted with slow-motion shots of very mundane activities such as spooning sugar into a coffee cup. There is a heavy emphasis on the isolated image rather than the continuity of a flow of images, coupled with the continuous use of wide-angle distorted perspective and a preoccupation with surreal images such as a close up of an eyeball.

There is a search for the bizarre, fantasy or evocative imagery that attacks cause and effect. Many music videos tease the viewer into attempting to find a narrative logic that is missing. Events are juxtaposed for their disturbing effect. Discontinuous editing is used to fracture any temporal or spatial coherence. There is a lack of narrative construction in the shots and sequences are constructed from isolated arresting images similar to fashion photography. The content of the shot emphasizes feeling or atmosphere with no narrative construction or a coherent 'message'.

Visual puzzles

Pop videos challenge the visual impulse to find order in diversity by using many more close-ups than long shots, which avoid revealing the context of a shot, and often the geography of the setting is not explained. There is often an emphasis on foreground with no information about background. This can be achieved either by long focal length lenses that flatten perspective or wide-angle lenses and crowded foreground with characters masking out background. The lighting treatment is often non-realistic using filters, and atmospheric locations are used to produce dream states and fantasy. The jump cut predominates, often with rapid cutting to generate pace.

Richard Lester

Richard Lester's films featuring the Beatles, 'A Hard Day's Night' (1964) and 'Help' (1965) were the first to move away from a continuous record of a performance to a more free-flowing stream of images that remained within the 'feeling' of the music. His technique included cinema vérité, jump cuts, multi-cameras on the performances, rapid cutting and whip pans. Energy, in this style, takes precedence over realism.

This style moved away from the musicians/singers performing a number such as in 'Singing in the Rain' (1952), in favour of movement and rapid changes in location. A series of diverse images unified only by a soundtrack were presented, uninhibited by traditional rules of continuity. The films were a vehicle for the music and not structured around a plot and characterization. The 'what happens next' method of classic storytelling is replaced by fast-cutting imagery to replicate pace, energy and atmosphere.

The Beatles played themselves, which allowed them to step in and out of character and speak to the audience. This use of parody to break down the barrier between audience and performer became a popular device. The style voids cause and effect plots and any consistency in time or place. It concentrates on mood, feelings or to evoke atmosphere of a surreal location. The general movement called Post-Modernism shares a key feature of this style by reflecting on itself. Participants step outside of their video persona to comment on their video performance or the media in general. They in effect join the audience who are watching the performance and comment on the performance. MTV style emphasizes that it's a film – it's not real.

In a sketch in the Monty Python TV programme, two or three characters are 'trapped' in a featureless studio set. They are unable to exit through a door or window because they then find themselves on a pre-recorded film. They cannot break out of a TV 'performance' even though the concept of a studio reality is proposed as having a greater reality than appearing on film. The comedy works for the studio audience because they can see the characters in the studio set but can only see their images protesting on the playback of the film. The performers acknowledge that they are being watched as opposed to maintaining an illusion that the performance is 'real'.

Uncertainty as a style

If MTV style seeks to be less 'realistic' there is another style of crime fiction that attempts to persuade its audience that they are watching an authentic event. Standard Hollywood camera technique emphasizes content – the development of the narrative rather than highlighting the methods of production. In Steven Boccho's 'NYPD Blue' TV series the shooting style appears to continuously draw the audience's attention to the camerawork.

Characteristics of this visual style:

- every dialogue close-up has a twitch in the framing as if the cameraman has accidentally knocked the camera;
- in a diagonal tilt to a hospital entrance, for example, the camera overshoots the door and rapidly pans back and centres up. The

camera appears to be uncertain of its final framing (see Figure 2.4);
- a fast pan with actor movement on a long focal length lens picks up another actor to follow moving in the opposite direction. The camera appears to be distracted or unsure of its priorities;
- a flash pan from an unimportant object picks up a moving subject that is immediately cut away from before their identity is fully established.

The viewer is continuously teased by random camera movement with very few static shots to establish or explain the 'geography' of the setting. This causes some viewers to complain of 'jerky' camera-work and distracting movement. They complain that they are distracted by the visual style and cannot lose themselves in the story. In effect, they are constantly being reminded that they are watching a film. 'NYPD' camera moves are fast, staccato and obtrusive. There appears to be no attempt to hide the mechanics of film making. How does the camerawork style of 'NYPD' differ from the dozens of other TV crime series or feature films?

Some people may imagine that a hand-held camera and random unstructured shots are more real or more immediate, but film makers have always been looking for ways of communicating their message with maximum effectiveness. The unsteady camera is simply a recent variation on the many ways realism has been attempted in film and TV programme making.

The camera surprised by the action

When camcorders came into widespread use in broadcasting in the early 1980s, they were first used for newsgathering before entering general programme making. On-the-shoulder 'wobblyscope' became the standard trademark when covering impromptu action. War reporting or civil unrest were presented in news bulletins with the nervous 'tic' of a hand-held video camera. Realism appeared to be equated with an unsteady frame.

Cinema vérité in the early 1960s linked on-the-shoulder camerawork with a new flexibility of movement and subject, but many film directors adopted the uncertainty of an unsteady picture to suggest realism and authenticity (see below, 'JFK' (1991), dir. Oliver Stone).

Many productions mimic the camera movement of ENG news coverage that, because the subject matter is unknown and unstaged, is frequently 'wrong footed' when panning or zooming. Holding unpredictable action within the frame results in a different visual appearance from the calculated camera movement of a rehearsed shot. The uncertainty displayed in following impromptu and fast-developing action has an energy that these productions attempt to replicate.

The same visual characteristics are used by commercials designed to suggest that a carefully calculated piece of promotion is spontaneous and 'real'. In one detergent commercial, for example, an unsteady camera follows a 'reporter' to the door of a house. A surprised 'housewife' opens the door and reacts to the reporter and film crew before endorsing the product. The style is a parody of a news 'doorstepping' sequence using the familiar ENG visual characteristics of unsteady camerawork and uncertain camera movement.

Hand-held camerawork became the signature for realism. Even costume dramas that had been meticulously researched for costume and setting and classically shot and lit would throw in an obligatory hand-held sequence to add pace and spontaneity to a scene ('Persuasion', BBC TV, 1994).

An example occurs in Stanley Kubrick's 'Dr Strangelove' (1964), which has a sequence where a deranged American air force officer is under siege by American soldiers in his office on an air base. With him in the office is an English liaison officer player by Peter Sellers. As bullets spray the office windows the two take cover on the office floor. The set is lit and the action staged to emphasize the identity and feeling of the main actors. It is what can be termed mainstream camera technique. As the American officer moves towards the window, a camera move accompanies him and its movement matches the actors movement – it starts when he starts and stops when he stops. This is a characteristic of invisible technique. The audience can observe, but it is not overtly made obvious that they are watching a controlled and structured action.

When Kubrick cuts from this standard treatment of the interior to the soldiers advancing on the office, the camerawork style changes. It is now shot like war reportage. The camera is carried on the shoulder and there is a constant unsteady frame. Many shots are on a very long focal length lens that compresses depth, and action is often masked by interposed objects. The camera appears to be constantly surprised by the action. It has the visual signature of actuality coverage and the audience consciously pick-up on this 'news' style. It appears as if this is spontaneous action. It is out of the control of the director. It is real and immediate.

Of course, just as Kubrick controls the staging of the interior action and the smooth invisible camerawork, the exterior is equally under his control and he can, if he wishes, place every actor/soldier in position for a 'well composed' shot. He chooses not to because the unsteady, random nature of the apparently ad-lib exterior shooting allows him to fabricate the ersatz realism of news coverage. The visual language has been changed to suit the message.

Oliver Stone achieves the same effect in his film 'JFK' (1991), when he creates the visual appearance of a surveillance/training film of the Cuban rebels. This change in visual language is in contrast to the mainstream technique he uses in the rest of the film.

Belief and disbelief

Film makers adopted the imperfections of hand-held camerawork as a style and also to symbolize an attitude to their material, but this 'uncertainty' style sends two conflicting signals to the audience.

There is the production attempt to recreate the authentic ' primitive' unstructured news footage – the feeling in the viewer that he or she is watching a real event that is beyond the control of the film maker and therefore the camera has a difficult time to capture the action. But the rapid and unsteady camerawork that provides this impression also draws attention to itself.

If the audience continuously becomes aware of the methods of presentation, that is, if camera movement draws attention to itself, then this denies the reality of the action and suggests that the film is a piece of fiction – a fabrication of reality. The audience will be constantly reminded that they are being told a story and never lose themselves in the action. This style has to overcome the viewer's irritation of random, unstructured camera movement and the continuous nervous 'tic' of an unsteady camera.

'Medium Cool'

One influence on this style may have been the feature film 'Medium Cool' (1968). The director of this film was Haskell Wexler, an ex-news cameraman. One of the characteristics of news camerawork is that it is seldom possible to rehearse camera movement. News, by definition, is unrehearsed although a great deal of movement can be anticipated by an experienced cameraman. The uncertainty of what is going to happen is reflected in the look of news coverage. Whereas, in a feature film, each camera movement is carefully pre-planned and calculated, news coverage requires almost a 'hose pipe' squirting of the lens to follow whatever is happening as it happens.

At the beginning of 'Medium Cool' there is a discussion between a group of people at a reception. Haskell Wexler shoots the discussion as if it is unrehearsed and the cameraman has had no opportunity to discover in what order the speakers will talk. They are all actors and the scene could just as well have been scripted and shot-listed as any similar scene in a conventional narrative film. Instead, Wexler imitates the look of a spontaneous news conference by his style of camerawork in order to make the discussion appear to be authentic and realistic.

The uncertain camerawork in 'NYPD' is similar to this news-style recreation in 'Medium Cool'; it is a fabricated style. It appears as if the camera is surprised by events. Like the audience, the camera never seems to know what will happen next. This replication of news coverage is constructed by a set of visual mannerisms.

Camcorder style

Ignorance of technique may seem to be a curious influence on a style but the growth of amateur use of the video camera has spawned a million holiday videos and the recording of family events that appear remarkably similar in appearance to some visual aspects of production shot in the 'camera surprised by events' style.

The user of the holiday camcorder is often unaware of main-stream camera technique and usually pans and zooms the camera around to pick up anything and everything that catches their attention. They have little or no knowledge of camera shot structure and rarely if ever are the tapes edited. The result is a stream of unconnected and fast-moving shots that never settle on a subject and are restlessly on the move (i.e., similar to the production style of 'NYPD Blue').

Amateur pans and zooms are often uncertain in their execution. Being unrehearsed, they frequently change direction and, when they settle on a subject, the shot is usually not held long enough for the subject to be established. The results are remarkable consistent across the world from Japan to Iceland. Most of them are very similar and with very little visual interest except to the immediate circle of family and friends.

This 'camcorder style' is a home-grown technique of innocent simplicity practised with no intellectual concept of the craft or technique
of professional camerawork. There are direct parallels with naive art,
where Sunday painters produce at times extraordinary paintings
because of their unawareness of main-stream art. Very accomplished
artists (e.g., Miro, Picasso, Klee, etc.) were impressed by this naivety
and the innocence of child paintings and primitive art and produced
work that was heavily influenced by the 'untutored' eye.

The maker of a holiday video has the same naive self-assurance that
their work is presentable and accomplished as the naive painter. They
assume that their work will engage their audience in the same way as
main-stream video production.

Video diaries

The appeal of this 'innocent eye' approach has been taken up by
broadcasting organizations who have loaned camcorders to the 'man
in the street' for them to make video diaries of their own lives. The
novice cameraman or woman is given a brief explanation of the
mechanics of the camera and then left to their own devices to film
whatever they wish.

The broadcasters claim that the appeal of this 'camcorder style' is its
immediacy, its primitive but authentic style. It eliminates the professional crew who, by their presence in a location, may have an undue
influence on the participants. The resulting untutored camerawork
provides an alternative to the standard styles inherited from the 'invisible technique' tradition.

Most European video diaries, however, are not the raw and rough
outpourings of an 'innocent eye'. Broadcasters usually make certain
that the material acquired by the amateur cameraman is carefully
structured and cut by professional editors. The transmitted material
uses very sophisticated editing techniques on very unsophisticated
camerawork.

There appears to be a stylistic confusion or mismatch between the
primitive 'honesty' displayed by unsophisticated amateur camerawork
that is cut using professional editing techniques in order to make the
video diary 'watchable' by a mass audience. If it is acceptable that the
camerawork can be crude and lack visual subtlety why not bring someone off the street to edit the tape and extend the principle to the
'innocent' editor?

Low-tech

There has been a style backlash against the high definition, high quality video images that are possible with digital television production.
These 'low-tech' stylists choose sub-broadcast equipment such as
Super-8 film and domestic DV video cameras to create grainy, sub-
standard pictures for their productions, in marked contrast with the
usual highly polished commercial images. They have defiantly chosen
to be a counter-culture to the over-crafted film and television product.
They are looking for another version of authenticity by suggesting that
image quality that is so good that it is invisible is masking reality.

Punk – the cult of the incompetent

There is a style of camerawork that falls between the innocence (or ignorance) of the domestic camcorder user and the conscious alternative technique created by groups such as cinema vérité. Its chief characteristic is an aggressive hose-piping of the camera that sprays backwards and forwards to follow anything that moves or speaks. This style of 'punk TV' can be seen in TV youth programmes, music videos and some 'people' shows.

The style is a bogus naivety similar to the punk musicians of the 1970s who were deliberately inept at singing and playing their instruments and used their inadequacy in technique to taunt their audience. They aggressively displayed their incompetence. Anyone can play in a band, they suggested: why do you have to be a musician? They rejected what they saw as snobbishness in the music establishment and rejected any concepts of musicality or 'quality'.

'Punk TV' camerawork also values the energy, spontaneity and 'bad taste' of the spray-can approach in camera coverage. These productions reject the standard visual conventions and attempt to provide their own individual language. It can be summarized as 'do your own thing – shout don't sing'. Punk music was almost a rejection of communication. Some bands hated applause. They wanted no confirmation that they had made a connection with their audience.

Some 'punk TV' camerawork and productions display the same nihilism with a disregard for clear communication, an ignorance of conventions moving into an aggressive display of lack of technique. It is an 'in your face' yobbish style with a deliberate avalanche of hand-held shots to zap the viewer.

These, of course, are deliberate production decisions in order to inject pace and texture into the narrative. The camerawork may appear anarchic but there is usually a precision to the cuts when music is shot. Unless the director is completely inept, the cuts come on the beat and match the mood and the pace of the number. In practise very few hand-held styles of camerawork used in productions will abandon narrative editing. The camerawork may be prized for its 'rawness' and spontaneity but it will almost certainly be organized and structured by conventional editing technique with just a few jump cuts thrown in for flavour.

Defocused 'blobs of colour' style

Staging in depth, the wide-angle look with deep focus, had been in vogue from the late 1930s to the mid-1950s but two innovations caused problems with this style of camerawork. Early CinemaScope (circa 1954) required a separately focused anamorphic supplementary lens attached to the front of a 50 mm lens, resulting in a reduced exposure. In addition, the widespread use of Eastman colour negative, which was less sensitive than the fastest black and white stock, prevented the large depth-of-field in studio interiors that had been obtained in such films as 'Citizen Kane'. As long focal length lenses became available for the new widescreen formats a new style gradually evolved.

A long focal length lens and appropriate camera distance not only compresses space but produces attractive defocused abstract background patterns. Andrejz Wajda using a 250 mm lens noted: 'The background, dotted with secondary elements, loses its aggressiveness. The image softens, the medley of colours melts into flat tints of colour... The foreground, however, is transformed into a coloured haze that seems to float' (*Double Vision: My Life in Film*).

The film maker who inspired and popularized this style of out-of-focus, misty blobs of colour was Claude Lelouche with his film 'Un homme et une femme' (1966). In fact, Wajda and his cameraman called the fuzzy foreground shapes they devised with a long focal length lens, 'lelouches'. The style has had a long and enduring influence both in commercials and feature films. Lelouche was not the first director to explore the abstract qualities of a long focal length lens; Antonioni's 'Il desert Rosso' (1964) was shot with lenses of 100 mm upwards but 'Un homme et une femme' captured the creative imagination of a number of film makers, e.g., the 500 mm zoom lens used on the cycle sequence in 'Butch Cassidy and the Sundance Kid' (1969).

The main characteristics of this style are the use of a very long focal length lens, shooting against the light and the use of heavy diffusion. Lelouche did not use diffusion but, because of the poor optical performance of long focal lenses at this time and his fondness for allowing subjects to move away or towards the lens without following focus, it appears, when shooting against the light, that diffusion had been used. Flare and light behind the actor had always been avoided by American cinematographers. One reason, given by Gordon Willis, was that studio bosses wanted a good, well-contrasted picture to cater for the drive-in audiences viewing outside with less than perfect film projection. With the move away from studio feature production to independent production, possibly cinematographers were free to use flare or very dark scenes, such as in 'The Godfather' (1972).

Heavy diffusion on a lens produces a scattering of white light over the whole frame as well as a loss of definition. Foreground and background defocused blobs of colour caused, for example, by flowers provide romantic, benevolent colourful 'nature' images that are still exploited to date. If, on a long focal lens, focus pulls are added through foreground leaves or shooting reflections in water against the light, a whole range of stylized effects are available. The reflections on moving water can, of course, be tweaked up for greater effect by the use of star filters.

The reconstruction of a period

Television versions of classic books such as the novels of Jane Austen involve a production quest for period authenticity with authentic costume, settings and characterization. But what constitutes an authentic film style of the period? What would be an authentic camerawork/production style when shooting any subject before the development of cinema?

A costume drama set in the eighteenth century used hand-held cameras on a banquet to replicate 1990s ENG style of camerawork. Is this an anachronism? Would the director accept a stylized acting performance (e.g., Marlon Brando 'method' acting) or would this be considered 'out of character' with the period? If costume and settings are in period for a decade in the twentieth century should the film style of the production be in the same period? The same arguments have raged for many years, for example when Shakespeare plays are performed in modern dress.

There is a paradox of the quest for authentic period costume dramas that seek authentic settings, food, locations, etc., but use contemporary styles in shooting. The interpretation of a past age may be completely bogus when translating from text to images. The construction of a Jane Austin novel is of its time. The television images of this novel are also of their time and may be in direct conflict. Audiences often dislike modern-dress versions of Shakespeare that seek to reinterpret the sixteenth century in terms that are relevant to twentieth-century audiences. But can Jane Austin be re-written in the style of Dashiell Hammett and remain true to the original author's intentions? Viewers may be image illiterate and be impressed by authentic settings while totally ignoring the anachronism of the shooting style. Should adaptations of Edwardian novels be staged in the style of early films?

The unconscious expression of contemporary fashion and attitudes can be seen in the set/prop design of science fiction films that are intended to be set in the future. Each decade's prediction of what the future will look like is heavily based on the current contemporary design ideas.

Sports coverage

Live sports coverage has a curious combination of factual and subjective camerawork. The broadcast of a sports event can be a reasonably accurate record of the event. Real people engaged in an activity with an unknown result. The camera coverage of the game can introduce a strong subjective influence. For example, the final of a tennis tournament will provide a point by point description of the match's progress. The big close-up of the participant's face is a production effort by the director to interpret the feelings of the player. A close-up in drama carries a great deal of emotional intensity. It is hoped that the story of the tennis match will have the same type of intensity when the visual grammar of fiction is used on a sporting event.

Changing styles

The American film academic David Bordwell proposed that there was continuity in film style over time with the occasional revision.

My research questions, focusing on the elaboration of norms, have led me to stress continuity. The lesson of this is quite general. Modernism's promoters asked us to expect constant turnover, virtually seasonal breakthroughs in style. In most artworks, however, novel devices of styles or structure or theme stand out against a backdrop of norm-abiding processes. Most films will be bound to tradition in more ways than not; we should find many more stylistic replications and revisions than rejections. Especially in a mass medium, we ought to expect replication and minor modifications, not thoroughgoing repudiation. We must always be alert for innovation, but students of style will more often encounter stability and gradual change. (Bordwell, 1997)

Summary of the history of style

Changes in style and technology do not confine themselves to a specific decade or country. Here are a few changes over the past 100 years.

- *1895–1910*: this was an age of invention and experiment in film technique. Style was not so much a considered application of technique as the result of the early pioneers' discoveries.
- *1910–1940*: by the end of the silent period the Hollywood studio system was in full operation and began to shape style. This resulted in the recognizable visual styles of the major studios. Warner Brothers had a gritty hard-edge realism; Universal had a moody darkness; MGM had the luxurious, high-key, glamorous look; at RKO, Van Nest Polglase oversaw the styling of the Astaire–Rogers musicals and 'Citizen Kane'; Paramount had a gloss influenced by European sophistication.
- *1940s*: saw staging in depth, on the street shooting, the long take and elaborate camera development shots.
- *1950s*: sci-fi and long focal length lenses, widescreen styles influenced by limitation of widescreen lenses and depth of focus. Most television was live until the end of the decade, which imposed limitation of camerawork and story lines.
- *1960s*: the development of the lightweight camera and Nouvelle Vague shooting; widescreen solved the shape and the limitations of the screen.
- *1970s*: television established with TV sitcoms, soaps and more sophisticated sports coverage. The break-up of the Hollywood system allowed independent productions to be more adventurous.
- *1980s*: the lightweight video revolution in television liberated drama from the studios.
- *1990s*: advances in video post-production allowed film and TV to achieve control of effects and purely electronic-generated images.

13
Lighting and composition

The key pictorial force

The many influences on composition already discussed, such as invisible technique, choice of lens/position, perspective, visual design elements and style, are all created or influenced by light. The most important element in the design of visual images is light. Apart from its fundamental role of illuminating the subject, light determines tonal differences, outline, shape, colour, texture and depth. It can create compositional relationships, provide balance, harmony and contrast. It provides mood, atmosphere and visual continuity. Light is the key pictorial force in film and television production.

The basic requirement to provide adequate light for an exposed picture with the required depth-of-field can fairly easily be achieved with contemporary film stock. Video cameras are sufficiently sensitive to provide an acceptable exposure under almost any found lighting condition. But whereas the technical requirements of exposure, appropriate colour temperature and contrast range may be readily satisfied, the resultant image may be a muddle of competing areas of light and shade that do not communicate the intended 'visual message' of the shot. The control of light to guide the audience's attention and to communicate production requirements plays a crucial part in the creation of any film or TV image. In almost every situation, visual communication can be more effective by choosing the camera position or staging participants with reference to found light and usually by adding some form of additional direct or reflected light.

Production lighting does a great deal more than simply enabling the viewer to recognize the content of the shot, but usually the first basic technical requirements are to supply sufficient light for the required exposure, at the appropriate colour temperature, and to help modify or create a suitable contrast range for the subject in order to meet the requirements of the recording medium.

Using light as a set of techniques to create tonal differences, outline, shape, colour, texture, patterns of colour, and to define and develop the space of the shot requires an understanding of how we perceive light, the nature of light and the contrast range of the recording medium.

Gradations of brightness

A basic understanding of how we see the world will help when devising the lighting and composition of a shot. There are significant differences between how the eye responds to a scene and how a camera converts light into an electrical signal or records it on film. Lighting must take account of these differences and make the appropriate adjustments.

The relative brightness of a reflective surface is a subjective perceptual construct depending on the brightness levels of surrounding surfaces. The eye perceives gradations of brightness by comparison. It is the ratio of one apparent brightness to another (and in what context) that determines how different or distinct the two appear to be. The just noticeable difference between the intensity of two light sources is discernible if one is approximately 8 per cent greater/lesser than the other, regardless of them both being of high or low luminous intensity. The amount of light entering the eye is controlled by an iris and it is also equipped with two types of cells; rods that respond to dim light, and cone receptor cells that respond to normal lighting levels. For a given iris opening, the average eye can accommodate a contrast range of 100:1, but visual perception is always a combination of eye and brain. The eye adapts fast to changing light levels and the brain interprets the eye's response in such way that it appears as if we can scan a scene with a very wide contrast range (e.g., 500:1), and see it in a single glance.

Every element in an image has a specific brightness. One area will be seen as bright, another will be perceived as dark. The visual 'weight' of different brightness levels will depend on proximity, area and contrast. The eye is naturally attracted to the highlight areas in a frame but the contrast and impact of an object's brightness in the frame will depend on the adjacent brightness levels. A shot of a polar bear against snow will require different compositional treatment than a polar bear in a zoo enclosure. A small bright object against a dark background will have as much visual weight in attracting the eye as a large bright object against a bright background.

How 'bright' one subject appears compared with another and the perceived changes in brightness is a function of perception. In an interior, a face against a window during the day will appear to be dark. With the same illumination on the face against a window at night, the face will appear to be bright. Colours appear to be lighter against a dark background and darker against a light backing.

The relationship between different brightness levels in the frame plays an important part in balancing the composition. The study of light and dark in composition is termed chiaroscuro – Italian for 'light–dark'.

For John Alton, the definitive Hollywood cameraman of the Film Noir genre, black was the most important element in the shot. The most important lamps for him were the ones he did not turn on. The relationship between the light and dark areas of the frame play a critical role in many interior and exterior shots. A large amount of black can be balanced with a small highlight deftly positioned. The high-key/low-key mood of the frame will dictate styles of composition as well as atmosphere. A few strong light/black contrasts can provide very effective visual designs.

Contrast range

The eye has a much greater ability than a video camera to see detail in shadows through to highlights. One aim of lighting is to create a range of tones either to conform to the contrast ratio of film/video or to express a production requirement. Although there is a reduction in the overall contrast range that can be reproduced in a visual medium, the depiction of strong contrasts can still be achieved by the use of light/dark comparisons.

High contrast creates a solid separation and good figure/ground definition. When size is equal, the light/dark relationship plays an essential part in deciphering which is figure and which is ground. Equal areas of light and dark can be perceived as either figure or ground.

The boundary area of a shape often relies on a light/dark relationship. A figure can be separated from its background by backlighting its edge. A highlight in the frame will attract the eye and, if it is not compositionally connected to the main subject of interest, it will compete and divert attention.

Exposure

When viewing a film or television image, it is often easy to accept that two-dimensional images are a faithful reproduction of the original scene. There are many productions (e.g., news, current affairs, sports coverage, etc.) where the audience's belief that they are watching a truthful representation unmediated by technical manipulation or distortion is essential to the credibility of the programme. But many decisions concerning exposure involve some degree of compromise as to what can be depicted even in 'factual' programmes. In productions that seek to interpret rather than to record an event, manipulating the exposure to control the look/composition of a shot is an important technique.

As we have discussed, human perception is more complex and adaptable than a video camera. The eye/brain can detect subtle tonal differences ranging, for example, from the slight variations in a white sheet hanging on a washing line on a sunny day to the detail in the deepest shadow cast by a building. The highlights in the sheet may be a thousand times brighter than the shadow detail. The TV signal is designed to handle (with minimum correction) no more than approximately 40:1.

But there is another fundamental difference in viewing a recorded image and our personal experience in observing a subject. Frequently, a film/TV image is part of a series of images that are telling a story, creating an atmosphere or emotion. The image is designed to manipulate the viewer's response. Our normal perceptual experience is conditioned by psychological factors and we often see what we expect to see; our response is personal and individual. A storytelling image is designed to evoke a similar reaction in all its viewers. Exposure plays a key part in this process and is a crucial part of camerawork. Decisions on what ranges of tones are to be recorded and decisions on lighting, staging, stop number – depth-of-field, etc., all intimately affect how the observer relates to the image and to a sequence of images. The 'look' of an image is a key production tool and a large element of that look is the lighting treatment.

Each shot is one amongst many and continuity of the exposure will determine how it relates to the preceding and the succeeding images. Factors that affect decisions on exposure include:

- the contrast range of the recording medium and viewing conditions;
- face tones and maintaining continuity of face tones and their relationship to other picture tones;
- the choice of peak white and how much detail in the shadows are to be preserved;
- subject priority – what is the principle subject in the frame (e.g., a figure standing on a skyline or the sky behind them?);
- what electronic/processing methods of controlling contrast range are used;
- the lighting technique applied in controlling contrast;
- staging decisions – where someone is placed affects the contrast range.

Characteristics of light

Like clay in a potter's hand, the four characteristics of light: quality (hard or soft), direction (frontal, side, back, underlit, top lit, etc.), source (available artificial or natural light, additional lights) and colour, can be manipulated by the lighting cameraman to achieve the precise requirements for a specific shot. The auto features on a video camera are often unable to discriminate the priorities of a shot and must be over-ridden, so likewise, to simply accept the effects of a found lighting situation is to disregard the most powerful part of image making. Available or 'found' light is any combination of daylight and/or artificial light that illuminates any potential location.

Quality

The quality of light produced by a natural or an artificial light source is often categorized as 'hard' or 'soft'. A 'point' source (i.e., a small area of light at a distance from the subject) produces a single hard-edged shadow of an object. An unobscured sun or moon is a hard light source. Hard lighting reveals shape and texture and, when produced by a lamp, can be shaped and controlled to fall precisely on the required part of the frame. Shadow areas of an image (the absence of light or very low light levels) often play an essential part in the composition and atmosphere of a shot. Lighter and darker areas within the frame help to create the overall composition of the shot and to guide the attention of the viewer to certain objects and actions. Shadows on a face reveal structure and character.

A soft source of light produced by a large area of light (relative to the subject) results in many overlapping soft-edged shadows of an object and tends to destroy texture. It is not so controllable as hard light but is often used to modify the effect of hard light. For example, by bouncing sunlight off a large area reflector to fill-in the shadow created by sunlight falling on the subject.

How much light is used and where it is focused also sets the 'key' of the image. A shot with a preponderance of high tones and thin shadows is termed a high-key picture and is usually considered cheerful and upbeat. An image with large areas of dark tones, strong contrast and deep shadows is termed a low-key image and appears sombre, sinister or mysterious.

Direction

The direction from which any part of an image is lit affects the overall composition and atmosphere of a shot. Frequently when setting lamps for a shot, the position and therefore the direction of illumination is controlled by the perceived 'natural' source of light (e.g., window or table lamp in an interior).

Source

Early film was lit by natural light. Artificial light sources were introduced for greater production flexibility and economic reliability (e.g., to keep filming whatever the weather). A system of lighting faces, often the most common subject in feature films, was known as three-point lighting. This used a key light to model the face, soft light to modify the key-light effect and a backlight to separate the face from its backing. Three-point lighting is still extensively practised, although the use of a backlight has fallen out of fashion in feature film making. The quest for a 'natural' look to an image produced a fashion for using large areas of bounced light. Modelling on a face was reduced or eliminated and the overall image produced was softer and less modelled. To heighten realism, and because of the availability of very sensitive cameras, many shots were devised using available light. This is often necessary when shooting documentaries because not only does rigging lights take time and unsettle participants but being filmed under bright lights is inhibiting and counter-productive to the aim of recording unmediated 'actuality'.

Colour

The fourth aspect of lighting is colour, which is discussed in the next chapter.

Lighting technique

The lighting director must fulfil a number of requirements when deciding the lighting treatment for a particular shot. These include:

- practical (explicit) script requirements such as time of day, interior/exterior, etc.;
- providing the right mood or atmosphere (implicit requirements) – interpreting the script and narrative requirements, e.g., high key/ low key, etc.;
- lighting the action and providing the compositional emphasis where it is required in the shot;
- fulfilling the technical requirements of the medium through the control of lighting levels for the required exposure, colour temperature and contrast range. This can be achieved by a number of techniques including base lighting – enough light on everything in the shot that is required to be seen, zone lighting of foreground, mid-ground and background, chiaroscuro (see below), etc.

Lighting and emphasis

Directing the viewer's attention, emphasizing what is important in the frame, is an essential part of the lighting treatment. The position of a small, isolated visual element within the frame will achieve dominance depending on its relationship to the frame edge, the nature of its background and its contrast to its background. Its location within the frame will depend on its movement or implied movement (e.g., direction of eye line). If the subject is offset on one of the intersections of thirds (see 'The Rule of Thirds' in Chapter 10) it can achieve compositional balance by its perceived direction moving into the frame. A more dynamic and dissonant arrangement is created by an off-centre location with movement towards the nearest edge of frame.

Usually a dead-centre framing drains the shot of any visual interest as there is no dynamic tension between the subject and the frame. Likewise, a very eccentric positioning close to the edge of the frame requires some compositional reason provided by the method of lighting the subject, or its background. Contrast with the background is also a compositional consideration either in colour, brightness level or texture to achieve pictorial unity. The tonal values of costume and location assist in this emphasis, plus selective focusing. The lighting treatment, as well as revealing information can also conceal information in order to realize a script requirement for mystery, uncertainty, confusion, etc.

Good lighting, like other craft techniques in film and television production, is not usually noticed by the audience but it enhances the mood and emphasizes the main subject/s whilst avoiding directing attention away from the subject. Location lighting treatment seeks to avoid being in conflict with the existing mood of the natural lighting of the shot.

Invisible lighting

In a more subtle but no less influential way, the use of light by its direction, coverage and intensity can be used for pictorial unity and subject emphasis as an invisible technique. Invisible in the sense that although the lighting direction, intensity and coverage may change between long shot and close-up, the lighting design has skilfully disguised the changes to maximize the strength of each image.

In long shot, the lighting emphasis may be on the atmosphere of the room and the subject's relationship with the interior. The lighting will help to integrate the composition of figure and background. In close shot, the lighting may emphasize features of the face and separate subject foreground from background. Broken shadow design on the background may be quite different in pattern between long shot and close shot in order to accommodate the competing emphasis in the individual shots but visual unity is sustained by other lighting controls.

The lighting effect suggested in each shot may match normal experience but, if carefully analysed, could not be achieved in that specific situation. The skill of this lighting treatment is to convince and persuade the viewer of the naturalness of the artifice.

Single shot, single camera technique allows the luxury of tailoring composition, lighting and staging to maximize the objective of each shot, provided lighting and other visual continuity detail appears consistent. An audience can be convinced of time continuity without an exact match of every visual element carrying over between each shot. A disguised lighting technique allows each shot to be lit to maximize effect and audience attention.

Multi-camera television

Continuous multi-camera shooting records an exact visual match between shots. Body position, lighting and setting carry over automatically between shots and therefore considerable compromise is often necessary between the ideal composition and what is available by shooting in real time. The perceived effect of light relates to the angle between the light source and the camera. Ideally a shot is lit for one viewpoint whereas multi-camera shooting produces a number of viewpoints. It does have the advantage of continuity of performance by the actors/presenters and allows the tempo and interpretation to unravel/unfold over time without the interruption for new set-ups.

The three functions of lighting – illumination (illuminance), interpretation and medium requirements, all have a bearing on composition. High contrast may provide punchy dynamic images but all productions do not require to communicate with the dramatic intensity of 'Hamlet'. Form follows function in lighting as it does in other creative activities.

In 1855, as the arguments raged about the quest for perfect mechanical reproduction, a photographer, Eugene Durieu, rejected the use of light simply as a means of obtaining an exposure. He proposed that light could be a means of expression to bring life, mood and modelling to an image. He rejected the mechanistic view of image reproduction and suggested that 'Imitation is neither the means nor the aim of art. The photographer should choose a viewpoint, concentrate interest on the principal subject, control the distribution of light and be as selective as an artist.'

The argument has continued ever since with the 'realists' attempting to close the gap between audience and action by allowing them to identify and become part of the action (e.g., TV soaps, etc.) and those who use subjective and fantastic imagery to move, alter or change the audience's disposition.

Harmony and contrast

As we discussed in Chapter 3, the Gestalt theories explain the act of perception as a continuous quest to resolve visual confusions, to reduce visual ambiguities and to rationalize and explain. The theories suggest there is a continuing human drive towards equilibrium – that is towards no visual uncertainties. We are unable to switch-off looking (except by closing our eyes) and therefore there is the constant need to understand what we see. The way we achieve understanding is to group and organize diversity, to simplify complex images into regular patterns and to eliminate, where possible, conflicting readings of an image (Figure 13.1). The lighting treatment of a shot has this objective.

But there is an equal and opposite force at work in this disposition towards visual simplicity. As we have seen, continuous perceptual attention requires continuous challenges. Perception requires visual puzzles to unravel and decode. If the challenge is too great, if the viewer is supplied with images that make no sense, like a too-difficult crossword puzzle, perceptual attention will be discarded once one or two clues have proved unsolvable. But if there is no ambiguity in a visual image, no uncertainty in the act of perception, if there is a surfeit of simplicity and symmetry, attention will drift and a visual condition close to sleep will be induced. Attention often requires unbalance, visual shock, stimulation and arresting images.

Although perception seeks visual unity, a detailed visual communication requires contrast to articulate its meaning. Morse code can be understood if the distinction between dot and dash is accentuated. A visual message requires the same accentuation of contrast in order to achieve coherent meaning. Light, by supplying contrast of tones, can remove visual ambiguity in a muddle of competing subjects but the wrong tonal contrast can produce a confused and misleading 'message' – the dots and the dashes come close to the same duration and are misread.

Communication

Communication is achieved by contrast. The communication carrier – sound or light – provides a message by modulation. There is a need for polarities whether loud or soft, dark or light, dot or dash. Meaning is made clear by comparison.

Light is the perfect medium for modulating contrast. It illuminates the subject and is therefore the carrier of the message. Lighting technique, as applied in film and television production, balances out and reduces the contrast ratio to fit the inherent limitations of the medium. It therefore contributes in the drive towards perceptual equilibrium by creating simplified images. But light is also needed to provide modelling, contrast and tonal differences. In this sense it introduces diversity and contrast whilst identifying meaning.

A dynamic image is one where a visual conflict or tension has been set up and then resolved. The ying/yang of visual design is harmony and contrast. Compositional harmony created by lighting, appeases the perceptual system and therefore facilitates the delivery of the message. Contrast, in a shot created by light, grabs the attention and ensures the perceptual system stays switched on to receive the message.

Hard and soft

Within a broad generalization, the two qualities of light that are used in film and television production are hard and soft. Usually, hard light produces the greatest contrast, modelling and texture. It creates depth, shape and relationships. All light, hard or soft, can reveal modelling, texture, contrast – it is a matter of shadow structure that determines the 'sharpness' of the effects. Diffused light is often applied to reduce the contrast introduced by a hard light source and to create an integrated harmony of tones.

Figure 13.2 *Office Party* (1977), Patrick Caulfield. Although perception seeks visual unity, a detailed visual communication requires contrast to articulate its meaning. A dynamic image sets out a visual conflict or tension and a resolution. There is a strong, underlying triangular shape in this painting which anchors the diversity of competing visual elements

Figure 13.2 *Office Party* (1977), Patrick Caulfield. Although perception seeks visual unity, a detailed visual communication requires contrast to articulate its meaning. A dynamic image sets out a visual conflict or tension and a resolution. There is a strong, underlying triangular shape in this painting which anchors the diversity of competing visual elements

Past influences

Artists have frequently been the most acute observers of the effects of light and its ability to create mood, atmosphere and depth. Film and television lighting cameramen have often been influenced by paintings, consciously or otherwise, when seeking guides to two-dimensional compositions.

Artists of all periods had sought solutions to the essential paradox of pre-contemporary painting, which was how to represent depth on a flat surface. They wished to create an illusion of three dimensions without revealing the techniques that achieved this deception. The successful illusionist persuades the viewer to concentrate their attention on what the magician wishes them to see whilst masking or ignoring the mechanics of how it has been achieved. Invisible technique in film and television production works on the same principle. Moving images are viewed on a flat surface that can be conceived, depending on the lighting and camera treatment, as a 'window' for the audience to look through or alternatively, as a flat surface design.

In art, there have been many solutions to this dilemma but two styles are useful in the study of light and composition – chiaroscuro and Notan.

Chiaroscuro

Chiaroscuro is the technique of depicting depth by balancing light and shadow in a picture. Particular attention is paid to the skill in the handling of shadow. Film and television lighting, on first thought, may be conceived as the process of directing light to different parts

Figure 13.3 *The Betrothal of the Arnolfini* (detail), Jan Van Eyck, 1434, London National Gallery. Jan Van Eyke's *The Betrothal of the Arnolfini* is a perfect example of how to handle soft bounced light. The camera right of the groom is much darker than the camera right side of the bride's face, which has more fill helped along by the light kicking up from her lace headdress and being angled towards the source of the light. There are many subtle lighting touches throughout the frame, from the highlights on the chandelier to the higher intensity tone of the joined hands – the central focus of this marriage painting

of the shot. From this perspective, the lit areas become the dominant consideration whereas artists for hundreds of years have known the importance of the shadow structure of an image when creating form and depth. Positioning lamps to create shadows and withholding light from parts of a subject can often be the most important part of a lighting treatment.

Two painters who excelled in chiaroscuro were Caravaggio in the early 1600s and Rembrandt van Rijn (1606–1669). In Rembrandt's paintings there is a dominant light source, often outside the frame, which only illuminates selected parts of the subject (see Plate 8). It is unsurprising that early on in film making, lighting cameramen borrowed Rembrandt's technique in the use of light on faces.

They adopted a few simple conventions that are still with us today and can be summarized as:

- the key light or main source of natural light is positioned to light the side of the face that is furthest from the camera. The side of the face to camera is in shadow but modified with a fill or reflected light;
- the subject is separated from background either by light or choice of background;
- preferably the background should contrast with the main subject (e.g., light foreground against dark background or dark foreground against light background) to maximize attention on the main subject;
- make the subject the brightest or most dominant area in the shot;
- Rembrandt lighting relies on an appearance of natural light which, in his paintings, frequently comes from outside the camera left of the shot;
- another 'trademark' was his penchant for placing a small triangle of light (produced by the shadow of the nose) on the cheekbone of the camera right side of face that had detail, although in shadow from the main source of light.

Other characteristics of lighting in his paintings often copied in film work include using only one apparent light source that selectively lights only part of the shot. Rembrandt favoured low overall illumination with the background darker than the main subjects of the picture. He achieved this by depicting the main source of light quickly falling away before it reached the background. This distribution of dark background and the higher intensity tones of the principal figures directs the attention to the main subject of the painting. Using highly directional light without the modifying effect of other light sources accentuates texture and form.

Rembrandt or chiaroscuro lighting enhances the three-dimensional properties of faces and setting and allows control of space depicted in the composition. Controlled light reaches those parts of the shot that are required to advance the story or to provide additional information about the main subject. It can be used to express a wide range of emotional qualities ranging from dark, sinister, threatening environments to the luxurious opulence of glittering glass and plush velvet interiors. When expertly used, it allows complete control of the image, providing only that which is required for the shot but still appearing natural and unstudied. Looking beyond the main subject in frame, good chiaroscuro lighting often subjectively sets the audience's response to the narrative. It works on the senses without being obvious and sets atmosphere and image intelligibility. Like music, it can create mood and meaning with a few carefully chosen highlights or a few well placed shadows.

Notan

Some artists abandoned shadow in the quest to define form. They rejected the illusion of depicting depth by the use of a few facile tricks in favour of the creation of a surface pattern created by two-dimensional outline, colour and tone. This emphasis on surface can only really be achieved in film and television by soft lighting with the minimum of cast shadows. This usually means high-key pictures where there is a predominance of light tones. Movement inevitability reveals some indication of depth and so true flat surface design in TV and film images is usually restricted to commercials or music videos, although many Technicolour musicals used very flat lighting relying on colour and dance to provide pattern. A variation of notan is often used when silhouettes are used to withhold information or to increase tension or mystery.

The studio look

For many years feature films, and later television dramas, were produced in studios. Large companies dominated film production up to the 1970s and they had a commercial requirement for a specific style and type of film they wished to make. A style of lighting developed over many decades which lit the subject in sympathy with the demands of the script and the demands of glamour. The resulting images may be at odds with the perceived lighting realism of the setting (e.g., a window as the only source and direction of light may be ignored in a close-up) but is sufficiently 'natural' to be accepted in a flow of images. One of the main influences on this style of lighting was the commercial pressure to exploit the glamour of the leading players.

The domination of the star actor/actress in Hollywood feature film production created a vocabulary of close-ups (CUs), medium close-ups (MCUs), and over-the-shoulder (O/S) shots to emphasize the star. The aim of the lighting cameraman was to make the artiste as handsome or as glamorous as possible. If you could photograph a star well, then the star would get you under contract to their particular studio.

The following quotes from cameramen indicate the influence lighting decisions could have. Cameraman Lee Garmes: 'If the scene average light level was 100 ft candles then Dietrich would be lit with 110 ft candles so that her face was the significant part of the frame.' Charles Lang: 'I had to use a high-key light to narrow Dietrich's cheek bones. Claudette Colbert could only be shot one side and therefore sets had to be designed for the action to keep that side of face to camera.'

The creation of the studio look in the 1930s was achieved by a strong apprenticeship of assistant cameramen following a specific studio style. Technicians worked on whatever they were allocated to but the studio system allowed them to work on many films and they therefore developed a range of techniques across a diversity of narrative styles. Major studios tended to be known for specific genre films and the look of their films followed the subject. MGM built a reputation for 'glamour', Paramount for 'gloss', Warners for 'hard-edge' gritty realism.

Multi-camera television broadcast production followed the same 'industrial' pattern, with television technicians allocated to work on a broad range of programmes and techniques, ranging from 'Play of the Month' to 'Playschool'. Although there was some specialism, most camera crews and lighting directors were expected to have the techniques required to embrace all the different television programme formats.

In the 1950s and 1960s, there was a pursuit for greater realism in the subject and appearance of many feature films. The story was filmed in its natural locations away from studio-built sets. This influenced the way the film was lit. There were competing lighting styles of expressionism and realism. Realism relied on found lighting at the location with the minimum of additional lamps. Expressionism was created by tight control of hard light sources in their intensity and position.

Expressionism

The fashion for high contrast, dynamic graphic images reached its apogee in the Film Noir style of the 1940s and 1950s, which had been heavily influenced by the earlier German expressionist cinema. This style of lighting with hard-edge shadows and high contrast has a powerful influence on the composition of the shot. Woody Bredell who photographed 'The Killers' (1946) suggested that the film was lit in order to reduce the detail in the images to the very basic visual information for storytelling. This was achieved by strong, single-source lighting, by slashes of light, low angles and dark shadows to produce stark imagery (see front cover).

An important function of a hard light source is to provide shadow as well as a lit surface. Dark shadows give an image visual weight. High contrast – deep blacks and highlights – strengthen the core meaning of an image. There is no uncertainty of the principal subject. Figure and ground cannot be mistaken. But strong contrast can tip over into a crude unappealing simplicity that runs out of interest once the initial impact has been absorbed. If the predominant tones of an image are dark and without highlights, the image can convey mystery and suspense and, as used in some television soaps, a form of ersatz realism by avoiding any visual indication that is out of keeping with the setting (e.g., bright highlights on hair provided by backlight). But a surfeit of low-key realism can also induce a visual sense of depression leading to indifference.

The Film Noir period ended with 'A Touch of Evil' (1958). It was shot by Russell Metty with extraordinary baroque touches, made at the same time as the New Wave was emerging in Paris. 'Touch of Evil' anticipated the fluid use of a hand-held camera when Welles had an Eclair Cameflex lightweight European camera imported, and it was hand-held to great effect in the high contrast interior lit by an external flashing neon sign when the Welles' character murders a small town criminal.

This graphic, hard edged, high contrast lighting style controlled the composition of the shot. Shadow can be used as mass in a framing to balance out other visual elements. The edges between shadow and lit areas can be used in the same way as line convergence is used to focus attention, create depth or to unite foreground and background.

Realism

Throughout the second half of the twentieth century film speeds continued to increase first with black and white negative and later with colour. This allowed filming in most locations without the need or requirement to add many additional lamps. To many film makers it seemed contradictory to carefully select a location for its atmosphere and realism and then try to obliterate the location ambience by using the same lighting techniques that were available in the studio.

The French cinematographer Raoul Coutard, when filming Jean-Luc Godard's 'A Bout de Souffle' in 1959, took advantage of the increased film speed available to shoot the film using natural or 'found' light. He took 18-m lengths of Ilford HPS negative sold for use in 35 mm still cameras, and cemented them together to make 120-m rolls for use in a Cameflex film camera. By pushing it in development he had a film that gave him an 800 ASA rating, which allowed Goddard to shoot all the location scenes with available light. Most lighting cameramen were not such 'available'-light purists but Coutard went on to develop the technique of bounced light.

In 'Le Petit Soldat' (1960) Coutard used rows of photoflood reflector bulbs attached to the tops of windows and door frames pointing at the ceiling. This even spread of soft light imitates natural light from a window in an all white room with the bonus of no lamp stands or polecats (scaffold bars) so that an interior can be shot 360°. This technique requires a fast film as the light is all reflected, plus there are difficulties in getting light into the actors eyes.

Bounced light was seen as more natural and realistic than the stylized three-point lighting of key, fill and backlight that was standard in many features. It was later adapted for studio work by using large polystyrene sheets to bounce light or diffusion was achieved by semi-translucent material across the top of the set.

The increasing use of soft lights as the main source of television lighting was facilitated by:

- increased CCD sensitivity. When a light is bounced off a poly-board, the effective candlepower is reduced by about one-fifth. It was therefore difficult to get the required lighting level with older, less sensitive cameras;
- a growing awareness and fashion for more natural, soft lit images, and the developing technique to handle 'soft' lighting;
- the increasing availability of equipment such as special soft lights, fluorescent lights, etc.

Controlled lighting and composition

One of the main values of light in relation to composition is the ability to accentuate tonal differences and provide balance or visual unity. Compositional design using light sources relies on control of light direction. Keeping light off surfaces in the field of view can be as important for the composition of the shot as controlling where the light will fall. With bounced light this becomes more difficult. Soft light by definition will spread a wash of light across all of the action and other visual design methods to control composition have to be used.

Modulating the light pattern of a shot introduces selective contrast and this is best achieved by a hard light source. But the degree and extent of the artificial contrast or range of tonal values in an image that is introduced by the selective positioning of lamps gives rise to arguments about styles of lighting.

'Realistic' lighting aims to replicate naturally occurring light sources, whether sunlight or light naturally found in interiors or exteriors. As an objective, it is nearly always compromised because of the technical considerations of the recording medium. Intercutting between a subject in full frontal sunlight facing a subject who has only naturally occurring reflected light will produce an obvious mismatch. Nearly all subjects illuminated by naturally occurring light sources will need some lighting modification, even if it is simply restaging their positions to reduce the worst excesses of uncontrolled light.

Naturalism and found light

Naturally occurring light sources do not discriminate between important and unimportant visual elements ascribed to them by individuals. It is the human mind in the act of perception that attaches relevance to one image as opposed to another. The quest by some lighting designers to replicate naturally occurring lighting effects is at odds with most visual communication such as scripted drama, information, etc., which aims, by selective production techniques, to focus on one aspect in order to communicate a specific message. 'Realistic' lighting (i.e., everyday random and haphazard illumination) will require modification not only to conform to the technical requirements of the medium (e.g., contrast range, minimum exposure, etc.) but also as part of the overall production strategy to be selective in the message produced.

Film and television production is selective in order to communicate. Naturally occurring light illuminates impartially every surface within its orbit, making no judgements and exercising no discretion. This is the visual equivalent of the image produced from an unmanned, static security camera. One victory for the advocates of natural light was the gradual disappearance of the strong, glossy hair backlight that had been a staple of Hollywood glamour lighting for so many years.

Diffused light technique was used in a move away from what many saw as the 'unrealistic' contrast introduced by hard light sources. These selectively lit aspects of a subject and setting, especially in what was considered the artificial and mannered three-point portrait lighting system where every face had a key, fill and backlight. Diffused light often eliminates strong modelling and the separation of planes that indicate depth. It may be difficult to separate foreground/ background without some form of backlight or hard light emphasis on selective areas of the frame and therefore the illusion of depth is diminished. The direction and selective coverage of soft light is more difficult to control and therefore inevitably there is less control of tone and mass in a composition. As we have discussed earlier, strong contrast can emphasize meaning and provide attention-grabbing dynamic images but at the cost of appearing mannered, artificial or, in a word, unrealistic. In normal everyday perception we seldom encounter strong, unequivocal visual statements but neither do we view the world within a frame, without normal binocular depth perception and being subjected to rapid changes of image size. Any two-dimensional depiction of reality begins with selection and the drive towards lighting 'realism' is only partly modifying the inherently artificial representation of a television or film image.

Television lighting

Television technology has been a constant quest to design equipment that would accurately reproduce the colour and contrast range of the subject in shot. For many years, video picture making avoided any technique that 'degraded' the image i.e., altered the fidelity of the electronic reproduction. The aim was to light and expose for the full range of the video signal and transmit pictures that had good blacks, detail in the highlights and with the highest resolution the TV system was capable of providing, particularly to viewers receiving pictures in poor reception areas. The technical constraints on both contrast range and resolution were the regulations governing the rationing of bandwidth. Attempts to improve resolution were by adding electronic enhancement, which gave video pictures their characteristic 'edge' appearance on dark-to-light and light-to-dark tonal transitions.

The production methods of the television industry had to be structured to provide endless hours of live and recorded programming. The majority of such programming was topical, instantly consumed and therefore had budgets to match the endless appetite of 24-hour television. Very fast shooting schedules, low budget production methods were added to the edgy, low contrast stereotypical TV image displayed on small receivers watched in conditions of high ambient light. Video images struggled to match film quality and the difference was reinforced by the engineering 'sanctity' of reproduction fidelity. This was in sharp contrast with the photographic and film mediums, which often attempted to customize the image to suit a particular emotional or aesthetic effect. In this approach, the camera was not a 'scientific' instrument faithfully observing reality, but the means of creating a subjective impression. Up to the introduction of digital television, this technique practised for many decades in film had made little impact on television programme making. Either production content was unsuitable for subjective images or the degree that an analogue signal could be customized to express mood or atmosphere was limited by the needs of terrestrial broadcasting.

Any two from cheap, good or fast – but not all three

Television lighting for many years concentrated on the need to satisfy the technical requirements of the medium because of the historical limitations of electronic pictures. Film lighting on small budgets was more adventurous. 'We used a lot of long focal length lenses, smoke and nets. That's the best, maybe the only way to make no money look interesting. You discount the background, focus on a long (focal length) lens, and isolate the subject.' This appears to sum up many of the difficulties and solutions that lighting has to deal with. No money, small budgets, limited time, means that lighting requires the imaginative use of available resources.

For most of the time, additional lamps are not required to achieve adequate exposure on exteriors. With claims of low-light cameras down to 1 lux, the proverbial black cat in a coal cellar can still be noisily seen by screwing up the gain and keeping the coal cellar door open. To over-generalize, in the past, film lighting concentrated on the need to interpret and give atmosphere to an image, whereas television lighting was often constrained by the demands of working in a low-cost, mass-produced market.

Expressing an idea through an image

The challenge to TV video production lighting is to match the film and photographic ability to customize the image to suit the message. The look of the shot is not just a good transmitter picture with every shot containing a reference black and a full contrast range up to a peak white. Video has progressed beyond the point where simply achieving a good engineering picture was the principle aim of lighting. Lighting to achieve the production aims has been the crucial objective for years but has often been difficult to achieve with a transmitted analogue signal.

The quest for video technological perfection is not quite accomplished, but single camera digital production allows the potential for customizing the image to match the production aims. We have reached a point where achieving a technically acceptable picture without imperfections is less a craft than a routine.

TV lighting is not an engineering activity and in that sense there is no objective 'right' way. There are formulas but, without doubt, lighting is much more of a craft than a science. With the potential to control and customize the video image through set-up cards, and with digital resolution good enough to almost dispense with image enhancement, there is every possibility that the elusive 'film look' will more and more depend on budget and production schedules than the inherent characteristics of the electronic image.

Decorative lighting

The move from tube to CCD cameras coincided with the development of a greater range of computer-controlled moving light sources. Many quizzes, pop music and variety programmes and some film musicals require very bold and decorative lighting treatments for the wide shots. Lighting directors were called upon, in effect, to design sets that were almost completely dependent on in-vision lamps and self-illuminating features built into the set. The digital CCD cameras could handle more saturated colours and more extreme contrasts. Moving lighting fixtures and moving mirror fixtures were initially used for live concert performances and discos and then waggling light beams gave way to using the gobos and projection features of the fixtures. A new high-tech lighting look emerged that was glitzy, smart and appeared expensive. The budget, of course, dictates how many fixtures can be hired, the time and manpower available for the rig and the time available to set, programme and exploit all of the lighting rig's potential. Another useful innovation was the auto pilot system allowing moving lights to follow a performer via a small transmitter around the stage. Decorative lighting is often the visual image of the shot rather than lighting the subject of the shot.

Summary

The most important element in the visual design of film and television images is light. Apart from its fundamental role of illuminating the subject, light determines tonal differences, outline, shape, colour, texture and depth. It can create compositional relationships, provide balance, harmony and contrast. It provides mood, atmosphere and visual continuity. Light is the key visual force and is therefore central to any consideration of visual composition.

Although perception seeks visual unity, a detailed visual communication requires contrast to articulate its meaning. Light, by supplying contrast of tones, can remove visual ambiguity in a muddle of competing subjects.

A dynamic image is one where a visual conflict or tension has been set up and then resolved. The ying/yang of visual design is harmony and contrast. Harmony, appeases the perceptual system and therefore facilitates the delivery of the message. Contrast grabs the attention and ensures the perceptual system stays switched on to receive the message.

Within a broad generalization, two qualities of light are used in film and television production – hard and soft. Hard light produces contrast, modelling and texture. It creates depth, shape and relationships. Diffused light is often applied to reduce the contrast introduced by a hard light source and to create an integrated harmony of tones.

14
Colour

How the eye sees colour

Colour vision is made possible by cones on the retina of the eye, which respond to different colours. The cones are of three types sensitive to certain bands of light – either green, red or blue. The three responses combine so that, with normal vision, all other colours can be discerned. There is a wide variation in an individual's receptor response to different colours but many tests have established an average response (see Figure 14.1).

Colour television adopts the same principle by using a prism behind the lens to split the light from a scene into three separate channels. Colour analysis in the camera will give the appropriate red, green and blue signals according to the spectral energy distribution of the colour being observed. A fourth signal, called the luminance signal, is obtained by combining proportions of the red, green and blue signals. It is this signal that allows compatibility with a monochrome display. The amplitude of the luminance signal at any moment is proportional to the brightness of the particular picture element being scanned. Colour film negative uses a similar filter technique to expose different layers of emulsion to the different colours of the spectrum.

A TV colour signal is an electrical representation of the original scene processed and reproduced on a TV display monitor. The fidelity of the displayed colour picture to the original colours will depend on the analysis characteristics of the light splitting block and the linear matrix of the video camera, which are designed and adjusted to be displayed on the appropriate phosphor characteristics of the display tube, all of which collectively take into account, and accurately reproduce the average human perceptual response to colour. In practice, the available phosphor compounds that are employed in tube manufacture determine the selection and handling of the television primary colour signals needed to provide accurate perceptual response to a displayed colour picture.

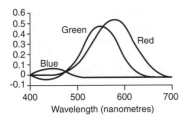

Figure 14.1 Thomas Young (1773–1829) was one of the first people to propose the three-colour theory of perception. By mixing three lights widely spaced along the spectrum he demonstrated that he could produce any colour (and white) visible in the spectrum by a mixture of three, but not less than three, lights set to appropriate intensities. The choice of suitable wavelengths to achieve this is quite wide and no unique set of three wavelengths has been established. The average three colour sensitive cones in the eye have the response curves displayed here, and all spectral colours are seen by a mixture of signals from the three systems

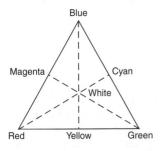

Figure 14.2 Additive colour system. Nearly the whole range of colours can be produced by adding together, in various proportions, light sources of the three primary wavelengths. This is known as additive colour matching. Some colours that the eye can perceive plot outside the triangle and can not be combined by the use of the three chosen primaries unless the application of 'negative' light is employed in the camera processing circuits. Given that the tube phosphor and the 'average' perceptual response to colour remains unchanged, the fidelity of colour reproduction will be determined by the design of the circuits handling the mixture of the three colour signals

White balance

In colorimetry it is convenient to think of white being obtained from equal amounts of red, green and blue light. This concept is continued in colour cameras. When exposed to a white surface (neutral scene), the three signals are matched to the green signal to give equal amounts of red, green and blue. This is known as white balance. The actual red, green and blue light emitted when white is displayed on a colour tube are in the proportion of 30 per cent red lumens, 59 per cent green lumens and 11 per cent blue lumens.

Although the eye adapts if the colour temperature illuminating a white subject alters, there is no adaptation by the camera and the three video amplifiers have to be adjusted to ensure they have unity output. Because the colour temperature of different light sources and mixtures of light sources varies, it is essential to select the correct filter and white-balance the camera whenever you suspect a change has occurred. When there is a change in the colour temperature of the light illuminating a potential shot it is necessary to adjust the white balance of the camera. The fidelity of colour reproduction is dependent on the white-balance procedure. If required, the white balance can be deliberately adjusted so that overall the pictures are warmed up to a straw colour or cooled to a bluish tint. This customizing is frequently irreversible and so more extreme colour effects should be left to post-production where the depth and appearance of the image can be assessed on Grade A monitors.

Colour correction

A fundamental problem with location work is dealing with a mixture of light of different colour temperatures. If the light remains uncorrected, faces and subjects may have colour casts that look unnatural and distracting. The two most common light sources on location are daylight, which has a range of colour temperatures but averages around 5600 K, and tungsten light, which is often produced by lamps carried to the location that are approximately 3200 K.

Colour correction filters

There are two basic types of correction filter used when attempting to combine mixed lighting of tungsten and daylight:

1. an orange filter, which converts daylight to tungsten and is most often seen attached to windows for interior shots;
2. a blue filter, which converts tungsten to daylight and is often used on tungsten lamps.

Any correction filter will reduce the amount of light it transmits and therefore a balance must be struck between colour correction and sufficient light for adequate exposure. A filter for full colour conversion from daylight to tungsten will have a transmission of only 55 per cent, which means nearly half of the available light is lost. A filter for full colour correction from tungsten to daylight has an even smaller transmission factor of 34 per cent – it cuts out nearly two-thirds of the possible light from a lamp. This is a more serious loss because whereas daylight is usually more than adequate for a reasonable exposure, reducing the light output of a lamp by blue filtering to match daylight may leave an interior lit by blue filtered lamps short of adequate light.

Altering the colour balance

As well as colour correction filters on lens or lamp, both film and video use filters to adjust colour response. These include filters that give an overall tint to the shot and graduated (grads) filters, which help to control bright skies by having a graduated neutral density from the top to clear filter at the bottom – the graduation can be obtained as a hard or a soft transition. There are also filters with a graduated tint to colour skies or the top part of the frame. They are positioned in the matte box for optimum effect but, once adjusted, the camera can rarely be tilted or panned on shot without disclosing the filter position. There are also skin tone warmers to improve close-ups of faces. This can also be achieved electronically.

Post-production

Both film and video can achieve significant changes in the colour appearance of images in post-production. Video has a huge range of post-production effects available. Film production can grade a negative or a print in processing or when dubbed to video for electronic post production.

Colour as subject

Twentieth-century painting has often employed colour as the primary means of visual communication. In their relationship within a frame, colours provide their own kind of balance, contrast, rhythm, structure, texture and depth, independent of any recognizable figurative subject that may be defined in terms of line or tone. Colour not only has a profound influence on composition, in many forms of image making it is the subject of the composition.

The importance of colour to express emotional states or to create sensations of movement and space has not always been recognized. Up to the early Renaissance period, colour was considered by many art patrons as an embellishment to a painting to be selected from a list of expensive pigments. Colour was added as a beautifying agent and priced accordingly. For many years, painters blocked in the main structure of a painting primarily in line and tone. Colour was used to supplement the linear and tonal expression of ideas. Although painters began to appreciate the expressive use of colour, the scientific investigation into colour theory by Goethe, Helmholtz, Chevreul and others in the nineteenth century provided the stimulus to reinforce or confirm many painter's intuitive understanding of the effects of colour. Eventually, the optical sensations of colour were fascinating enough to be able to provide the very subject matter of a picture.

Monochrome

Both film and TV began as a black and white medium. In fact, film began with no colour, no sound and with very little if any camera movement. The ability to record infinite detail mechanically and the novelty of its 'realism' compensated the photographic image for its lack of colour. Television, by adding the ability to witness an event as it occurred, wherever it occurred, could also compensate for the absence of colour.

The legacy of monochrome television

The gradual transition in the 1960s to colour broadcasting and the gradual replacement of black and white receivers with near universal colour reception left behind one legacy of monochrome television. Nearly all broadcast television cameras are fitted, as standard, with monochrome viewfinders. There are exceptions, but the majority of cameras in daily use up to, and including the introduction of high-definition equipment, use monochrome viewfinders to acquire the basic material for colour television.

Camera manufacturers explain this paradox as their inability, so far, to provide a 1.5″ monocular colour viewfinder with sufficient resolution, added to their claim that the cost of doing so would be prohibitive. Despite the vast technological changes that have occurred with the development of television cameras in the last 50 years, the one consistent technique that has remained unchanged has been the need for cameramen to use a monochrome viewfinder even when composing colour pictures.

The spread of the DV camera into broadcasting has brought with it the colour liquid crystal display (LCD) viewfinder, which is often fitted as standard. With these viewfinders, colour can now be seen as integral to the composition of the shot instead of the need for a mental note to remind oneself to take colour into consideration when framing up using a monochrome viewfinder.

Optical viewfinders on film cameras have always provided the opportunity to check the influence of colour on the shot.

Problems associated with monochrome viewfinders

One of the most common misconceptions with this situation is that there is no need for a colour viewfinder except where colour differentiation is necessary, for example sports coverage, snooker, etc. The camera manufacturers believe that the viewfinder is simply there to be used for focus and what they term 'the adjustment of the picture angle'.

The fact that colour plays a significant part in picture composition is either ignored or conveniently becomes the responsibility of other technicians in the television production chain. After 30 years of transition from monochrome to colour, cameramen remain the last group of black-and-white viewers.

The result of framing a composition in monochrome often results in the over-reliance on tone, mass and linear design as the main ingredient of the composition. If a colour monitor is accessible, then adjustment can be made for the colour component of the shot but only too often, the frame of reference for the composition is the monochrome viewfinder or a small portable low quality colour monitor. Colours of similar brightness such as red and the darker shades of green merge and may be indistinguishable in the monochrome viewfinder and yet, as separate hues, they exercise a strong influence on the composition (see Plates 4 and 5). Saturated red and blue appear much darker in a monochrome viewfinder than their brightness value in colour. A small saturated colour against a complementary background has a much greater impact in colour than its viewfinder reproduction.

To some extent monochrome pictures are more abstract than colour and the effect of the image is different from our normal colour perception. The image can be more streamlined if only tone and line are considered as compositional elements. Many years ago, film cameramen, after years of black-and-white photography, had difficulty in adjusting to the complexity of colour composition compared with the simplicity and control of monochrome. When using orthocromatic black and white film stock, they would often use a pan glass when converting to panchromatic film to assess how the colour tones would reproduce in monochrome. Some still photographers prefer to avoid colour in order to emphasize the form and shape of an image.

Using a monochrome viewfinder, video operators have the reverse problem. They must assess how a monochrome viewfinder image is converting a colour image and if there are colour components in the image unseen in colour in the viewfinder that will disrupt a monochrome composition.

It is possible to demonstrate that a video image has been composed in monochrome by switching out the colour on the receiver. It is surprising how much strength is reintroduced into a shot that was originally composed in black and white when the colour content is removed. The reverse can also be seen when a shot could have been improved if a colour viewfinder had been available in order to actively use colour in the composition in addition to line and tone.

A flat lit scene viewed in black and white gives the impression of lack of contrast and punch whereas the same scene in colour may be much more acceptable than the monochrome rendering suggests. A shot lit with predominantly red light has very little contrast and low modulation when viewed through a monochrome viewfinder. This often provokes an unnecessary struggle by the cameraman using a monochrome viewfinder to provide dynamic compositions using mass and line, which is quite unnecessary when the same shot is viewed in colour (see Plates 6 and 7).

Contrasty lighting may provide compositions with more impact whereas overcast light may give flat black-and-white pictures, although the colour content may help to separate subject material. In a monochrome viewfinder the lack of contrast dilutes the visual strength and without strong light/dark relationships the composition may often appear to be lacking balance or emphasis. If reliance is placed on monochrome viewfinder compositions, some colour combinations may have a striking dissimilarity to the balanced black-and-white compatible image.

Composing with a monochrome viewfinder results in emphasizing contrast, mass and usually the convergence of lines. Colour becomes simply the accidental effect of individual objects within the frame rather than the conscious grouping and locating of colour within the frame. The weight of colour elements are not used to balance the composition and can frequently unbalance the considered monochrome composition of tone and line.

Colour and composition

The faithful reproduction of colour requires techniques to ensure that the specific colours of a scene are reproduced accurately and colour continuity requires that the same colours are identically reproduced in succeeding shots. This is often a basic requirement in most types of camerawork but colour as an emotional influence in establishing atmosphere or in structuring a composition, also plays a vital role in visual communication.

Terms used to describe colour can sometimes lead to confusion. In this account:

- *hue* refers to the dominant wavelength – the colour we see;
- *value* is a measurement of reflectivity on a scale of 1–10;
- *saturation* is the purity of the colour.

The perceived hue of any coloured object is likely to vary depending on the colour of its background and the colour temperature of the light illuminating it. Staging someone in a yellow jacket against green foliage will produce a different contrast relationship to staging the same person against a blue sky (see Plates 2 and 3).

There appears to be a reduction in the perception of 'colourfulness' under a dull overcast sky. The muted effect on colour under diffused light can often allow colours to blend and provide a softer pastel relationship and a satisfactory picture, whereas the lack of contrast may produce flat, drab monochrome images.

Sunlight raises the general level of illumination and provides a directional light that, reflected off coloured objects, tends to increase the 'colourfulness' of a scene compared with the diffuse light of an overcast sky. A proportion of directional light is reflected as white specular from glossy surfaces and increases the impact of colour. The hard modelling and greater contrast make the scene look more 'alive'.

The perceptual impact of a coloured object is not consistent but is modified by the quality of the light illuminating it, by reflection, shadow and by its relationship with surrounding colours.

Balancing a composition with colour

Balance in a composition depends on the distribution of visual weight. Mass, relative brightness, line and the psychological importance of a visual element can all be structured to provide visual unity in an image and to provide a route for the eye to travel in order to emphasize the most important element. Colour can be used to balance and to unify an image in many ways (see Plate 7).

An out-of-focus single hued object within the frame (e.g., red), often exerts a strong influence in the composition and may distract attention from the main subject.

Light/dark relationships

As we have seen, the eye is attracted to the lightest part of an image or that part of the image which has the greatest contrast and if colour is reproduced as a grey scale, yellow, after white, is the brightest colour. Depending on their backgrounds, a small area of yellow, for example, will carry more visual weight than a small area of blue. When balancing out a composition attention should be paid to the relative brightness of colour and its location within the frame.

Cold/warm contrast

Many colours have a hot or a cold feel to them. Red is considered hot and blue is thought of as cold. People disagree about how hot or how cold a particular colour may be but the general perceptual consensus is that hot colours advance and cold colours recede. This has a compositional significance of colour as a depth indicator and affects the control of the principal subject. It will take other strong design elements within a shot to force a foreground blue object to exist in space in front of a red object.

The eye naturally sees red as closer than blue unless the brightness, shape, chroma value and background of the blue is so arranged that in context it becomes more dominant than a desaturated, low brightness red. Colour effects are relative and no one set of guidelines will hold true for all colour relationships. For example, the intensity of a hot colour can be emphasized by surrounding it by cool colours. The intensity of the contrast will affect balance and to what part of the frame the eye is attracted.

Strong prolonged stimulation of one colour has the effect of decreasing the sensitivity to that colour but sensitivity to its complementary is enhanced. Looking at a saturated red, for example, for some time and then shifting the gaze to a grey area will provoke a sensation of blue-green. This effect of successive contrast is a result of a process of adaptation by the cones and rods in the eye. Intercutting with shots containing strong saturated primaries may give rise to 'after' images of complementary colours (see Plate 1).

Colour symbolism

There have been a number of theories based on general colour association concerning the symbolism of colour. Hollywood cameraman Villorio Storaro used his own colour theory in shooting 'The Last Emperor' (1987), where he equated different colours with different moods or atmospheres. The shots at the beginning of the Forbidden City and the family were predominantly orange. He used yellow for personal growth of the young emperor and the realization of personal identity. Yellow was also the royal colour of the Chinese. Yellow dissolved to green with the arrival of the tutor – the arrival of knowledge.

Nestor Almendros used the 'magic hour', that moment of the day when the sun has left the sky and the earth and the sky are bathed in a golden light. There were barely 25 minutes each day of this quality of light to shoot the film 'Days of Heaven' (1978) but it was considered that the contribution of the emotional quality of the light was worth the extra budget required.

Summary

Balance in a composition depends on the distribution of visual weight. Colour can be used to balance and to unify an image in many ways.

If the weight of colour elements is ignored (or unseen), it can frequently unbalance the considered monochrome composition of tone and line.

A composition framed in monochrome may result in the over-reliance on tone, mass and linear design as the main ingredients of the composition.

Colour not only has a profound influence on composition, in many forms of image making, it is often the subject of the composition.

The perceptual impact of a coloured object is not consistent but is modified by the quality of the light illuminating it, by reflection, shadow and by its relationship with surrounding colours.

The individual response to colour may be a product of fashion and culture, or it may be an intrinsic part of the act of perception.

15
Staging

Introduction to staging

If light is the dominant influence on picture composition, staging performance, action, actors and props in relationship to a setting is at the heart of all film and television production. What people do as well as what they say is equally important in a visual medium. The interpretation of a narrative is initially the combined task of writer, director and performer. Making it all meaningful within a frame is often achieved by the combined skills of director and cameraman. It is difficult to separate out the distinctions between a performance and the visual treatment of a production. A successful project is seen as a succession of significant images and action but there are also many other craft skills in the realization of a production such as editing, sound, design, costume, make-up, etc. They all have a essential input in staging and composition and to adequately cover their role would require many books.

The relationship between people can be established quickly by their position in a frame and how they are staged in depth. In many ways, using pictures to tell a story is the quickest and most effective way to establish motive, response, mood, point of view, and all the other myriad feelings that can be expressed by the face or body attitude. All these aspects of staging are in the director's domain but camera movement, camera position and choice of lens all influence production decisions. This chapter deals with a few considerations when staging for shot composition, but it far from exhausts all aspects of production decisions when staging action.

Where shall I stand?

Throughout this book, phrases have been used such as pictorial unity, balanced composition, emphasizing the main subject of interest, etc. Nowhere is this search for picture integration more commonplace and exacting than in the figure/background staging dilemma. As many film and television images consist of faces or figures in a setting, much of the time, cameramen are involved in finding solutions to the visual problem of combining a foreground subject with its background.

We discussed in the figure/ground section (Chapter 13) how the main subject of interest in an image cannot exist without a background and that often there must be some visual design method to connect the main subject to its 'ground' even though this may be featureless. A plain backing may be sufficient to emphasize the subject, but more usually there is a need to set the subject in context – to provide a setting that will reinforce or comment on the subject. The content of the setting provides atmosphere, mood and information and acts as a powerful reinforcer of the presentation of the main subject of interest. A low camera angle often helps to make the foreground subject dominant and cuts the presenter away from his/ her background but it can be unflattering. Equally important is the integration of the background with the main subject to provide a unified image.

What is staging?

Blocking movement or staging action refers to the initial setting up of a shot where actor/presenter position and movement is plotted. With the single camera/single shot technique, the complete action for the shot can be seen before camera position, camera movement and lens is decided and the final framing agreed. This should achieve the precise composition that is required because a great deal of control can be exercised in the positioning of actor/presenter to background and the control of background. Essentially, the visual elements that make up the shot can be arranged to achieve the objective of the shot.

This is not dissimilar to the methods painters use to achieve an integrated image. Apart from those few artists who strive for a perfect replication of the scene in view, the design of a painting is achieved by control of the chosen visual components, placing every element where it works for the complete composition.

Although there has always been a great deal of discussion on what constitutes good design, artists have more control over the design of their painting than a cameraman because they have the ability to fashion each visual element to enhance the unity of the image.

Unless the style of painting requires a literal record of the field of view, artists have the ability to arrange and rearrange the painted area so that overall, they achieve the composition they are searching for. Although a great deal of image manipulation can be achieved with lens and camera position, in general, cameramen have to deal with a 'found' visual situation and attempt by lighting and actor positioning to achieve visual control of the whole frame.

In the mid-nineteenth century, early photographers had ambitions to control all the elements of a photographic image and spent a great deal of time setting up and copying academic compositions borrowed from painting. The results were unconvincing, posed freeze frames that soon dropped out of fashion along with the style of paintings they were attempting to emulate.

Film and television have the added compositional element of subject movement and the tradition of recording the 'real' world. With a few exceptions, the majority of narrative film and television productions stage the dreams, fantasies and desires of the protagonists in the dramas against recognizable slices of location or set. Even though the plots may involve bizarre and fantastic developments, in general, they are played out against settings that contain solid, known objects easily identified by the audience.

Visual storytelling therefore has the requirement for tightly designed images created in the choice of set design, costume, makeup, staging, lighting and camera angle. With such a degree of control, the implication is that every image chosen is the result of a production decision. There should be no lucky accidents, although the history of film and television camerawork has numerous examples to the contrary.

The American cinematographer Conrad Hall, for example, noticed when setting up a shot for 'In Cold Blood' (1967), that light passing through artificial rain dripping down a set window threw a shadow of a 'tear' rolling down the cheeks of the artiste in close-up who was remembering his past (sad) life. This simple visual accident was immediately incorporated into the shot. Gordon Willis shooting 'The Godfather' (1972) used top lighting to help reduce Brando's heavy jowls. This resulted in Brando's eyes being in shadow and intensified the menace of the character.

Staging action for a number of television cameras to shoot continuously, however, often requires a great deal of compromise between the ideal for each shot and what in practice can be achieved. Multi-camera television coverage requires pre-planning of set or location set design, lighting and a camera script with details of all planned shots. For complex programmes such as drama, there will also be extensive pre-rehearsal of artistes involved where interpretation and action is devised and plotted.

Once in the studio or at the location, each shot will be blocked and then a run through of the scene will test the practicalities and the problems of the camera script. With continuous multi-camera shooting, there is not a great deal of adjustment available for the optimum positioning of actor and background. Any repositioning of the actor for one camera will affect the framing of another camera. Reasonable compromises are sought but the perfection of the single shot/single camera framing are often not a practical option. A dozen small corrections that would have been made for single camera shooting such as lighting, background set changes and artist positioning are not always possible if continuous action is covered by multi-cameras. The tendency in multi-camera television shooting is for shot size to have greater importance and precedence over the search for the integrated image that is possible with single shot recording.

Framing up a shot of inanimate objects is easier and involves finding the right position in space for the lens with the right lens angle and then devising the lighting, balance and frame. If the visual elements in the frame are small enough to rearrange, then good composition can be achieved by placing each item in an optimum position for visual unity.

Staging people and staging action

If good composition can only be achieved by control of the visual elements, how is it possible to reorder the visual elements in a shot to create a dynamic composition? In the chapter on perspective (Chapter 4), we discussed ways of adjusting the camera-to-subject relationship in order to produce dynamic compositions. Control of the skeleton of the picture can be ordered by choice of lens, camera position and camera distance from subject.

Frequently, in television and film, the principal subjects in the frame are people. In a controlled situation where the artiste can be positioned in relationship to the lens, there is frequently an optimum position that gives the best composition with that specific background and artiste. Best in this context means the most appropriate relationships for the message that is to be communicated.

A common relationship in television news/factual programming is the reporter with the 'over my left shoulder World War Three has just broken out' shot. This combination of reporter delivering a piece to camera with the suggestion or flavour of the content of the piece in the background is commonplace but frequently produces awkward framing.

If the reportage concerns a civil catastrophe or strong visual activity in the background, then a combined image will result in divided interest between reporter and the background event. What may be intended as background 'atmosphere' for the 'piece to camera' often develops into a split screen with a double shot obliging the viewer to constantly shift their attention between foreground and background. The two centres of interest – reporter and background – are usually caused because of the tight framing of the reporter. The close size of shot and the talking to camera creates a separation, a detachment from the glimpsed events taking place outside the intimacy established between reporter and viewer. Talking to the lens creates the effect of standing outside the situation being reported, of taking a detached, objective view of the type of extraordinary event that would normally have overwhelmed and involved an observer.

Journalistic values are claimed to be based on the search for objectivity, of the seeking after fact as opposed to comment or opinion but paradoxically, this 'objectivity' is often accompanied by powerful, emotional images that are intended to grab and involve the audience's attention. The subjective, emotionally involving images of human suffering or despair are sometimes combined, in an uneasy alliance, with a 'factual' piece to camera.

The most neutral and objective image would appear to be the fashion for posing the journalist against a sign or logo. Over the shoulder of the reporter is seen a notice which may say 'Home Office', 'Scotland Yard', 'Treasury', etc.

This type of shot often fails to work as the background rectangle sign fights the foreground reporter as the main subject of interest. Divided interest seems to appeal to literal minded journalists accustomed to working with print. The background sign appeals to them because they believe it reinforces the story whereas in fact a divided interest image is often a distraction to the viewer.

The same divided interest is carried over into the news bulletin where the newsreader is pushed out of the frame by a programme logo or generic title. This stale visual arrangement is an awkward composition that has achieved acceptability by constant repetition (see Figure 6.4).

Interviews

A recurring news and feature item is the location interior interview. It usually requires shots of the interviewee seated in their office or house being questioned by a presenter. There are a number of factors in deciding camera position and interview position including:

- Does the interview position allow variation in shot size to sustain a long interview if required?
- Can the participants positional relationship be established?
- Is the environment around the interviewee important to the interview? Does the background to the shot give more information?
- Is there a comfortable distance between participants for them to relate to each other?
- Avoid the bottom frame line coinciding with someone seated – i.e., seat of chair and frame line correspond so that it looks as if the person is sitting on the bottom frame. This also applies to leaning on a vertical that coincides with right/left frame edge.
- Is there sufficient space and how convenient is it to relight and reposition for reverses? Before cross-shooting on a subject ensure that all angles have compositional potential. When setting up an interview, eyeball the reverses before deciding on the main shot.
- Do windows need to be in shot?
- The colour temperature difference and balance between daylight entering from windows and the light provided by added lamps.

If there is complete control over the subject position then look for a background that will draw attention to the subject, will balance out the main subject (e.g., offset framing) and will hint at an explanation of the subject either by mood, atmosphere or information.

Control of background

A small area of background can be controlled by lighting or by limiting the depth-of-field by an ND (neutral density) filter in the camera, but the greatest control is by choice of camera position, lens angle, camera distance and foreground subject position. Consideration must also be given to how the shot will be intercut and often a matching background of similar tonal range, colour and contrast has to be chosen to avoid a mismatch when intercutting.

Too large a tonal range between intercut backgrounds will result in obtrusive and very visible cuts. Visual continuity of elements such as direction of light, similar zones of focus and the continuity of background movement (e.g., crowds, traffic, etc.) in intercut shots have also to be checked.

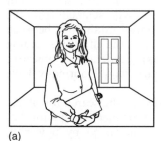
(a)

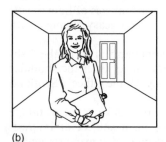
(b)

Figure 15.1 The same size of foreground subject achieved with a narrow angle lens **(a)** and a wide angle lens **(b)**

Figure composition

Single figure composition

The single figure occurs constantly in film and television framing. There appear to be two aspects that affect its relationship with the setting (other elements will be discussed in the appropriate sections). With a simple or plain background, the figure should be in contact with one or two edges of the frame in order to achieve unity with the image. With a shot closer than full figure this is obviously inevitable. If the context of the shot allows, a side-lit portraiture enables the darker side of the face to set up a relationship with the background. Another visual solution is to find a balancing relationship with background forms or light (using shadow), similar shapes or colour. A single figure is often used to show scale in a landscape and will be identified by movement even if the figure is dominated by the location.

The most useful staging to integrate offset figures with their background is to get the presenter to stand with his or her body turned into the frame rather than square-on to camera. If the shoulder line points into the background then there is a natural lead-in that connects background to foreground.

Two figure composition

Two people in a frame can quickly lead to a 'divided interest' composition unless one of them is made more dominant. This can be achieved by unequal size or position in frame or simply having one person with their back to camera. There are many standard two shot stagings ranging from a larger foreground figure contrasted with a smaller background figure, over-the-shoulder two shots, three-quarter two shot, etc. Other methods of switching attention between two figures in the same frame is by dialogue, movement or lighting.

Multi-figure compositions

Circles, pyramid and oval groupings are classical solutions to binding together three, four or more subjects. Five subjects are often easier to combine into a composition than four. Using the outline shapes of heads and arms and legs to guide the eye around the simple geometric forms, individuals are merged into a coherent composition. It is important to set a focus point (the main subject) within the group and then build the most appropriate shape to emphasize that point.

Individuals in the group may be active or passive in their relationship to the overall composition. Staging people with their backs to camera or in three-quarter profile weakens their importance. Placing people on the focus of a leading line formed by the group's outline shape or other strong directional line, will strengthen their importance. Balancing two people against one within a pyramid grouping is another standard solution to control attention.

Working at speed

Because of the wide range of techniques that are employed in film and television production it is not possible or desirable to itemize a set of compositional do's and don'ts that will cover all situations. Certain basic conventions can be identified that are in use across a wide spectrum of camerawork but in general, as with the choice of camera equipment, it is 'horses for courses'. One specialist area of programming or film making will evolve a certain way of working which suits the requirements of that technique. Other types of production would find these conventions restricting or superfluous.

Actuality programming – working live or recording as live (i.e., no retakes) – have one technique in common. Live action demands a stream of continuous pictures, which means that each cameraman is required to frame up their shots at speed. Occasionally they may have time to reposition the camera without haste and to take time out to consider the precise framing of a shot. This is a rare and infrequent luxury in many types of programming such as sport, music or group discussions. Most productions require a continuous variety of shots often linked to a specific event.

The live multi-camera coverage of an orchestral concert, for example, will be camera scripted in sympathy with the piece performed. Depending on the nature of the music and the television treatment decided by the director, there may be in excess of 200–300 shots shared between five or more cameras.

Each shot has its designated function in the score and must be ready and framed at the precise bar that it is required. The speed of the camerawork will therefore be synchronized with the music and at times this will entail rapid and continuous shot change. The tempo of the camerawork varies between extremely quick reactions 'off-shot' to find the next instrument, to slow camera movement 'on-shot' that reflects the mood of the music. Panning movements have to be synchronized with the number of bars allocated to that shot and must finish exactly on the instrument or group of instruments agreed because possibly, at that point in time, a solo or change of tempo may occur.

This reflex framing by the camera operator with no time to consciously consider composition, is achieved by relying on habit and the developed feeling for a good picture that instantly oversees the eye/hand coordination. If there is no time to consider the image, the only thing to do is to rely on experience and training. Live television continuously requires quick compositional decisions.

Camerawork that is carried out in the real time of the event covered often allows no time for any thoughtful consideration about the precise way of framing. There is no opportunity to re-order the visual elements. The most that can be done in the time available is to trim the shot by way of the zoom and a slight jiggle of the framing points.

An example of the instinctive response to movement can be seen in slow-motion replays of fast sporting action. In the UK, the square-on 'slo mo' camera position in cricket coverage is required to follow the ball as soon as it leaves the bat. Sometimes even the batsman does not know which way the ball went. Continuously during the game, the slow-motion replays reveal that the cameraman has instinctively followed the ball to a fielder who has gathered the ball and aimed it at the stumps in one fluid movement. The framing seen in slow motion belies the real speed and technique required to follow and keep the ball in the frame and the players involved. It has been judged that the speed of the action is sometimes too fast for the umpires on the field to assess what has happened and they call upon a third umpire in the stadium to adjudicate. He is able to do this by relying on the slow-motion replay of the debated incident. High technology does not provide this aid – simply the fast reflexes of cameramen.

In unscripted multi-camera working, one eye has to be kept on what other cameras are offering (through mixed viewfinder or a monitor) in order to provide alternative shots to the shot on transmission. Although most television sports coverage has designated roles for each camera, there are often accompanying incidents such as presentations at the end of the event or 'celebrating' spectator shots that require an *ad lib* coverage. In group discussion programmes, size of shot must be matched and alternatives available for cutaways.

Summary

Many film and television images consist of faces or figures in a setting. Much of the time, cameramen are involved in finding solutions to the visual problem of combining a foreground subject with its background.

The internal space of the shot is a subtle but important part of the look, mood and atmosphere of the shot. When three-dimensional objects are converted into a flat two-dimensional image, size relationships will be controlled by camera distance to subject and lens angle. The choice of the lens angle is therefore dependent on how the action is to be staged and the visual style that is required.

16
Movement

Camera movement

When I was 12 years old, I stood in a film studio at Elstree near London watching a camera crane following an actress, Ingrid Bergman, walk down a very large curved staircase set in the centre of the studio. Apart from a location shot filmed in Acton, London, for 'Kind Hearts and Coronets' (1949), this was the only film making I had ever seen. I was intrigued by the crane's movement as it floated parallel to, and in perfect synchronization with, the actress's movement, down the stairs and across a hall. Jack Cardiff was the cinematographer on the film 'Under Capricorn' (1949) and he wrote many years later about the problems involved with this production. The director, Alfred Hitchcock, was experimenting with the ten-minute take, which he had introduced in 'Rope' (1948). The scenery was designed to be moved aside to allow the crane to move between rooms and up the stairs to the bedroom all in the same continuous shot. I was amazed at how many takes it took but only later did I understand why a ten-minute shot requires so much planning and choreography between actor and camera. I think the crane was a Mole Richardson, one of a pair that Hitchcock had imported from the USA, although ten years later, when I worked on the same crane at the BBC, I noticed that it also had MPRC on the side – Motion Picture Research Council, Hollywood.

The crane movement I witnessed that day had all the hallmarks of a classic camera movement. It combined the functional purpose of keeping the main subject in frame in a development shot that took her from A to B, with a visual interpretation of the character's grace and style as she descended the staircase. The rich visual texture of this movement through space did all these things and yet it was probably unnoticed by the audience.

Invisible movement

The camerawork technique practised by the professional cameraman –
such as stop/start camera movement on action; matching camera
movement to subject movement; pivot points on zooms and tracks;
matched shots on intercuts – is designed to make 'invisible' the
mechanics of programme production. The intention is usually to
emphasize subject – picture content – rather than technique.

An old cliché of Hollywood is that 'a good cutter cuts his own
throat'. It refers to the invisible technique (discussed in Chapter 1)
employed by film editors to stitch together a series of shots so that
the audience is unaware that any artifice or craft has been employed.
The transition between images is so natural that the techniques used
flow past unnoticed. The editor has done such a good job in disguising
his or her contribution to the film that their expertise is invisible. If the
viewer is unaware of the camerawork then quite often the cameraman
has achieved his objective. Like the old Hollywood saying, expert
camerawork, whether single or multi-camera, renders the cameraman
anonymous.

The antithesis of this is seen in many home videos where hose-piping
the camera and unsteady zooming draws attention to the method
of recording the subject and zaps the viewer into visual stupefaction.
The drawback of practising an invisible technique is that, to the
uninitiated, there is no obvious 'craft'. The cameraman is not only
anonymous, he or she appears to have made little contribution to
the production.

Camera movement and invisible technique

There is the paradox of creating camera movement to provide visual
excitement or visual change whilst attempting to make the movement
'invisible'. Invisible in the sense that the aim is to avoid the audience's
attention switching from programme content to the camerawork. As
we have discussed, intrusive and conspicuous camera movements are
often used for specific dramatic or stylistic reasons (e.g., music videos),
but the majority of programme formats work on the premise that the
methods of programme production should remain hidden or invisible.

Synchronized movement

Two basic conventions with camera movement are firstly to match the
movement to the action so that the camera move is motivated by the
action and is controlled in speed, timing and degree by the action.

Secondly, there is a need to maintain good composition throughout
the move. A camera move is a visual development that provides new
information or creates atmosphere or mood. If the opening and closing frames of a move, such as a zoom in, are the only images that are
considered important, then it is probably better to use a cut to change
shot rather than a camera move. A camera move should provide new
visual interest and there should be no 'dead' area between the first and
end image.

A camera move is usually prompted by one of the following:

- to add visual interest;
- to express excitement, increase tension or curiosity;
- to provide a new main subject of interest;
- to provide a change of viewpoint;
- to interpret an aspect of the narrative;
- to follow the action.

Movement that is not motivated by action will be obtrusive and focus attention on the method of recording the image. It will make visible the camera technique employed. It is sometimes the objective of obtrusive camera movement to invigorate content that is considered stale and lacking interest. If there is a lack of confidence in the content of a shot, then possibly it is better to rethink the subject rather than attempting to disguise this weakness by moving attention on to the camera technique employed.

Obtrusive camera movement

Early films were often conceived by the audience as moving photographs and dubbed 'the movies'. Movement always captures attention and interest and there has been a continuous demand for fast-moving productions and fast-moving camerawork accentuating the pace of the action.

As we discussed in Chapter 12, in the development of music videos, pace became the source of energy that drove the audience's interest forward, not the 'what happens next in the story?' technique of classic Hollywood narrative style. Music videos are similar to commercials with many images combined in a very short time. A characteristic of this style is continuous camera movement and very fast cutting – almost single frame – to inject pace.

This is using camera movement in a very different way to the disguised, unobtrusive changing image of much film and television production. But continuous, obtrusive movement has moved from music videos/commercials to much mainstream popular programming. There is a modern emphasis on continuous camera movement that appears to obey the dictum that it is not visually interesting unless the image is on the move. Some suggest that this rapid change of view is a product of reduced attention span or, on the other hand, an example of greater visual literacy that allows the audience to understand visual information in a much shorter time than their parents.

Single camera and multi-camera movement

Film is a record of an event edited and assembled after the event occurs. Live television is a presentation of an event as it occurs. Although camera movement in single and multi-camera shooting share many similarities, they are to some extent conditioned by the differences imposed by the practice of recording a single shot and the practicalities of recording or transmitting a number of shots continuously.

Live, or recorded as live, multi-camera coverage presents an event in real time and requires flexible camera mounts able to provide a variety of shots. In the studio, camera movement can be maximized on- or off-shot by tracking over a level floor. Film and single camera coverage can break the action into single shots and lay tracks and devise movement without the need to compromise or be inhibited by other camera movement.

Staging action for multi-camera continuous coverage requires a great deal more visual compromise than action that is conceived for a single shot. There are limitations on set design and lighting for multi-camera shooting which are easily overcome or simply not a consideration in single shot/single camera recording. In general, because of the constraints of time/budget, multi-camera operation often requires constant minor adjustments to the frame in order to accommodate actor position or staging that could have been replotted if time/budget (and the ever-present need for multi-camera compromise) was available.

Two types of movement

Camera movement can be conveniently grouped as functional movement and interpretive movement. This over-simplified division will often overlap but if functional movement is reframing to accommodate subject movement, then interpretive movement can be defined as a planned, deliberate change of camera position or zoom to provide visual variety, narrative emphasis or to reflect mood, atmosphere or emotion. Subject movement is often designed to motivate camera movement so in practice there is often no simple demarcation.

Camera movement also includes change of size of shot motivated by dialogue or narrative demands. Frequently, the importance or emotional intensity of a line of dialogue will naturally draw the camera closer but the move has to be handled with sensitivity and feeling, and timed to exactly match the emotions expressed. Just as camera movement will be synchronized with the start/stop points of action, movement motivated by dialogue or emotional expression, will be controlled by the timing and nuances of the performance.

One of the weaknesses of television camerawork is that there is a tendency to cover action by small zoom movements or camera movement. Single-camera film or video usually settle on either staging the action so that it can be contained in a static frame or have tracks laid down and devise a positive camera movement to contain the action. In television productions, continuous small minor adjustments of framing detract from content and become an irritant, although with unrehearsed action there is no way of avoiding constant frame adjustment. As subject movement is frequently unplanned, the composition of the shot will need continuous adjustment. This requires a pan and tilt head that can be instantly adjusted in discrete movements.

Multi-camera coverage requires maximum flexibility with camera movement to follow often unrehearsed action. A common dilemma is when to reframe a subject who is swaying in and out of reasonable framing. The shot may become too tight for a subject who needs to emphasize every point with hand gestures. It is seldom possible to constantly pan to keep someone who is swaying in frame as, inevitably, an anticipated movement does not happen and the composition becomes unbalanced. If the shot cannot be contained without continuous reframing then the incessant moving background will eventually become a distraction from the main subject of the shot. The only solution is to widen the shot. If the viewer is unaware of the camerawork then quite often the cameraman has achieved his objective. Expert camerawork, whether single or multi-camera, provides invisible camera movement by matching movement to action.

The pan

The simplest camera movement on a static subject is the pan. It is often used in the mistaken idea that it gives visual variety among a number of static shots. Usually, the main use of a pan, apart from keeping a moving subject in frame, is to show relationships.

There is obviously the need to begin a pan with a well-balanced shot that has intrinsic interest in its own right. The second requirement is to find visual elements that allow the pan to flow smoothly and inevitably to the end framing. The end frame must be well balanced and again of intrinsic interest. The pan alerts the viewer that the camera is moving to reveal some image of importance or interest. If this anticipation is denied and the end framing is quickly cut away from because it contains no visual interest, then the movement is an anti-climax.

Using dominant lines and movement

The speed of a panning shot must be matched to content. Panning fast over complex detail produces irritation – it is impossible to take in the information. Panning slowly over large, unbroken, plain areas may provoke boredom. It is almost always necessary to help with the visual change by finding some visual connection between first and last composition. Panning with movement, along lines, edges or any horizontal or vertical visual link usually disguises the transition and leads the eye naturally to the next point of interest. Use dominant horizontal, vertical or angled lines to pan along in order to move to a new viewpoint. Panning on lines in the frame allows visual continuity between two images and appears to provide a satisfactory visual link. The same visual link can be achieved by using movement within the frame to allow a pan or a camera movement from one composition to another. A common convention in an establishing shot is to follow a person across the set or location, to allow new information about the geography of the setting as the shot develops. The person the camera follows may be unimportant but is used to visually take the camera from a starting composition to possibly the main subject.

The reverse of unobtrusive technique is frequently seen in the 'pan and scan' conversion of widescreen films to 4:3 television screens. The 4:3 framing oscillates from one side of the original widescreen to the other with no visual motivation other than change of dialogue location. This ersatz 'panning' is intrusive and clumsy.

The speed of a pan across a symphony orchestra playing a slow majestic piece will be at a different speed to a pan across the orchestra when it is playing at full gallop. Speed of movement must match mood and content. If it is required to be discrete and invisible then movement must begin when the action begins and end when the action ends. A crane or tilt up with a person rising must not anticipate the move neither must it be late in catching up with the move. Any movement

Figure 16.1 Preselect one or two adjacent sides of the frame to the main subject of the zoom and, whilst maintaining their position at a set distance from the main subject of the zoom, allow the other two sides of the frame to change their relative position to the subject. Keep the same relationship of the adjacent frame edge to the selected subject during the whole of the zoom movement

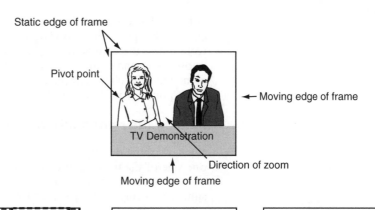

Static edge of frame

Pivot point

Moving edge of frame

Direction of zoom

Moving edge of frame

TV Demonstration

TV Demonstration

TV Demonstration

that is bursting to get out of the frame must either be allowed camera movement to accommodate it or there is a need for a cut to a wider shot.

It is an old truism that still photography deals with space relationships whilst film and television camerawork deal with space, time and movement to accommodate a constantly changing visual pattern. Composition is not just the shape of subjects but also the shape of motion. As well as camera movement, there is also movement within the frame when either dialogue or action switches the audiences attention between the main subjects.

Pivot points

A common mistake with users of domestic camcorders is to centre the subject of interest in the frame and then to zoom towards them keeping the subject the same distance from all four sides of the frame. The visual effect is as if the frame implodes in on them from all sides.

A more pleasing visual movement is to keep two sides of the frame at the same distance from the subject for the whole of the movement. This is achieved in a track or a zoom by preselecting a pivot point in the composition which is usually the main subject of interest and, whilst maintaining their position at a set distance from two adjacent sides of the frame, allow the other two sides of the frame to change their relative position to the subject. This allows the subject image to grow progressively larger (or smaller) within the frame whilst avoiding the impression of the frame contracting in towards them (Figure 16.1).

The point that is chosen to be held stationary in the frame is called the pivot point. Using a pivot point allows the subject image to grow progressively larger (or smaller) within the frame whilst avoiding the impression of the frame contracting in towards them.

It may be necessary on a combined track and crabbing movement to change this pivot point during the move but again, as in all camera techniques, the changeover to a different pivot point must be subtle, unobtrusive and controlled by the main subject of interest. The movement must be choreographed so that there are no violent swings on pivot points from left to right of frame.

Finding the right tracking line

We saw in the description of zooming that keeping two sides or even one side of the frame at a constant distance from the principle subject throughout a zoom or track creates a more pleasing visual result than simply allowing all four sides to implode in on the subject.

In zooming, the control of the pivot point is achieved by panning and/or tilting to adjust the frame during the zoom. Control of the framing during tracking (to keep a constant distance between one side of the frame and the subject) can also be achieved by panning/ tilting but it is more effective if it can be controlled by the line of the track (see Figure 16.2).

Finding the right camera height when tracking

The same technique can be used to maintain a pivot point at the top of the frame when tracking in or out, for example, on a singer. When tracking-in, the camera is craned up at a rate that holds the pivot point at the top of the frame without the need to reframe the camera. The lens height automatically arrives at the more flattering position, slightly above eye height, for the closer shot whilst avoiding crossing the key light and shadowing the artiste! Tracking-out, the camera is craned down at a rate that maintains the top-of-the-frame pivot point arriving at a lower angle wide-shot that compresses the amount of floor area in shot.

The development shot

Tracking or crabbing the camera to emphasize another visual element in the frame is a standard convention that has been used for many years. A development shot, as the name implies, is a shot that smoothly and unobtrusively moves towards a new viewpoint. It can start with a composition that emphasizes one set of visual elements and then moves, motivated by action or driven by the audience's curiosity, to an image that emphasizes another set of visual elements. In dramatic terms, it has no real equivalent in theatre or literature and when staging, pace and execution are fully integrated it can provide the most visually exciting images.

To achieve its greatest impact, a development often requires foreground elements to wipe across frame to emphasize movement; it requires a progressive change of viewpoint from its starting position; and it needs a main subject of interest that can be followed through various dynamic compositions. Although the movement must be fluid and changing, it requires a continuing revelation of dynamic images.

Many development shots require either a wide opening to the move or they end wide. As we have discussed, camera movement is accen-

Figure 16.2 A tracking line to produce an end frame of presenter plus scoreboard. The tracking line chosen requires no constant reframing during the move and no change in the direction of the pedestal wheels to maintain the preselected pivot point. It is the tracking line angle that maintains the pivot point. Operationally it is simpler and smoother and visually unobtrusive – the motivation for selecting a pivot point

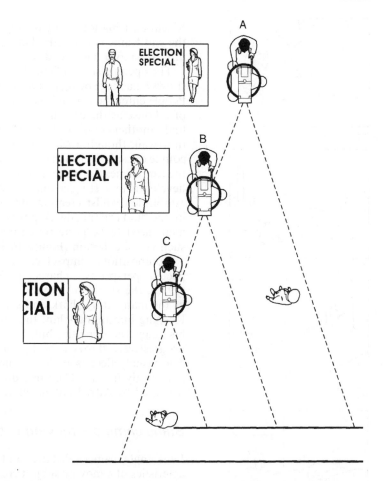

tuated when using the wide-angle end of the zoom (plus appropriate set design) but if part of the development involves a medium close-up or close-up of a face, then at some stage, on a wide angle (< 40°) there will be unacceptable distortion and probably camera shadow.

This can be avoided by starting the move on the wide angle and then, at some point in the development, continue the move on the zoom. The transition between track and zoom needs careful selection but usually the movement can be carried over by continuing with a slight crab whilst ending in a tight shot on the zoom. This obviously involves 'blind zooming' with no opportunity to pre-check focus. Critical focus will occur in close-up just at the point when subtle control of framing is required. On a crane or a dolly, the camera lens can be tracked to a predetermined position whilst the cameraman controls framing, pivot and focus. The same type of development shot on a pedestal may require the assistance of a tracker to 'sweeten' the move. The reverse development shot of zoom first–track later requires even more precise focus and attentive camera control.

A development shot moves from one set of visual elements on to another viewpoint. This visual transition requires reframing, using pivot points, tracking, crabbing and zooming and therefore it is essential that the cameraman anticipates what the final frame will be in order to smoothly progress the move to achieve that objective.

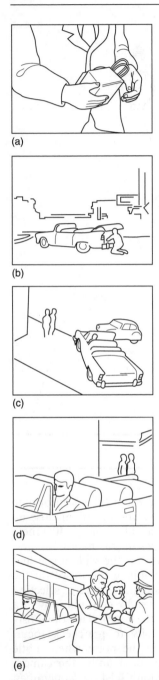

(a)

(b)

(c)

(d)

(e)

Figure 16.3 An extended development shot in the opening sequence of 'Touch of Evil' (1958). **(a)** Close-up of timer of bomb being set in someone's hands; **(b)** bomb being placed in boot of car; **(c)** camera cranes up to see couple walk to the car; **(d)** the car passes the principal characters and the camera follows them; **(e)** to the frontier post where the car with the bomb draws alongside

Visual anticipation is organizing all the necessary adjustments before the end frame is reached. 'Tidying up' the composition cannot be left until the move has ended.

The opening shot of 'Touch of Evil' (1958) directed by Orson Welles shows a package being placed in the boot of a parked car (Figure 16.3). People enter the car and the camera cranes up and away over the roof of a house as the car pulls away. Tracking across a street the camera finds another couple walking and then follows the car and the couple as they walk though a Mexican frontier town. The car and the walking couple constantly switch positions as the main subject of interest before the car reaches the frontier customs post and explodes. This continuous development lasting a minute of screen time allows the plot to be established whilst creating atmosphere and excitement all contained in one fluid exciting development. Actor movement and camera movement need to be perfectly choreographed by the director to achieve such visual cohesion (Figure 16.3(a)–(e)).

Compositional impact can also be achieved by combining unexpected perspective characteristics. In Stephen Spielberg's 'Jaws' (1975), the sheriff of a seaside town has been anticipating the return of the man-eating shark and suddenly hears screams from the beach. Keeping him in mid-shot, the camera tracks and zooms, which keeps his image the same size but, because of the changing camera distance, progressively shows a background to foreground size ratio change. The visual effect is to freeze him in space while the background is apparently in flux. The same double movement of camera and zoom was used by Alfred Hitchcock in 'Vertigo' (see Figure 16.5).

Static camera – moving subject

Lens angle, camera distance and camera height will dictate the characteristics of a moving subject composition. On a long focal length lens with the subject at a distance from the camera, space will be compressed and movement will appear disproportionately small compared with image size. For example, a subject can walk ten paces on a long focal length lens in mid-shot and hardly register a change in size. This contradicts our normal perception of perspective change and sets up a surreal 'running on the spot' feel to the image.

A close position with a wide-angle lens will accentuate movement, and any movement towards the camera will make the subject change size disproportionately to the actual movement taken. Action that is corner to corner will be more dynamic than action that sweeps horizontally across the frame.

Moving camera/moving subject

One of the most common forms of moving camera/moving subject shot is to follow, in the same size shot, a subject walking or driving. A popular convention is the parallel tracking shot where two people in conversation walk with the camera crabbing with them often slightly ahead so that both faces are seen. For this technique to be 'invisible' the frame must be steady, horizontally level and the same size shot maintained over most of the move. The effect is as if the audience was a third person walking with them and listening in to their conversation.

A number of visual variations are to be found, which rely on what is a static foreground of main subject whilst the background moves. People in cars, trains even glass lifts can be held framed in static shot while the background moves behind them.

Moving the camera whilst the subject size alters can be more difficult to handle. Unless there are other visual elements moving in and out of the frame, the change in size of the subject can appear as if the camera is unable to keep up or is gaining on the subject. When the movement is across the frame as in a crabbing shot then change of size may not be so apparent and is visually acceptable.

Frame adjustment whilst tracking

One of the compositional conventions of camerawork with profile shots, where people are looking out of frame, is to give additional space in the direction of their gaze for 'looking room'. Similarly, when someone is walking across frame, to give more space in front of them than behind.

This space in the frame to 'walk into' needs to be maintained throughout a development. This can be difficult if the subject, for example, is standing to the left of frame and moves to camera left (i.e., towards the left-hand side of the frame; see Figure 16.4). This requires an accelerated rapid pan left in order to provide space on the left (the direction of movement) before settling down to match the speed of the pan with the walk. The appropriate framing for the end composition must be achieved before the subject stops to avoid the camera reframing after the action has ended. If the subject is walking to take up a similar left of frame position with another 'results board', then the camera must stop the pan when the board is correctly framed making certain there is sufficient space on left of frame for the subject to walk into. In general, anticipate any change in frame size whilst on the move and do not leave the reframing until the subject has settled. Come to rest with the subject.

As we have seen in the section on perspective, moving the camera towards or away from the subject alters the size relationships between foreground and background objects. The perspective of mass changes in a similar way to our own perceptual experience when we move towards or away from an object. Tracking the camera therefore not only conforms to our normal visual expectations but sets up interesting re-arrangements of all the visual elements in the camera's field of view. Changing the camera distance alters all the image size relationships apart from very distant objects near or on the horizon. The size of a range of hills remains unaffected no matter how far we travel towards them until we reach a critical distance where we have a part of the hills as foreground with which to compare a background.

Movement within the shot and lens angle

A two-dimensional film or television image of three-dimensional space can involve compromise between action and the requirements of the camera. A common adjustment is the speed of the actor movement to the size of the shot or the lens angle in use.

A small movement in a close-up can be the equivalent of a big movement in long shot. A full figure, three-pace walk towards a

(a) Static frame

(b) 123

Accelerate the pan as the subject moves to provide space in the frame 'to walk into' and begin to zoom out to anticipate the final frame

(c) 125 123

Pace the zoom out to match walk and hold the pan when the end frame is reached and allow subject to move into final position

(d) 123 125 123

Correct final framing anticipated and made invisible by the walk

Figure 16.4

wide-angle lens will create a much bigger change in size than the equivalent full figure walk towards a 25° lens. The 'internal space' of the lens in use becomes a critical consideration when staging action for the camera (see Figure 15.1).

Actor movement that is motivated by the story line is often required to be modified by the demands of the specific lens in use. One of the most common adjustments is the speed of a rise from a chair, which may need to be covered in close-up. A normal rise will often appear frantic contained in a tight shot and is frequently slowed down. This also helps with the problem of achieving good framing when covering a fast-moving subject on a tight lens.

Another common development shot is keeping a foreground artiste or object in shot while crabbing to follow the background movement of another actor. This is fairly straightforward using a wide-angle lens if the camera position is tight to the foreground subject, as this allows the arc of the crab to be relatively short. A few feet of camera movement will accommodate a 10-ft change of position of a background artiste. If a longer focal length lens is used, for the same size foreground image, the camera is much further back and the arc of the crabbing line now becomes considerably extended in order to keep the same background actor movement in shot (Figure 16.5(a) and (b)). Using a narrower angle lens also alters the apparent movement of the camera as less background scenery is covered by the sweep of the lens.

Camera movement must have visual elements that change their relationship depending on camera position. A crab around a subject set against a featureless background will provide slight indication of change of viewpoint. The same movement with the subject set against a varied and broken background now has markers to indicate the change of viewpoint. If foreground features sweep across the frame there are even more indicators that the viewpoint is changing and the movement (if that is what is required) becomes more dominant and visual.

Camera movement using a narrow-angle lens has a distinct visual quality but requires greater operational precision than wide-angle lens movement. Moving the camera using a wide-angle lens is smoother and provides a great deal more movement in the frame for the distance covered compared with using a narrow-angle lens.

The internal space of a shot often underlines the emotional quality of the scene. 'Normal' perspective (see Chapter 4) for establishing shots is often used where the intention is to plainly and straightforwardly describe the locale. A condensed or an expanded space, on the other hand, may help to suggest the mood or atmosphere of the action.

The choice of lens angle and resulting composition should not be accidental unless, as is frequently the case, camera position and angle are *fait accompli* created by a multi-camera compromise.

Accentuating the effect of camera movement

The greatest impression of movement can be observed by using a wide-angle lens and tracking between similar size objects such as a row of trees on each side of a road. The apparent size of each tree to its neighbour changes dramatically as it approaches the lens. There is

Figure 16.5 (a) A common development shot is to hold a two shot of foreground actor (C) while actor A walks to B. If the camera position is tight to the foreground subject (C) the arc of the crab is relatively short. **(b)** If a longer lens is used, for the same size foreground image, the camera is much further back and the arc of the crabbing line now becomes considerably extended in order to keep the same background actor movement in shot

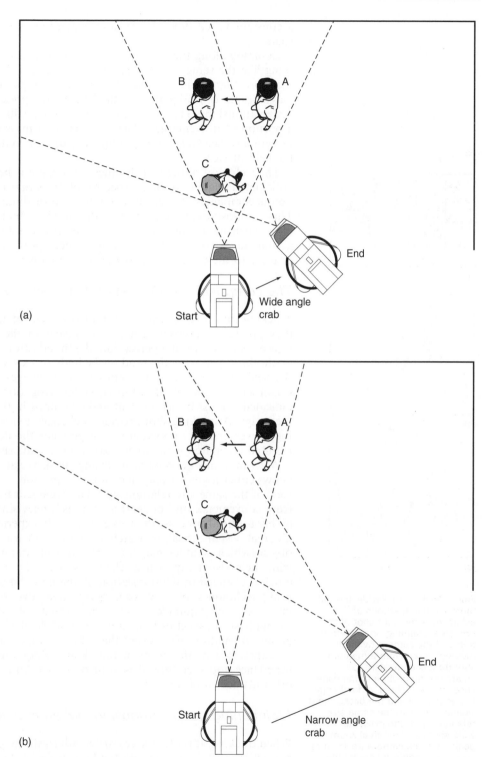

(a)

(b)

a constant visual flow of size ratio expansion as we track down the road.

Zooming along the road between rows of trees does not have anything like the same visual dynamics. The camera does not move and therefore there is no change in size relationships. The zoom simply magnifies the central portion of the field of view preserving the existing size relationships. They remain unaltered as in a still photograph when a portion of it is enlarged. The perspective of mass is decided by the camera distance and zooming simply expands or contracts a portion of the field of view.

The feeling of flatness or deadness of a zoom is because there is no anticipated change to the perspective of mass that in normal perception accompanies changes in magnification or diminution of subject. This compositional inertia can be disguised by building in a camera move such as a pan with action or even a crabbing movement to accompany a zoom. The camera movement provides some relational changes to the visual elements that the zoom is magnifying.

The compositional distinction between zoom and track

Tracking into a scene extends the involvement of the viewer in that they are being allowed visually to move into the two-dimensional screen space. In normal perception, depth indicators can be appraised or checked by moving the head or the body to seek a new viewpoint of the field of view. Viewing a series of static images on a two-dimensional screen does not allow this visual 'interrogation'. If depth is to be indicated it must be self-evident and contained in the composition of the image. A tracking shot provides a change in viewpoint and allows the viewer greater opportunity to experience the depth of the space pictured compared with either a zoom or a static shot.

A zoom in or out contains no change in size relationships, it simply allows either a greater magnification of a portion of the shot or wider view of the same size relationships. The argument for zooming (apart from convenience and budget) is that, as a television production is a highly artificial process, the viewer is already experiencing a radically different visual sensation watching a two-dimensional image of an object (which is either magnified or extremely diminished) compared with their visual experience when observing the actual event. If so much is changed in the translation by the film and television medium using techniques of shot size, perspective, two dimensions, small image, etc., why quibble about zooming that fails to reproduce some small physical aspect of human perception? A television production is an approximation of an event that often includes attempts to induce an experience of the event in the viewer. Zooming creates a visual experience and therefore, it is argued, is as valid a technique as any other artifice employed.

Maintaining good composition when moving

When tracking, it is often necessary to adjust the height of the camera, particularly when moving into the human figure. In shots closer than full figure, lens height is often eye-height, but when the camera is further away, depending on the shot, the lens height is usually lower to reduce the amount of floor/ground in shot. A low lens height places

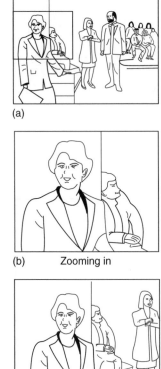

(a)

(b)   Zooming in

(c)   Tracking in

Figure 16.6 From a wide shot **(a)** there are two methods of achieving a medium shot of the presenter standing on the left of frame. If the camera (without moving) zooms into a medium shot **(b)** it is equivalent to enlarging the portion of the wide shot outlined. There is no change in perspective and the background seated man is in the same size relationship to the presenter in the wide shot as in the final zoom position. If the camera tracks in to arrive at a medium shot **(c)** the size relationship changes and also more of the background is in the medium shot than in the same size shot achieved by zooming in

emphasis on the subject by avoiding distracting foreground level surfaces such as roads, grass or floor. Like all 'rules of thumb', this convention is probably ignored more than it is employed but changes in lens height often accompany tracking movements in order to bring emphasis on to the main subject.

Another reason for altering the lens height when tracking into the subject is to enhance the appearance of artistes by shooting slightly down on faces, rather than shooting up and emphasizing jaw lines and double chins, etc.

Hot heads and remotely controlled cameras

One of the limitations of development shots that attempted to cover a wide range of movement in space was the need for the camera to be manned. This required the crane to carry the weight of the cameraman and camera on a boom arm that was counterbalanced and positioned in space by a tracker. The whole of this weight was mounted on a moving platform often driven by a motor. This type of crane was a large and sometimes limited device to produce camera movement.

The development of the remotely controlled lightweight camera mounted on a much lighter dolly using a remote controlled 'hot head' (a generic title for a remotely controlled pan/tilt head) allowed camera developments that were not possible with the traditional crane design. The range of the lightweight boom arms were much greater and could be swung into formerly inaccessible positions such as over the top of audiences or in high angle positions within a set. A greater speed of movement in shot development became possible and a whole new range of fluid compositions became commonplace.

Lightweight video cameras have also allowed the widespread use of Steadicam. This torso harness camera mount separates body movement from the camera and has revolutionized 'hand-held' operation. Steadicam has enabled a whole new range of visual development shots over any surface without the need to lay tracks. Movement of 360° around the subject, following action up/down stairs, through doorways, into transport, and following sports events by running the touch line are just some of the camera movements that are possible. In the hands of a skilful operator, the camera can be smoothly moved to any point in the space accessible to a person.

Remotely controlled cameras and pedestals were introduced into news studios and allowed one individual to control a number of cameras from a control room position. Robotic cameras could be pre-programmed to provide a range of shots at the touch of a button and to reposition in the studio. A timed preset zoom movement could be created that reframed the shot utilizing pivot points. The 'remoteness' of this type of camera operation precludes some types of production contribution provided by a manned camera.

Summary

Camerawork technique – such as stop/start camera movement on action; matching camera movement to subject movement; pivot points on zooms and tracks; matched shots on intercuts – is designed to make 'invisible' the mechanics of programme production. The objective is usually to emphasize the subject – picture content – rather than camera technique.

Two basic conventions with camera movement are firstly to match the movement to the action so that the camera move is motivated by the action and is controlled in speed, timing and degree by action. Secondly, there is a need to maintain good composition throughout the move. A camera move should provide new visual interest and there should be no 'dead' area between the first and end image of the movement.

Functional movement is reframing to accommodate subject movement. Interpretive movement can be defined as a planned, deliberate change of camera position or zoom to provide visual variety, narrative emphasis or new information. Just as camera movement will be synchronized with the start/stop points of action, movement motivated by dialogue or emotional expression will be controlled by the timing and nuances of the performance.

17
Shooting for editing

Invisible stitching

The nineteenth-century painter Whistler suggested that a work of art can be said to be finished when all traces of its construction are eliminated. Film and television productions are often much more of a craft than an art but editing is one skill where this observation seems most apt.

The skills and craft employed by the film/video editor to stitch together a sequence of separate shots persuades the audience that they are watching a continuous event. They are unaware of the hundreds of subtle decisions that have been made during the course of the production. The action flows from shot to shot and appears natural and obvious. The editing skills and techniques that have achieved this are rendered invisible to the audience, and therefore the unenlightened may ask, 'but what has the editor done? What is the editor's contribution to the production?'.

This invisible visual manipulation can only be achieved by the director/cameraman providing the appropriate shots for the production. An essential requirement for the editing process is a supply of appropriate visual and audio material. The cameraman, director or journalist need to shoot with editing in mind. Unless the necessary shots are available for an item, an editor cannot cut a cohesive and structured story. A random collection of shots is not a story, and although an editor may be able to salvage a usable item from a series of 'snapshots', essentially editing is exactly like the well known computer equation which states that 'garbage in equals garbage out'.

It is part of broadcasting folklore that the best place to start to learn about camerawork is in the edit booth. Here, the shots that have been provided by the cameraman have to be previewed, selected and then knitted together by the editor into a coherent structure to explain the story and fit the designated running time of the item in the programme. Clear storytelling, running time and structure are the key points of editing and a cameraman who simply provides an endless number of unrelated shots will pose problems for the editor. A cameraman returning from a difficult news/magazine shoot may have a different version of the edit process. A vital shot may be missing, but then the editor was not there to see the difficulties encountered by the news cameraman. And how about all the wonderful material that was at the end of the second cassette that was never used? With one hour to transmission there was no time to view or to cut it, claims the editor.

In some areas of news and magazine coverage this perennial exchange is being eliminated by the gradual introduction of portable field editing. It is no longer a case of handing over material for someone else 'to sort out'. Now the cameraman is the editor or the editor is the cameraman. This focuses under 'one hat' the priorities of camerawork and the priorities of editing. The cameraman can keep his favourite shot if he can convince himself, as the editor, that the shot is pertinent and works in the final cut.

Selection and structure

Editing is selecting and coordinating one shot with the next to construct a sequence of shots that form a coherent and logical narrative. There are a number of standard editing conventions and techniques that can be employed to achieve a flow of images that guide the viewer through a visual journey. A programme's aim may be to provide a set of factual arguments that allows the viewer to decide on the competing points of view; it may be dramatic entertainment utilizing editing technique to prompt the viewer to experience a series of highs and lows on the journey from conflict to resolution; or a news item's intention may be to accurately report an event for the audience's information or curiosity.

A crucial aspect of the composition of a shot is to consider how it will relate to the preceding and succeeding shots. If a production allows pre-planning, a camera script or storyboard will have been blocked out and the structure of each sequence and how shots are to be cut together will be roughly known or even precisely planned. Additional cover shots will be composed and devised with the original scripted shots in mind.

In factual programming, however, the order of a particular sequence of shots may be unknown at the time of recording. The editor requires from the cameraman maximum flexibility with material supplied and the nucleus of a structure. A 'ground plan' of a potential sequence of shots is often mentally sketched out in order to assist in the edit. Edit-point requirements, such as change in angle and shot size, subject movement, camera movement and continuity, have to be considered and provided for to enable the footage to be assembled in a coherent stream of images. Shooting with editing in mind is therefore essential.

Basic editing conventions

A cameraman or director, when setting up a shot, should consider the basic editing conventions to be satisfied if the viewer is to remain unaware of shot transition. It would be visually distracting if the

Figure 17.1

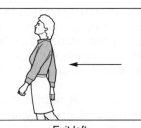
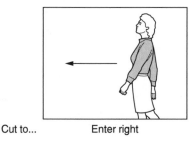

Exit left   Cut to...   Enter right

Rise from chair: hold static frame   Cut to...   The rise is repeated in static frame wide shot

Medium shot holding object   Cut to...   Close-up of object must be held in the same way as position of hand in medium shot

audience's attention was continually interrupted by every change of shot.

Moving images in film or television are created by the repetition of individual static frames. It is human perception that combines the separate images into a simulation of movement. One reason this succeeds is that the adjacent images in a shot are very similar. If the shot is changed and new information appears within the frame (e.g., what was an image of a face is now an aeroplane), the eye/brain takes a little time to understand the new image. The greater the visual discrepancy between the two shots the more likely it is that the viewer will consciously notice the change of shot.

A basic editing technique is to find ways of reducing the visual mismatch between two adjacent images. In general, a change of shot will be unobtrusive if:

- the individual shots (when intercutting between people) are matched in size, have the same amount of headroom, have the same amount of looking space if in semi-profile, if the lens angle is similar (i.e., internal perspective is similar) and if the lens height is the same;

- the intercut pictures are colour matched (e.g., skin tones, background brightness, etc.) and if in succeeding shots the same subject has a consistent colour (e.g., grass in a stadium);
- there is continuity in action (e.g., body posture, attitude) and the flow of movement in the frame is carried over into the succeeding shot;
- there is a significant change in shot size or camera angle when intercutting on the same subject or if there is a significant change in content;
- there is continuity in lighting, in sound, props and setting, and continuity in performance or presentation.

The basis of all invisible technique employed in programme production and specifically in continuity editing is to ensure that:

- shots are structured to allow the audience to understand the space, time and logic of the action so each shot follows the line of action to maintain consistent screen direction to make the geography of the action completely intelligible;
- unobtrusive camera movement and shot change directs the audience to the content of the production rather than the mechanics of production;
- continuity editing creates the illusion that distinct, separate shots (possibly recorded out of sequence and at different times), form part of a continuous event being witnessed by the audience.

Summary of perennial technique

These editing techniques form the basics of an invisible craft that has been developed over nearly 100 years of film and video productions. There is innovation and variation on these basic tenets, but the majority of television programme productions use these standard editing conventions to keep the viewer's attention on the content of the programme rather than its method of production. These standard conventions are a response to the need to provide a variety of ways of presenting visual information coupled with the need for them to be unobtrusive in their transition from shot to shot. Expertly used, they are invisible and yet provide the narrative with pace, excitement, and variety.

An alternative editing technique, such as, for example, used in music videos, uses hundreds of cuts, disrupted continuity, ambiguous imagery, etc., to deliberately visually tease the audience and to avoid clear visual communication. The aim is often to recreate the 'rave' experience of a club or concert. The production intention is to be interpretative rather than informative.

Selection and editing

The primary aim of editing is to provide the right structure and selection of shots to communicate to the audience the programme maker's motives for making the programme and, secondly, to hold their attention so that they listen and remain watching.

Editing, in a literal sense, is the activity of selecting from all the available material and choosing what is relevant. Film and video editing require the additional consideration that selected shots spliced together must meet the requirements of the standard conventions of continuity editing.

A clear idea of the aims of the piece that is being cut must be understood by the director or cameraman. Choosing what is relevant is the first set of decisions to be faced. Sometimes this is completely controlled by what it is possible to shoot. This is why a clear understanding of the function of a shot in a sequence must be understood and the appropriate composition supplied at the moment of recording.

In the golden age of the Hollywood studio production system, most studios did not allow their directors to supervise the editing. It is said that John Ford circumvented this restriction by simply making one take of each shot whenever possible, and making certain that there was very little overlap of action from shot to shot. This virtually forced the editor to cut the film as planned by the director. Alfred Hitchcock storyboarded each shot and rarely looked through the camera viewfinder. The film was already 'cut' in his head before the shooting started.

Providing the editor with only the bare essential footage may work with film craftsmen of the quality of Ford and Hitchcock, but in the everyday activity of news and magazine items it is simply not possible. News, by definition, is often an unplanned, impromptu shoot with a series of information shots that can only be structured and pulled together in the edit suite. Selecting what is relevant is therefore one of the first priorities when recording/filming.

Good editing technique structures the material and identifies the main 'teaching' points the audience should understand. A crucial role of the editor is to be audience 'number one'. The editor will start fresh to the material and he/she must understand the story in order for the audience to understand the story. The editor needs to be objective and bring a dispassionate eye to the material. The director/cameraman/reporter may have been very close to the story for hours/days/weeks – the audience comes to it new and may not pick up the relevance of the setting or set-up if this is spelt out rapidly in the first opening sentence. It is surprising how often, with professional communicators, that what is obvious to them about the background detail of a story is unknown or its importance unappreciated by their potential audience. Beware of the 'I think that is so obvious we needn't shoot it' statement.

The edited package needs to hold the audience's attention by its method of presentation (e.g., method of storytelling – what happens next, camera technique, editing technique, etc.). Pace and brevity (e.g., no redundant footage) are often the key factors in raising the viewer's involvement in the item. Be aware that visuals can fight voice-over narration. Arresting images capture the attention first. The viewer would probably prefer to 'see it' rather than 'hear it'. A successful visual demonstration is always more convincing than a verbal argument – as every successful salesman knows.

The strongest way of engaging the audience's attention is to tell them a story. In fact, because film and television images are displayed in a linear way, shot follows shot, it is almost impossible for the audience not to construct connections between succeeding images whatever the real or perceived relationships between them. Image follows image in an endless flow over time and inevitably the viewer will construct a story out of each succeeding piece of information.

Telling a story – fact and fiction

The editing techniques used for cutting fiction and factual material are almost the same. When switching on a television programme mid-way, it is sometimes impossible to assess from the editing alone if the programme is fact or fiction. Documentary makers use storytelling techniques learned by audiences from a lifetime of watching drama. Usually, the indicator of what genre the production falls into is gained from the participants. Even the most realistic acting appears stilted or stylized when placed alongside people talking in their own environment. Another visual convention is to allow 'factual' presenters to address the lens and the viewer directly, whereas actors and the 'public' are usually instructed not to look at camera.

The task of the director, journalist, cameraman and editor is to determine what the audience needs to know, and at what point in the 'story' they are told. This is the structure of the item or feature and usually takes the form of question and answer or cause and effect. Seeking answers to questions posed, for example, 'what are the authorities going to do about traffic jams?' or 'what causes traffic jams?', involves the viewer and draws them into the 'story' that is unfolding. Many items can still be cut following the classical structure of exposition, tension, climax and release.

The storytelling of factual items is probably better served by the presentation of detail rather than broad generalizations. Which details are chosen to explain a topic is crucial both in explanation and engagement. Many issues dealt with by factual programmes are often of an abstract nature, which at first thought have little or no obvious visual representation. Images to illustrate topics such as inflation can be difficult to find when searching for precise representations of the diminishing value of money. Newsreels of the 1920s showing Berliners going shopping pushing prams filled with bank notes, graphically demonstrated inflation, but this was a rare and extreme visual example. The camera must provide an image of something, and whatever it may be, that something will be invested by the viewer with significance. That significance may not match the main thrust of the item and may lead the viewer away from the topic. Significant detail requires careful observation at location and a clear idea of the shape of the item when it is being shot. The editor then has to find ways of cutting together a series of shots so the transitions are seamless and the images logically advance the story. Remember that the viewer will not necessarily have the same impression or meaning from an image that you have invested in it.

Because the story is told over time, there is a need for a central motif or thread that is easily followed and guides the viewer through the item. A report, for example, on traffic congestion may have a car driver on a journey through rush-hour traffic. Each point about the causes of traffic congestion can be illustrated and picked up as they occur such as out-of-town shoppers, the school run, commuters, traffic black spots, road layout, etc. The frustrations of the journey through-out the topic will naturally link the 'teaching' points, and the viewer can easily identify and speculate about the story's outcome.

Time

With the above example, as the story progresses over time, the attitude of the driver will probably change. He/she may display bad-temper, irritation with other road users, etc. There will be a difference over time and without time there is no story. Finding ways of registering change over time is one of the key activities of director, cameraman or editor. Shots that register the temperament of the driver by using small observational details reveal the story to the viewer. The main topic of the item is traffic congestion and its wear and tear on everyday life. It can be effectively revealed by focusing on one drive through a narrated journey rather than generalizations by a presenter standing alongside a traffic queue.

Real time and compressed time

The editor can shape and manipulate time by the editing methods we have discussed, but any action continuously shown within a shot will run its actual time. Apart from slightly speeding up or slowing down the replay of the image, there is no way to reorganize the actual time of an action shown in full. Slightly adjusting the speed of the replay machine can sometimes allow an over-long action to fit the required time slot, but the time adjusted must be small otherwise the wrong tempo of a shot will become obvious to the viewer. Another method of extending the length of a shot is to freeze the last frame of the shot. This technique again is dependent on shot content.

Structuring a sequence

The chosen structure of a section or sequence will usually have a beginning, a development and a conclusion. Editing patterns and the narrative context do not necessarily lay out the events of a story in simple chronological order. For example, there can be a 'tease' sequence, which seeks to engage the audience's attention with a question or a mystery. It may be some time into the material before the solution is revealed and the audience's curiosity is satisfied.

Whatever the shape of the structure, it usually contains one or more of the following methods of sequence construction.

- A narrative sequence is a record of an event such as a child's first day at school, an Olympic athlete training in the early morning, etc. Narrative sequences tell a strong story and are used to engage the audience's interest.
- A descriptive sequence simply sets the atmosphere or provides background information. For example, an item featuring the retirement of a watchmaker may have an introductory sequence of shots featuring the watches and clocks in his workshop before the participant is introduced or interviewed. Essentially, a descriptive sequence is a scene setter, an overture to the main point of the story, although sometimes it may be used as an interlude to break

up the texture of the story, or act as a transitional visual bridge to a new topic.

• An explanatory sequence is, as the name implies, a sequence that explains either the context of the story, facts about the participants or event, or explains an idea. As mentioned before, abstract concepts such as inflation, land erosion or a rise in unemployment usually need a verbal explanatory section backed by 'visual wallpaper' – images that are not specific or important in themselves, but are needed to accompany the important narration. Explanatory sequences are likely to lose the viewer's interest and need to be supported by narrative and description. Explanatory exposition is often essential when winding-up an item in order to draw conclusions or make explicit the relevance of the events depicted.

The shape of a sequence

The tempo and shape of a sequence, and of a number of sequences that may make up a longer item, will depend on how these methods of structuring are cut and arranged. Whether shooting news or documentaries, the transmitted item will be shaped by the editor to connect a sequence of shots either visually, by voice-over, atmosphere, music or by a combination of any of them. Essentially the cameraman or director must organize the shooting of separate shots with some structure in mind. Any activity must be filmed to provide a sufficient variety of shots that are able to be cut together following standard editing conventions (e.g., avoidance of jump cuts, not crossing the line, etc.), and that there is enough variety of shot to allow some flexibility in editing. Just as no shot can be considered in isolation (what precedes, what follows, always have an effect), every sequence must be considered in context with the overall aims of the production.

The available material that arrives in the edit suite has to be structured to achieve the clearest exposition of the subject. Also the edited material has to be arranged to find ways of involving the viewer in order to hold their interest and attention. Structure is arranging the building blocks – the individual unconnected shots, into a stream of small visual messages that combine into a coherent whole. For example, a government report on traffic pollution is published which claims that chest ailments have increased, many work hours are lost though traffic delay and urges car owners to only use their vehicles for essential journeys.

A possible treatment for this kind of report would be to outline the main points as a voice-over or text graphic, interviews with health experts, motorist pressure-group spokesman, a piece to camera by the reporter and possibly comments from motorists. The cameraman would provide shots of traffic jams, close-ups of car exhausts, pedestrians, interviews, etc. The journalist would decide the order of the material while writing his/her voice-over script, whilst the editor would need to cut bridging sequences that could be used on the more 'abstract' statistics (e.g., increase in asthma in children, etc.). Essentially these montages help to hold the viewer's attention and provide visual interest on what would otherwise be a dry delivery of facts. A close-up of a baby's face in a pram followed by a cut to a shot of a lorry exhaust belching diesel fumes makes a strong, quick, visual point that requires no additional narrative to explain. The juxtaposition of shots, the context and how the viewer reads the connections is what structures the item, and allows the report to have impact. The production team in the field must provide appropriate material, but the editor can find new relationships and impose an order to fit the running time.

News – unscripted shot structure

There are a number of editing requirements that will have a bearing on the composition of a shot if a camera script has not been prepared (e.g., news and some documentaries). Most of the 'magazine' type item location work will not be scripted. There may be a rough treatment outlined by the presenter or a written brief on what the item should cover but an interview may open up new aspects of the story. Without pre-planning or a shot list, camera technique will often revert to tried and trusted formulas. Telling a story in pictures is as old as the first efforts in film making.

A standard convention in building up a sequence of shots is to move from the general to the particular. A wide general view (GV) to show relationships and show the individual elements in the scene. The closer shots of the individual subjects provide more information and involvement of the audience. The old Hollywood cliché of 'it's the close-up that tells the story, it's the wide shot that sells the picture (show them where the money is)' may have structured thousands of popular, conventional films but it does form the basis of an obvious truth. Unless the film maker wishes to deliberately deceive or confuse the audience, there is inevitably going to be a mixture of wide and close shots to explain, interpret and depict the narrative. The rhythm and arrangement of size of shot independent of content (which it never is) is a three-way creative arrangement between director, cameramen and editor. Creating the right framing, viewpoint, size of shot and visual style will often be the cameraman's contribution.

A close-up will give more information than the same subject in long shot. But the close-up is also a heavy accent – an emphasis that strongly draws the attention of the audience to a specific subject – either a face or even more strongly to an object. The emotional significance of a close shot of a pistol on a table is stronger than a throw-away shot of a car arriving in front of a house.

The narrative 'weight' of a shot is dependent on the size of the shot and also on the composition. Emphasis can be strengthened or lightened depending on the reason for the shot. Visual communication in this sense is similar to language where a shot can be loaded with strong colourful 'adjectives' underlining its significance or can be casually thrown away in neutral tones and left to the audience to judge its significance or make predictions and guess as to its role in the narrative.

The context of the shot will control the composition. The 'weight' of its impact has to be carefully considered and the detail and treatment tailored to its role in the production.

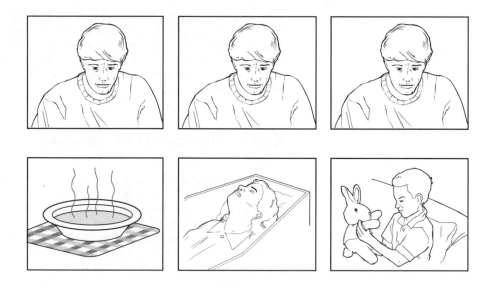

Information and decorative shots

Most TV news/magazine location items will have a mixture of informative and decorative shots. It is part of the cameraman's craft to
provide the editor/presenter with a variety of options but to keep the
shooting ratio in proportion to the editing time available. Information
shots are usually straightforward records of the incident or object. If it
is technically competent, the information shot requires no more than
variety in size and reasonable framing. Decorative shots require a
knowledge of television technique and the ability to exploit video
and lens characteristics.

Information shots are specific. They refer to a unique event – the
wreckage of a car crash, someone scoring a goal, a political speech.
They are often non-repeatable. The crashed car is towed away, the
politician moves on. The topicality of an event means that the camera
technique must be precise and reliable, responding to the event with
quick reflexes. There is often no opportunity for retakes.

Decorative shots are non-specific. They are often shot simply to
give visual padding to the story. A typical example is a shot of an
interviewee walking in a location before an interview. This shot
allows the dubbed voice-over to identify who the interviewee is and
possibly their attitude to the subject. The duration of the shot needs
to be sufficiently long to allow information that is not featured in the
interview to be added as a voice-over. The interviewee leaves the
frame at the end of the shot to provide a cutting point to the interview.

Solving continuity problems is one reason why the location production unit need to provide additional material to help in the edit. It is a
developed professional skill to find the happy medium between too
much material that cannot be previewed in the editing time available,
and too little material that gives the edit no flexibility if structure,
running time or story development changes between shooting and
editing the material.

News values and objectivity

Hard news is by its nature seldom, if ever, pre-scripted, and therefore material is recorded without a written plan. The editor, sometimes with a journalist, needs to shape and structure the raw material supplied as a sequence of unconnected shots.

It is essential for the news unit to shoot with editing in mind. A series of shots have to be meaningfully edited together and this relies on the cameraman anticipating edit points. As we have emphasized before, nothing is more time-consuming than an attempt to edit a pile of cassettes of ill-considered footage into some intelligent and intelligible form. To avoid this, the editor requires from the cameraman maximum flexibility with the material supplied, and the nucleus of a structure.

News reportage attempts to emphasize fact rather than opinion, but journalistic values cannot escape subjective judgements. What is newsworthy? What are news values? These questions are answered and shaped by the prevailing custom and practices of broadcasting organizations. Magazine items can use fact, feeling, atmosphere, argument, opinion, dramatic reconstruction and subjective impressions. These editing techniques differ very little from feature film storytelling. For a more detailed account of objective and subjective reporting see Chapter 11, 'News and documentary'.

News values are usually related to the intended audience. People are more interested in news that affects either their lives, emotions or income. They give a higher priority to news that is local, immediate (i.e., it is 'new' to them), has dramatic content (crime, rescues, real-life crisis), involves well-known personalities and is entertaining or humorous.

Even news editing tries to avoid reminding the audience that they are watching an edited version. For example, a typical news item where a politician steps off a plane is followed by a cutaway shot of cameramen, followed by the politician in the airport being interviewed. The news item ostensibly deals with fact, while the technique is derived from film fiction. Screen time and space has been manipulated and the technique employed is invisible to the audience. Whenever selection of material is exercised, objectivity is compromised. In news coverage a number of choices have to be made in subject, choice of location, choice of camera treatment, and selection and arrangement of shots in editing.

It is a news cameraman's complaint that when the editor is up against a transmission deadline, he/she will only quickly preview the first part of any cassette, often missing the better shots towards the end of the tape. The cameraman can help the editor, wherever possible, by putting interviews on one tape and cutaways and supporting material on another cassette. This allows the editor to quickly find material without shuttling backwards and forwards on the same tape.

Variety of shot

In order to compress an item to essential information, the editor requires a variety of options. This means a variety of relevant shots

Figure 17.3 Parts (a) to (f) illustrate a news story reporting a collision at sea between a container ship and a cruise ship. Figure **(a)** shows the container ship on fire. Access is vital in news coverage and the cameraman must attempt to get to a position where the vital shot that summarizes the story can be recorded. Figure **(b)** is shot on the container ship showing the 'geography' of the item of cargo and fire tender. Figure **(c)** shows the damaged cruise ship in port and **(d)** the disappointed holidaymakers leaving the ship while it is repaired. Figure **(e)** is an interview with one of the passengers giving his experience of the collision and **(f)** is a piece-to-camera by the reporter (with an appropriate background) summarizing the story and posing questions of who/what was to blame

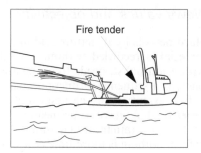

(a) Container ship on fire

(b) Container ship and fire tender, closer view

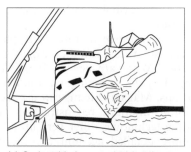

(c) Cruise ship in port, showing damage

(d) Disappointed holidaymakers

(e)

(f)

in order to restructure a continuous event (e.g., a football match, a conference speech) and to reduce its original timescale to the running order requirement. A continuous 20-minute MCU of a speaker without audience or relevant cutaways will inevitably lead to a jump cut if more than one portion of the speech is required. Take the opportunity during a pause, which may signal a new topic, or on applause to change the size of shot. Only 'keynote' sentences will be used and a difference in shot size at these points will avoid irrelevant cutaways to shorten the item. Pans, zooms and tilts can be used in a number of ways if the shot is held for five seconds or more before the start and at the end of the camera movement.

Brevity and significance

The pressure of cutting an item down to a short running time for news will impose its own discipline on shooting and editing in selecting only what is significant and using the shots that best sum up the essence of the story. The length of a shot depends on its function. The value of a shot is its relevance to the story in hand. One single 15-second shot may sum up the item but be superfluous in any other context. Check that the vital shots are provided and at the right length before offering visual decoration to the item. Editing for news means reducing to essentials. Make certain that shot length allows for brevity in editing and the relevant cutaways are provided for interviews. The viewer will require longer on-screen time to assimilate the information in a long shot than to absorb the detail in a close shot. Moving shots require more perceptual effort to understand than static shots. The skill in news shooting/cutting can be summarized as:

- each shot must be relevant to the story;
- shoot more detail than geography shots or scene setting;
- shoot more close, static shots than ones with camera movement;
- if possible, use short pans (no more than two seconds long) to inject pace into a story;
- devise a structure that contains pace, shot variety, and dynamic relevant images.

An appropriate shot

Every shot should be recorded for a purpose. That purpose is at its weakest if it simply seemed a good idea at the time to the cameraman or director, etc., to record a shot 'just in case' without considering its potential context. No shot can exist in isolation. A shot must have a connection with the aim of the item and its surrounding shots. It must be shot with editing in mind. This purpose could be related to the item's brief, script, outline or decided at the location. It could follow on from an interview comment or reference. It could be shot to help condense time or it could be offered as a 'safety' shot to allow flexibility in cutting the material.

There is very little point in providing a number of shots if they are unusable because of wrong exposure or if they are out of focus or the colour temperature is incorrect or if they are shaky and badly framed and important action begins before the recording is sufficiently stable to make an edit.

Continuity

Be aware of possible continuity mismatch between shots in background as well as foreground information. As well as changes over time (weather, light, face tones) watch for changing background action that will prevent intercutting. Avoid staging interviews against significant movement (e.g., a crowd emptying from an arena or a prominent working crane) as background continuity mismatch may prevent the interview being shortened. If possible, have different parts of the background in the singles and two shots if there is significant continuity of movement in the background or choose a static, neutral background. Keep a check on the position of coats, hats, clip-on microphones, attitudes of body and head on singles so that they can be matched on two shots.

The style and structure of the composition of a shot also requires a measure of continuity. It was mentioned earlier that the internal space of the shot created by very wide or a very narrow lens angles must be consistent within a sequence of shots to avoid a mismatch of apparent scene perspective. There is also the need to match shots that have strong line convergencies created by a wide-angle lens and a close camera-to-subject distance.

An individual style of camerawork can be seen as an individual's preference for a certain type of compositional 'look'. Some cameramen will favour a larger proportion of low-angle shots than average. Others devise complex camera movement or seek ambiguous images that tease the viewer into detecting and unravelling the image. In such instances, there is no problem with the compositional match during a sequence of shots because the individual preferences or style will or should remain consistent throughout the production. Problems only occur where someone is dabbling with a number of different 'looks' and a sequence of shots have no visual continuity.

Shot size

Avoid similar sized shots, whether in framing, scale, horizon line, etc., unless you provide a bridging shot. For example, a medium shot of an interviewee will not cut with a tight over-the-shoulder favouring the interviewee in the same medium-size shot. Wide shots of sea and boats need to be intercut with closer shots of boats to avoid the horizon line jumping in frame. Make certain that the all-over geometry of a shot is sufficiently different from a similar sized shot of the same subject (e.g., GVs of landscapes). In general, television is a close-up medium. Big wide-angle shots do not have the same impact they might have on a larger screen.

Crossing the line

To recap about the convention of crossing the line (see Figure 1.3). To intercut between individual shots of two people to create the appearance of a normal conversation between them, three simple rules have to be observed. If the interviewee in a single is looking from left to right in the frame then the single of the interviewer must look right to left. Secondly, the shot size and eye line should match (i.e., they should individually be looking out of the frame at a point where the viewer anticipates the other speaker is standing). Finally, every shot of a sequence should stay the same side of an imaginary line drawn between the speakers unless a cutaway is recorded that allows a re-orientation on the opposite side of the old 'line' (e.g., either the speakers re-group or the camera moves on shot).

It is easy to forget eye line direction when recording questions or 'noddies' after an interview has been recorded, particularly with a three-hander or when equipment is being demonstrated or explained. Make certain that the camera stays on one side only of the imaginary line drawn between the interviewer and interviewee.

Leaving frame

Do not always follow the action, especially on 'VIP' items where the temptation is to keep the 'notable' in shot at all times. It can some-times help in editing if the subject leaves the frame, but hold the empty frame for a few seconds and, on the new shot, hold the empty frame before the subject enters as it enables the editor to choose between cutting or not on a moving subject (see Figure 17.1).

Five-second module

News items tend to be constructed on an approximate five-second module. An example of a running order of a news story might be:

12″ voice-over establishing shots
10″ presenter to camera
10″ voice-over
25″ interview (with cutaways)
 7″ voice-over

running time of item: 1 minute 04 seconds.

To allow maximum flexibility for the editor, try to shoot in multiples of five seconds. Keep zooms and pans short. For example:

10″ hold at start of zoom (or pan)
5/10″ zoom (or pan)
5/10″ hold at end of movement.

This allows the editor a choice of three shots.

Length of pan

Avoid long panning or development shots. Although it may be difficult, depending on the circumstances, try to begin and end a camera movement cleanly. It is difficult to cut into a shot that creeps into or out of a movement. Be positive when you change framing. Use a tripod whenever possible as unsteady shots are difficult to cut and a distraction to the viewer.

Cutaway and cut-in

A cutaway literally means to cut away from the main subject or topic, either as a reaction to the event (e.g., cutting to a listener reacting to what a speaker is saying) or to support the point being made (e.g., a speaker discussing slum property is cutaway from to see the type of building they are talking about).

A cut-in usually means to go tighter on an aspect of the main subject. For example, an antiques expert talking in mid-shot about the manufacturer's mark on a piece of pottery she is holding would require a cut-in close shot of the pottery for the item to make sense to the viewer.

Clichéd visual metaphor

Just as there are stale and worn-out verbal metaphors, so there are visual clichés that have been over-used. These include weak attempts at copying mainstream feature film genres and techniques such as humour, suspense or shock effects. Attempt visual connections that are original and fresh. Rethink first, obvious thoughts and attempt to find fresh visual or audio relationships. Avoid using superimposed text to describe what is visually plainly obvious (e.g., a shot of a village signpost identifying the location has it name superimposed over the signpost).

Recap on basic advice for shooting for editing

There must be a reason in editing to change shot and the cameraman has to provide a diversity of material to provide a cutting point. In general a change of shot will be unobtrusive:

- if there is a significant change in shot size or camera angle when intercutting on the same subject;
- if there is a significant change in content (e.g., a cut from a tractor to someone opening a farm gate);
- when cutting on action – the flow of movement in the frame is carried over into the succeeding shot (e.g., a man in medium shot sitting behind a desk stands up and, on his rise, a longer shot of the man and the desk is cut to, see Figure 17.1);
- when intercutting between people, if their individual shots are matched in size, have the same amount of headroom, have the same amount of looking space if in semi-profile, if the lens angle is similar (i.e., internal perspective is similar) and if the lens height is the same;
- if the intercut pictures are colour matched (e.g., skin tones, background brightness, etc.) and if in succeeding shots the same subject has a consistent colour (e.g., grass in a stadium);
- if there is continuity in action (e.g., body posture, attitude);
- if there is continuity in lighting, in sound, props and setting, and continuity in performance or presentation.

On unscripted items such as news and TV magazine items:

- provide the editor with a higher proportion of static shots to camera movement. It is difficult to cut between pans and zooms until they steady to a static frame and hold;
- try to find relevant but non-specific shots so that voice-over information to set the scene or report can be dubbed on after the script has been prepared.

Interviews

The interview is an essential element of news and magazine reporting. It provides for a factual testimony from an active participant similar to a witness's court statement; that is, direct evidence of their own understanding, not rumour or hearsay. They can speak about what they feel, what they think, what they know, from their own experience. An interviewee can introduce into the report opinion, beliefs and emotion as opposed to the reporter who traditionally sticks to the facts. An interviewee therefore provides colour and emotion into an objective assessment of an event and captures the audience's attention. A first-hand account by people involved in an incident are facts in themselves. It is often spontaneous and vivid in its description and delivery. Because of the nature of some personal testament, its emotional impact can overwhelm other factual comments. The structure of such an item needs careful consideration to avoid distortion when using interviews that contain strong emotional appeals if these are balanced against more low-key reasoned argument.

Use of 'Vox Pops', random street interviews, is another method to provide the mood and opinions of the public. Its weakness is that, to some extent, the participants are self-selecting and it favours only those willing to talk to a reporter and a camera on a street corner. These people's opinions may be eccentric and not an accurate representation of the majority view.

Cutting an interview

A standard interview convention is to establish who the interviewee is by superimposing their name and possibly some other identification (e.g., farmer, market street trader, etc.) in text across an MCU of them. The interview is often cut using a combination of basic shots such as:

- an MS, MCU or CU of the interviewee;
- a matched shot of the interviewer asking questions or reacting to the answers (usually shot after the interview has ended);
- a two shot, which establishes location and relationship between the participants or an over-the-shoulder two shot looking from interviewer to interviewee;
- the interviewee is often staged so that their background is relevant to their comments.

The interview can follow straightforward intercutting between question and answer of the participants but, more usually, after a few words from the interviewee establishing their presence, a series of cutaways are used to illustrate the points the interviewee are making. A basic interview technique requires the appropriate basic shots:

- matched shots in size and lens angle;
- over-the-shoulder (o/s) shots;
- intercutting on question and answer;
- cutaways to referred items in the interview;
- 'noddies' and reaction shots (*note:* reaction shots should be reactions – that is, a response to the main subject);
- cutaways to avoid jump cuts when shortening answers.

How long should a shot be held?

The simple answer to this question is as long as the viewer needs to extract the required information, or before the action depicted requires a wider or closer framing to satisfy the viewers curiosity or a different shot (e.g., someone exiting the frame) to follow the action. The on-screen length is also dependent on many more subtle considerations than the specific content of the shot.

As discussed above, the rhythm of the editing produced by rate of
shot change, and the shaping of the rate of shot change to produce an
appropriate shape to a sequence, will have a bearing on how long a shot
is held on screen. Rhythm relies on variation of shot length, but should
not be arbitrarily imposed simply to add interest. As always with editing, there is a balance to be struck between clear communication and
the need to hold the viewer's interest with visual variety. The aim is to
clarify and emphasize the topic, not to confuse the viewer with shots
that are snatched off the screen before they are visually understood.

The critical factor controlling on-screen duration is often the shot
size. A long shot may have a great deal more information than a close
shot. Also, a long shot is often used to introduce a new location or to
set the 'geography' of the action. These features will be new to the
audience, and therefore they will take longer to understand and absorb
the information. Shifting visual information produced by moving
shots will also need longer screen time.

A closer shot will usually yield its content fairly quickly, particularly
if the content has been seen before (e.g., a well known 'screen' face).
There are other psychological aspects of perception that also have a
bearing on how quickly an audience can recognize images that are
flashed on to a screen. These factors are exploited in those commercials that have a very high cutting rate, but are not part of standard
news/magazine editing technique.

Although news/magazine editing is always paring an item down to
essential shots, due consideration should always be given to the subject
of the item. For example, a news item about the funeral of a victim of a
civil disaster or crime has to have pauses and 'quiet' on-screen time to
reflect the feelings and emotion of the event. Just as there is a need to
have changes of pace and rhythm in editing a piece to give a particularly overall shape, so a news bulletin or magazine running order will
have an overall requirement for changes of tempo between hard and
soft items to provide balance and variety.

Cutting on movement

A change of shot requires a measurable time for the audience to adjust
to the incoming shot. If the shot is part of a series of shots showing an
event or action, the viewer will be able to follow the flow of action
across the cut if the editor has selected an appropriate point to cut on
movement. This will move the viewer into the next part of the action
without them consciously realizing a cut has occurred. An edit point in
the middle of an action disguises the edit point.

Cutting on movement is the bedrock of editing. It is the preferred
option in cutting, compared with most other editing methods, provided the sequence has been shot to include action edit points.
When breaking down a sequence of shots depicting a continuous
action there are usually five questions faced by the editor:

1. what is visually interesting?
2. what part of a shot is necessary to advance the 'story' of the topic?
3. how long can the sequence last?
4. has the activity been adequately covered on camera?
5. is there a sufficient variety of shots to serve the above require-
    ments?

Figure 17.4

(a)   Crossing the line

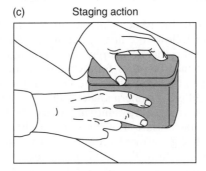

These shots (a) and (b) will need a
cutaway between them to avoid a jump cut

(b)   Making a cup of tea

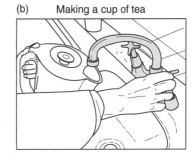

Action can be staged to avoid
continuous cutting. The shot
demonstrating the difficulty of
opening the tea caddy can be
developed to demonstrate the
difficulty of picking up the tea bag
(**d**) and left to form a continuous
shot unless there is a need to
condense time.

(c)   Staging action

(d)   Making a cup of tea

Watch for continuity mismatch.
There is milk in the mug in (**e**)
(figure demonstrates difficulty in
handling a teaspoon) which may
be picked up if the shot showing
the problems opening a milk
container (**f**) follows.

(e)   Check continuity

(f)

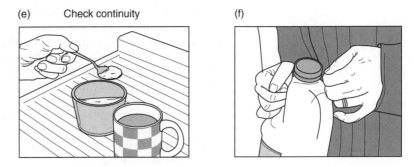

For example, a story to be edited concerns the difficulties disabled
people have with normal everyday domestic appliances. A sequence
was shot where the subject of the report was making a cup of tea (see
Figure 17.4) to illustrate these problems. The intention was for the
reporter, on a voice-over commentary, to identify each hazard.

The editor has a guide to the length of the sequence which equals the
running time of the relevant voice-over. Next he has a guide to what is
significant – what will advance the story. The voice-over may mention
for example, difficulties in turning on a tap, pouring boiling water into
a tea pot, pouring out the tea, opening a milk carton, etc. The vital
factor, of course, is whether shots covering these activities have been
provided by the location crew, and crucially, if they can be cut
together.

With this kind of sequence, the editor needs to be economic with the
use of screen time using only so much of a specific action (e.g., turning

on a tap), to provide the viewer with the necessary visual information whilst advancing the point of the 'story'. The total running time of the recorded event has to be pared down by selecting only essential parts of necessary shots to fit the voice-over. Cutting on movement, such as hands coming in and out of frame, will allow the whole activity to be collapsed into half-a-dozen close shots, wasting no screen time on irrelevant action (for example – searching the kitchen for the tea pot). Cutting on action such as movement in the frame, will provide the motivation for the cuts and allow compression of the activity without the viewer being aware that the event has been considerably speeded up.

Cutting on exits and entrances

One of the basic principles of perennial editing technique is that each shot follows the line of action to maintain consistent screen direction so that the geography of the action is completely intelligible. A sequence of shots following someone walking down a street can be cut so that they enter and leave frame in suitable changing size of shot or different camera angle, following their walk from one frame into the next frame, always moving across the frame in the same direction until an appropriate shot shows the audience that they have changed direction (e.g., walked around a corner and into a new street). For the novice editor, the problem is to decide at what point in each shot they should make the cut to the next shot.

Cutting on exits and entrances into a frame is a standard way of reducing the amount of screen time taken to traverse distance. The usual convention is to make the cut when the subject has nearly left the frame. It is natural for the viewer, if the subject is disappearing out of the side of the frame, to wish to be shown where they are going. If the cut comes after they have left the frame then the viewer is left with an empty frame and either their interest switches to whatever is left in the frame or they feel frustrated because the subject of their interest has gone. Conversely, the incoming frame can have the subject just appearing, but the match on action has to be good otherwise there will be an obtrusive jump in their walking rhythm or some other posture mismatch.

Allowing the subject to clear the frame in the outgoing shot and not be present in the incoming shot is usually the lazy way of avoiding continuity mismatches. An empty frame at the end of a shot is already 'stale' to the viewer. If it is necessary, because there is no possibility in the shots provided of matching up the action across the cut, try to use the empty frame of the incoming shot (which is new to the viewer) before the action begins to avoid continuity problems. This convention can be applied to any movement across a cut. In general, choose an empty frame on an incoming shot rather than the outgoing shot unless there is the need for a 'visual' full stop to end a sequence. Ending on an empty frame is usually followed by a fade-down or mix across to the new scene.

Perception and shot transition

Film and television screens display a series of single images for a very short period of time. Because of the nature of human perception (persistence of vision), if these images are displayed at an effective rate of 48/50 times a second, flicker is reduced and there is the illusion of continuous motion of any subject that changes position in succeeding frames.

It takes time for a change of shot to be registered and, with large discrepancies between shot transitions, it becomes more apparent to the viewer when the composition of both shots is dissimilar. If the programme maker aims to make the transition between shots to be as imperceptible as possible in order to avoid visually distracting the viewer, the amount of eye movement between cuts needs to be at a minimum. If the incoming shot is sufficiently similar in design (e.g., matching the principal subject position and size in both shots), the movement of the eye will be minimized and the change of shot will hardly be noticeable. There is, however, a critical point in matching identical shots to achieve an unobtrusive cut (e.g., cutting together the same size shot of the same individual where possibly there is only the smallest difference in the angle of the head), where the jump between almost identical shots becomes noticeable.

Narrative motivation for changing the shot (e.g., What happens next? What is this person doing? etc.), will also smooth the transition. A large mismatch between two shots, for example, where action on the left of frame is cut to when the previous shot has significant action on extreme right of frame, may take the viewer four or five frames to catch up with the change and may trigger a 'What happened then?' response. If a number of these 'jump' cuts (i.e., shot transitions that are noticeable to the audience), are strung together, the viewer becomes very aware of the mechanics of the production process and the smooth flow of images is disrupted. This 'visual' disruption, of course, may sometimes be a production objective.

Matching visual design between shots

When two shots are cut together, the visual design, that is the composition of each shot, can be matched to achieve smooth continuity. Alternatively, if the production requirement is for the cut to impact on the viewer, the juxtaposition of the two shots can be so arranged to provide an abrupt contrast in their graphic design.

The cut between two shots can be made invisible if the incoming shot has one or more similar compositional elements as the preceding shot. The relationships between the two shots may relate to matching shape, same position of dominant subject in the frame, colours, lighting, setting, overall composition, etc. Any equivalent aspects of visual design that are present in both shots will help the smooth transition from one shot to the next.

With intercut dialogue shots (especially noticeable in widescreen format), often the protagonists are framed in separate shots on either side of the screen to indicate they are spatially linked. The empty space on one side of the frame indicating the presence of the other. On each cut the incoming image fills the space left in the outgoing image.

A popular use of this in news/current affairs programmes is the Vox Pop sequence where members of the public are asked their opinion on a subject and their answers intercut with those positive about the subject on one side of the frame, and those negative about the subject are framed in their individual shots on the other side of the frame.

Depending on the questions and answers, the cut sequence has the appearance of a dialogue between the participants even though they have never met and conversed amongst themselves.

Matching rhythm relationships between shots

The editor needs to consider two types of rhythm when cutting together shots: the rhythm created by the rate of shot change, and the internal rhythm of the depicted action.

Each shot will have a measurable time on screen. The rate at which shots are cut creates a rhythm that affects the viewer's response to the sequence. For example, in a feature film action sequence, a common way of increasing the excitement and pace of the action is to increase the cutting rate by decreasing the duration of each shot on screen as the action approaches a climax. The rhythms introduced by editing are in addition to the other rhythms created by artiste movement, camera movement and the rhythm of sound. The editor can therefore adjust shot duration and shot rate independent of the need to match continuity of action between shots; this controls an acceleration or deceleration in the pace of the item.

By controlling the editing rhythm, the editor controls the amount of time the viewer has to grasp and understand the selected shots. Many productions exploit this fact in order to create an atmosphere of mystery and confusion by ambiguous framing and rapid cutting that deliberately undermines the viewer's attempt to make sense of the images they are shown.

Another editing consideration is maintaining the rhythm of action carried over into succeeding shots. Most people have a strong sense of rhythm as expressed in walking, marching, dancing, etc. If this rhythm is destroyed as, for example, cutting together a number of shots of a marching band so that their step becomes irregular, viewers will sense the discrepancies and the sequence will appear disjointed and awkward. When cutting from a shot of a person walking, for example, care must be taken that the person's foot hits the ground with the same rhythm as in the preceding shot, and that it is the appropriate foot (i.e., after a left foot comes a right foot). The rhythm of a person's walk may still be detected even if the incoming shot does not include the feet. The beat of the movement must not be disrupted. Sustaining rhythms of action may well override the need for a narrative 'ideal' cut at an earlier or later point.

Matching spatial relationships between shots

Editing creates spatial relationships between subjects that need never exist in reality. A common example is a passenger getting into a train at a station. The following shot shows a train pulling out of the station. The audience infers that the passenger is on the train when they are more probably on an entirely different train or even no train at all. Cause and effect patterns occur continuously in editing. A shot of an apple falling off a tree followed by a shot of Isaac Newton rubbing his head, must inevitably lead the viewer to conclude that Newton has been hit by the very same apple. This assumption is a combination of what the viewer knows (an apple apocryphally fell on Newton) and what is shown, and then mentally connecting the two shots in a cause/

effect relationship. For example, a reporter in medium close-up nods her interest in what the interviewee is saying. The viewer's assumption is that the reporter at that moment is listening to the interviewee when, in fact, the 'noddies' were shot some time after the interviewee had left the location.

Any two subjects or events can be linked by a cut if there is an apparent graphic continuity between shots framing them, and if there is an absence of an establishing shot showing their physical relationship. Portions of space can be cut together to create a convincing screen space provided no shot is wide enough to show that the edited relationship is not possible. For example, a shot of a person leaning against a signpost can be cut with a shot of a person sitting on a wall; these shots can be intercut and, to the viewer, hold a believable conversation together provided there is no shot that either reveals that there is no wall by the signpost, or no signpost by the wall.

Matching temporal relationships between shots

The position of a shot in relation to other shots (preceding or following) will control the viewer's understanding of its time relationship to surrounding shots. Usually a factual event is cut in a linear time line unless indicators are built in to signal flashbacks or, very rarely, flashforwards. The viewer assumes the order of depicted events is linked to the passing of time.

The standard formula for compressing space and time is to allow the main subject to leave frame or to provide appropriate cutaways to shorten the actual time taken to complete the activity. While they are out of shot, the viewer will accept that greater distance has been travelled than is realistically possible. Provided the main subject does not in vision leap from location one immediately to location two, and then to three and four, there will be no jump in continuity between shots. The empty frames and cutaways allow the editing-out of space and time to remain invisible. News editing frequently requires a reduction in screen time of the actual duration of a real event. For example, a 90-minute football match recording will be edited down to 30 seconds to run as a 'highlights' report in a news bulletin.

Screen time is seldom made greater than the event time, but there are instances, for example in reconstructions of a crime in a documentary, where time is expanded by editing. This stylistic mannerism is often accompanied by slow-motion sequences.

Matching tone, colour or background

Cutting between shots of speakers with different background tones, colour or texture will sometimes result in an obtrusive cut. A cut between a speaker with a bright background and a speaker with a dark background will result in a 'jump' in the flow of images each time it occurs. Colour temperature matching and background brightness relies on the cameraman making the right exposure and artiste positioning decisions. Particular problems can occur, for example, with grass that changes its colour between shots. Face tones of a presenter or interviewee need to be consistent across a range of shots when cut together in a sequence. Also, cutting between shots with in-focus and defocused backgrounds to speakers can produce a

Figure 17.5 The duration of an event can be considerably shortened to a fraction of its actual running time by editing if the viewer's concept of time passing is not violated. For example, a politician enters a conference centre and delivers a speech to an audience. This whole event, possibly lasting 30 minutes or more, can be reduced to 15 seconds of screen time by cutting between the appropriate shots.

In the first shot **(a)**, the politician is seen entering the building with a voice-over giving details of the purpose of the visit. A cutaway to an audience shot with a pan to the politician on the platform (**(b)** to **(c)**), allows all the intervening time to be collapsed without a jump cut, and also allows the voice-over to paraphrase what the politician is saying. A third, closer, profile shot of the politician **(d)**, followed by a shot of the listening audience **(e)**, continues with the voice-over paraphrase, ending with a MCU of the politician **(f)**, with his actuality sound, delivering the key 'sound bite' sentence of his speech. A combination of voice-over and five shots that can be cut together maintaining continuity of time and place allows a 30-minute event to be delivered in 15–20 seconds

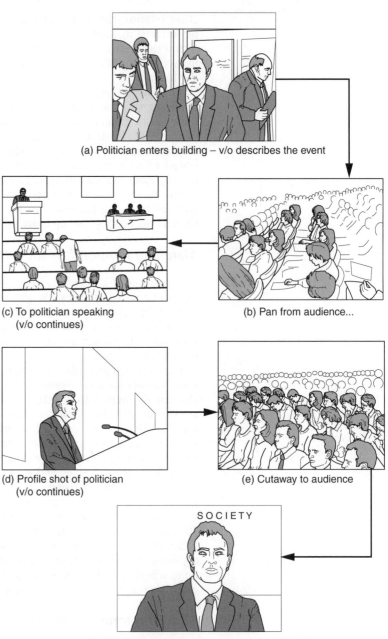

(a) Politician enters building – v/o describes the event

(c) To politician speaking (v/o continues)

(b) Pan from audience...

(d) Profile shot of politician (v/o continues)

(e) Cutaway to audience

(f) MCU of politician – actuality sound of speech

mismatch on a cut. Continuity of colour, tone, texture, skin tones and depth-of-field, will improve the seamless flow of images.

Rearranging time and space

When two shots are cut together the audience attempts to make a connection between them. Expanding the example given above, a man on a station platform boards a train. A wide shot shows a train pulling out of a station. The audience makes the connection that the man is on the train. A cut to a close shot of the seated man follows, and it is assumed that he is travelling on the train. We see a wide shot of a train crossing the Forth Bridge, and the audience assumes that the man is travelling in Scotland. Adding a few more shots would allow a shot of the man leaving the train at his destination with the audience experiencing no violent discontinuity in the depiction of time or space. And yet a journey that may take two hours is collapsed to 30 seconds of screen time, and a variety of shots of trains and a man at different locations have been strung together in a manner that convinces the audience they have followed the same train and man throughout a journey.

Basic editing principles

This way of arranging shots is fundamental to editing. Space and time are rearranged in the most efficient way to present the information that the viewer requires to follow the argument presented. The transition between shots must not violate the audiences sense of continuity between the actions presented. This can be achieved by:

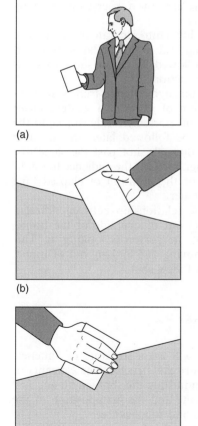

(a)

(b)

(c)

Figure 17.6

- *Continuity of action:* action is carried over from one shot to another without an apparent break in speed or direction of movement. In a medium shot, for example, (Figure 17.6(a)), someone places a book on a table out of shot. A cut to a closer shot of the book (Figure 17.6(b)), shows the book just before it is laid on the table. Provided the book's position relative to the table and the speed of the book's movement in both shots is similar, and there is continuity in the table surface, lighting, hand position, etc., then the cut will not be obtrusive. A close shot that crosses the line (Figure 17.6(c)), will not cut.
- *Screen direction:* if the book is travelling left to right in the medium shot, the closer shot of the book will need to roughly follow the same direction. A shot of the book moving right to left will produce a visual 'jump' that may be apparent to the viewer.
- *Eye line match:* the eye line of someone looking down at the book should be in the direction the audience believes the book to be. If they look out of frame with their eye line levelled at their own height, the implication is that they are looking at something at that height. Whereas if they were looking down, the assumption would be that they are looking at the book. An interviewer and an interviewee in separate shots must be eye line matched in order to cut between them. Their eye line out of frame must match with the audience's expectation of where the person they are talking to is positioned.
- *There is a need to cement the spatial relationship between shots:* a subject speaking and looking out of the left of frame will be assumed by the viewer to speaking to someone off-camera to the left. A cut to another person looking out of frame to the right will confirm this audience expectation. Eye line matches are decided by position, and there is very little that can be done at the editing stage to correct shooting mismatches except flipping the frame to

reverse the eye line, which alters the continuity of the symmetry of the face and other left/right continuity elements in the composition such as hair partings, etc.

- *Shot size:* another essential editing factor is the size of shots that form an intercut sequence of faces. A cut from a medium close-up to another medium close-up of a second person will be unobtrusive provided the eye line match is as above. A number of cuts between a long shot of one person and a medium close-up of another will jump and be obtrusive.

Types of edit

There are a number of standard editing techniques that are used across a wide range of programme making. These include:

- *Intercutting editing* can be applied to locations or people. The technique of intercutting between different actions that are happening simultaneously at different locations was discovered as early as 1906 to inject pace and tension into a story. Intercutting on faces in the same location presents the viewer with changing viewpoints on action and reaction.
- *Analytical editing* breaks a space down into separate framings. The classic sequence begins with a long shot to show relationships and the 'geography' of the setting followed by closer shots to show detail, and to focus on important action.
- *Contiguity editing* follows action through different frames of changing locations. The classic pattern of shots in a western chase sequence is where one group of horsemen ride through the frame past a distinctive tree to be followed later, in the same framing, of the pursuers riding through shot past the same distinctive tree. The tree acts as a 'signpost' for the audience to establish location, and as a marker of the duration of elapsed time between the pursued and the pursuer.
- *Point-of-view shot* establishes the relationship between different spaces. Someone on-screen looks out of one side of the frame. The following shot reveals what the person is looking at. This can also be applied to anyone moving and looking out of frame, followed by their moving point-of-view shot.

Emphasis, tempo and syntax

Just as a written report of an event will use a structure of sentence, paragraph and chapter, a visual report can structure the elements of the storytelling in a similar way. By adjusting the shot length and fine tuning the rate and rhythm of the cuts and the juxtaposition of the shots, the editor can create emphasis and significance.

A piece can be cut to relate a number of connected ideas. When the report moves on to a new idea there is often a requirement to indicate visually – 'new topic'. This can be achieved by a very visible cut – a mismatch perhaps or an abrupt change of sound level or content (e.g., quiet interior is followed by a cut to a marching band on parade) to call attention to a transitional moment.

Teasing the audience

A linear, logical progression of the story is not the only way to hold the viewer's attention. Often, a puzzle is set up or a question is posed to draw the audience into the story. Like a mystery novel, clues are given before the denouement at the end. This is obviously a fairly lightweight treatment and would be inappropriate in many hard-news stories.

Be sparing with editing structures that visually tease the audience with sequences that are ambiguous or mystifying. The technique of withholding the connection between succeeding shots until the link shot is shown, risks losing the audience's attention and interest. Too complicated a clue to a crossword puzzle may alienate the salver's interest. However, a montage that puzzles the viewer may also engage his interest.

The viewer will always believe that the programme maker has some reason for putting a shot on the screen – unless a production continually misleads them.

Sort it out in the edit

Lastly, as we have already stressed, a location shoot for a two-minute item that results in ten 20-minute cassettes with no thought to its eventual structure other than a misguided belief that it can all be sorted out in editing, can end in a long and inefficient trawl through inappropriate material. Transcribing the random letters produced by a monkey and a keyboard into meaningful words, then sentences, then an article, is probably easier. TV production requires planning, thought and structure from shooting right through to the master tape.

Sound and picture

The importance of audio may be overlooked in acquisition but any shortcomings will become increasingly obvious in editing. In nearly every type of production, sound and picture interweave and are mutually dependent. It is vital that the range of audio recorded (apart from being technically perfect) matches the visual coverage in providing the editor with flexibility and creative choice.

Multi-camera camerawork

The value of multi-camera technique is its ability to simultaneously observe a continuous event from a number of different camera positions. A continuous actuality event such as sport, music, state and public events, audience discussion, etc., can be transmitted live or continuously recorded to be transmitted later. Traditional multi-camera technique required each camera's picture to be selected through the vision mixing panel and cut to 'line' (i.e., transmitted or recorded) in accordance with a pre-rehearsed camera script detailing all agreed shots, or as a mixture of *ad lib* shots and pre-planned shots.

In order to comprehensively cover a continuous event such as sport, each camera is assigned a role. Covering a football match, for example, one camera will mostly stay wide as a master or safety shot that can be cut to at any time, whilst the other cameras will stay close for 'personality' close-ups of individual players. Cameras stick to their assigned role in order to provide the director with a guaranteed appropriate shot at all times, otherwise duplication of the same shot occurs.

With the expansion in the use of 'iso' (isolated) feeds, that is an individual camera's output is continuously recorded as well as being available at the mixing panel, a great amount of flexibility is available in post-production to re-edit the recorded material. Iso feeds began as a technique to provide variation of shot for instant 'slo mo' playback at live sports events. Now, some non-sport multi-camera productions 'iso' each camera and use post-production to complete the edit.

The basis of multi-camera techniques of composition is very similar to single camera operations except that:

- cameramen need good communications between producer and crew and, if possible, exposure needs to be centrally controlled to match pictures;
- the shots are instantaneously edited and therefore need to be matched in size;
- the shots need to be coordinated to avoid duplication and to provide variety and cutting points;
- with a live transmission a shot has to be ready and executed at the instant it is required – not when the cameraman is ready to record;
- there can be no retakes – camerawork problems are not edited out, they are transmitted.

Working as a team

As we have discussed in the section on the legacy of film technique, the skills and techniques used to make a TV programme should not be apparent to the average television viewer. If the viewer becomes aware of technique it will usually distract from the content of the programme. Camera technique should be invisible and this requires matched and consistent camerawork between all cameras on a multi-camera shoot. Unlike single camerawork where an operator may have his own idiosyncratic ways of framing and personal preferences of shot size, multi-camera work requires cameramen to coordinate their framing and composition to avoid 'jump cuts' between shots. The description and the framing of the shot needs to be understood by cameraman and director (see Figure 12.2) but also:

- headroom should be consistent and adjusted to suit the size of shot;
- the amount of looking room should match for similar sized shots (see Figure 17.7);
- each camera should have the same lens perspective and same camera height when involved in cross-cutting on interviews, etc.;
- the pace of camera movement and style of composition should match.

Figure 17.7

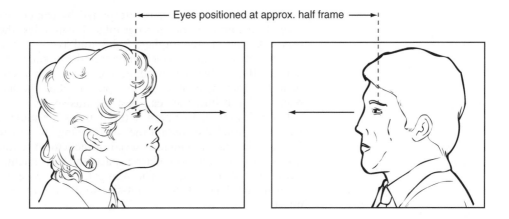

Balanced 'looking room' on intercut shots

As well as matching the style of camerawork there needs to be a technical match between the cameras. A grey-scale line-up before transmission ensures a colour match between cameras – for example, the skin tones of a face on different cameras needs to be the same. Also remote control of exposure and black level ensures a better match when intercutting cameras.

Matched shot size and the position in the frame of the subject can be observed and easily adjusted in a multi-camera shoot to allow smooth and 'invisible' cutting. In single camera/single shot coverage there is obviously the need to keep careful records of eye lines, body position, shot-size and other visual indicators in order to achieve visual continuity in post-production.

Dance and composition

As in every type of production, there are many ways of covering dance on film and television. There are tried and trusted basic conventions and there are innovations and visual experiments that reject and oppose the following generalizations about dance composition. As was said in another context, an orgy of self-expression can sometimes be no more productive than the blind obedience of rules. The following observations are offered as a basis for development.

Dance features the whole figure and therefore the majority of shots will include the whole figure. The dance 'shape' can be emphasized by keeping the camera low and therefore reducing the amount of floor in shot and emphasizing the figure in relationship to the backing.

Let the dancers move within the frame. Be wide enough for the dancers to make their own shapes within the frame. Avoid constant panning to keep the dancer within the frame. The fidgety background will work against the dancer's movement and keeping the dancer in centre frame while they are moving can work against the intentions of the choreographer.

If the dance movement is interpreted by camera movement, there could be a confusion of choreographic design unless there is collaboration with the choreographer. Spins and twirls can be extended by mixing between shots, which enhances the intended movement of the dancer. If possible, let the dancer choreograph to the frame. Show them the amount of studio floor space in shot and let the choreographer work out how they can best use this space.

Use a low-angled camera if the dancers are moving across frame. Use a high-angled camera if they are moving away or towards camera. Use a wide-angle to enhance speed of movement to and from camera. Use a narrow-angle to collapse space and movement. Use a close-up cut-in to disclose details of movement, to increase or express excitement in the dance. Devise shot-size to allow cuts on movement and music.

Summary

One aspect of the composition of a shot is to consider how it will relate to the preceding and succeeding shots. There must be a reason in editing to change shot and the cameraman has to provide a diversity of material to provide a cutting point. Edit-point requirements such as change in angle and shot size, subject movement, camera movement and continuity have to be considered and provided for to enable the footage to be assembled in a coherent stream of images. Shooting with editing in mind is therefore essential. It is part of the cameraman's craft to provide the editor/presenter with a variety of options but to keep the shooting ratio in proportion to the editing time available.

The narrative 'weight' of a shot is dependent on the size of the shot and also on the composition. Emphasis can be strengthened or lightened depending on the reason for the shot.

A good cut needs a change in shot size or significant change in content to be invisible.

Endnote

It is natural, when training for a craft or a new skill, to search for underlying rules and guidelines – to look for certainties in order to master and to measure the amount of progress achieved.

Camerawork is basically a craft but with its top practitioners it shades into a highly original, creative activity. Between learning by rote and the wilder excesses of individual subjective expression, a balance has to be struck between the dogma of 'always do it this way' and the anarchy of 'I don't quite know what I am trying to achieve, but out of this creative muddle new, original work will materialize. I hope!'.

This book has discussed the constituent parts of composition. From the theory of perception to the inherited values of previous 'visual problem' solvers there is a wide range of advice and opinion on how to achieve good communication. Composition is central to this process and touches nearly all aspects of film and television production. To rewrite Marshall McLuans' media catch-phrase – the image is frequently the message.

What has not been discussed so far, is the part played by individual innovation in the act of framing up a shot. The imaginative leap made in the early days of film making when cameramen and directors devised and invented new visual ways of telling a story has been continuously expanded and added to by many cameramen following in their footsteps.

The television pioneers faced similar challenges with the need to adapt and develop multi-camera technique. The unpredictability of the early electronic camera created a demand for reliability and certainty. The engineering quest was for equipment of high specification coupled with a cost-effective life before being superseded by the next innovation.

Cameramen also have a keen interest in reliable equipment but frequently need to add another ingredient to the mixture. Good camerawork, as well as requiring a technique that guarantees a quality product, also, at times, involves taking risks. There are occasions when no previous experience or guidelines can help in resolving a particular visual problem.

In live television camerawork, operational decisions have to be made in seconds. The cameraman chances his arm and goes with what he feels is the relevant action. If he/she is right, then the result on screen is so obvious, that a viewer is not even aware that a split second decision has been made. If he/she is wrong, the same viewer may be critical of the blunder. These visual decisions are made in seconds. The critic of these activities frequently have days, weeks or even months to make their own crucial decisions – and they can still get them wrong!

Cameramen have to live with uncertainty. It is part of the job. The programme may not be as good as they hoped, the film does not quite come off, etc., but stepping into the unknown – risk taking – is part of the everyday activity faced by production crews. There can never be absolute certainties about TV and film production technique and frequently, the new and the original are resisted until they achieve critical or financial endorsement.

Innovation, original work, is often the product of maverick thinking. A particular craft technique continues to be practised until someone demonstrates that it is based on unexamined assumptions. There are other ways of doing it.

It may have been implied in this discussion on composition that there is a clear, unequivocal method of work, but the creative urge to experiment, to try something different is as valuable as the need to have knowledge about the bricks and mortar of camerawork. Usually, innovation only succeeds if it takes off from an established craft skill. Genius is a commodity that is always in short supply.

The ability to create interesting and arresting compositions lies at the heart of the cameraman's expertise. The range and variety of outstanding camerawork testifies to the individuality present in the practice of the craft of camerawork. It would seem presumptuous to attempt to lay out principles and guidelines that would embrace such a diversity of practice. Technique changes too rapidly to attempt to set a discussion on composition in 'tablets of stone'.

Perhaps an eminent writer on the subject, Sir Charles Holmes (*Notes on the Science of Picture Making*), should have the last word:

It cannot be too definitely stated at the outset that a knowledge of principles is no substitute for invention. Principles themselves cannot create a work of art. They can only modify and perfect the vague pictorial conception formed in the artist's mind, which are the foundation upon which he builds.

Bibliography

Arnheim, Rudolph, *Art and Visual Perception*. Faber & Faber, London, 1967.

Barthes, Roland, *Mythologies*. Jonathan Cape, London, 1972.

Bell, Martin, *The Widescreen Book*. BBC Resources & BBC Broadcast, London, 1998.

Belton, John, *Widescreen Cinema*. Harvard University Press, Cambridge, MA, 1992.

Bordwell, David, *Narration in the Fiction Film*. Routledge, London, 1994.

Bordwell, David, *On the History of Film Style*. Harvard University Press, Cambridge, MA, 1997.

Bradley, D.R. and Perry, H.M., Organisational determinants of subjective contours, *American Journal of Psychology*, **90**, 253–62, 1977.

Cook, David, *A History of Narrative Film*. W.W. Norton, New York, 1996.

Cook, Pam, *The Cinema Book*. The British Film Institute, 1995.

Crowther, Bruce, *Film Noir*. W.H. Allen & Co., London, 1988.

Dancyger, Ken, *The Technique of Film and Video Editing*. Focal Press, Oxford, 1997.

Gardiner, Paul, *Evolution of Wide Screen Broadcasting in the United Kingdom*. ITC, London, 1999.

Gombrich, E.H., *Art and Illusion*. Phaidon Press, London, 1960.

Gombrich, E.H., *The Image and the Eye*. Phaidon Press, London, 1982.

Gregory, R.L, *Eye and Brain*. Weidenfeld and Nicolson, London, 1967.

Hill, J. and Gibson, P.C., *The Oxford Guide to Film Studies*. Oxford University Press, Oxford, 1998.

Holmes, Sir Charles, *Notes on the Science of Picture Making*.

Itten, Johannes, *The Art of Colour*. Reinhold, New York, 1962.

Kepes, Gyorgy, *Language of Vision*. Paul Theobald & Co., Chicago, 1961.

Mascelli, Joseph, *The Five C's of Cinematography*. Silman-James Press, Los Angeles, 1965.

Monaco, James, *How to Read a Film*. Oxford University Press, New York, 1981.

Neale, S. and Smith, M., *Contemporary Hollywood Cinema*. Routledge, London, 1998.

Phillips, William, *Film*. Bedford, St Martins, Boston, 1999.

Poynton, Charles, *The Current State of High Definition Television*, Poynton@inforamp.net, 1989.

Pudovkin, V.I., *Film Technique and Film Acting*. Lear Publishing Inc., New York, 1939.

Reisz, K. and Millar, G., *Technique of Film Editing*. Focal Press, Oxford, 1999.

Rogers, Pauline, *Contemporary Cinematographers on their Art*. Focal Press, Oxford, 1998.

Salt, Barry, *Film Style and Technology: History and Analysis*. Starword, London, 1983.

Scharf, Aaron, *Art and Photography*. The Penguin Press, London, 1968.

Ward, Peter, *Digital Camerawork*. Focal Press, Oxford, 2000.

Ward, Peter, *Basic Betacam Camerawork*, 3rd edition. Focal Press, Oxford, 2001.

Ward, P., Bermingham, A. and Wherry, C., *Multiskilling for Television Production*. Focal Press, Oxford, 2000.

Index

Focal Press

www.focalpress.com
Join Focal Press on-line
As a member you will enjoy the following benefits:

- an email bulletin with **information on new books**

- a regular **Focal Press Newsletter**:

    - featuring a selection of new titles

    - keeps you informed of **special offers, discounts and freebies**

    - alerts you to **Focal Press news and events** such as author signings and seminars

- complete access to **free content** and reference material on the focalpress site, such as the focalXtra articles and commentary from our authors

- a **Sneak Preview** of selected titles (sample chapters) *before* they publish

- a chance to have your say on our **discussion boards** and **review books** for other Focal readers

Focal Club Members are invited to give us feedback on our products and services.
Email: worldmarketing@focalpress.com – we want to hear your views!

Membership is **FREE**. To join, visit our website and register. If you require any further information regarding the on-line club please contact:

> Lucy Lomas-Walker
> Email: l.lomas@elsevier.com
> Tel: +44 (0) 1865 314438
> Fax: +44 (0)1865 314572
> Address: Focal Press, Linacre House,
> Jordan Hill, Oxford, UK, OX2 8DP

Catalogue
For information on all Focal Press titles, our full catalogue is available online at www.focalpress.com and all titles can be purchased here via secure online ordering, or contact us for a free printed version:

USA
Email: christine.degon@bhusa.com
Tel: +1 781 904 2607 T

Europe and rest of world
Email: j.blackford@elsevier.com
el: +44 (0)1865 314220

Potential authors
If you have an idea for a book, please get in touch:

USA
editors@focalpress.com

Europe and rest of world
focal.press@repp.co.uk

Also available from Focal Press ...

Media Manuals

- Combine practical advice, technical know-how and professional skills
- Contain only the essential information you need to know
- Act as 'on-the-job guides' for everyday use

The Media Manual series provides hands-on information for beginning professionals in TV production. The guides contain practical, step-by-step information broken down into two pages per topic with numerous diagrams, checklists and technical terms explained. Written by experienced television trainers, the manuals offer guidance on professional practice, explanations of technology, operational techniques and background theory for easy on-the-job reference.

Media Manual Titles:

16MM FILM CUTTING
John Burder, Gerald Millerson

AUDIO FOR SINGLE CAMERA OPERATION
Tony Grant

AUDIO TECHNIQUES FOR TELEVISION PRODUCTION
Roger Laycock

BASIC BETACAM CAMERAWORK (Third edition)
Peter Ward

BASIC FILM TECHNIQUE
Ken Daley

BASIC STUDIO DIRECTING
Rod Fairweather

media
MANUAL

*To order your copies call +44 (0)1865 888180 (UK) or +1 800 545 2522 (USA)
or visit the Focal Press website: www.focalpress.com*

Also available from Focal Press ...

Multiskilling for Television Production

Peter Ward
Alan Bermingham
Chris Wherry

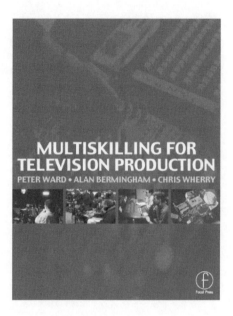

Written by television trainers who run their own courses on multiskilling, this book offers a comprehensive introduction to the broad range of skills and technical knowledge required in this industry. It details all the essential information you need to know, acting as an on-the-job reference source for everyday use. Anyone baffled by the range and scope of skills to be mastered will find this book invaluable.

2000 • 424pp • 450 illustrations • 246 x 189mm • paperback
ISBN 0 240 515579

For more details visit www.focalpress.com

To order your copy call +44 (0)1865 888180 (UK) or +1 800 545 2522 (USA)
or visit the Focal Press website: www.focalpress.com

Also available from Focal Press ...

Digital Cinematography
Paul Wheeler

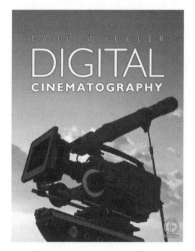

A guide for practising and aspiring cinematographers and DoPs to digital cinematography essentials – from how to use the cameras to the rapidly emerging world of High Definition cinematography and 24p technology.

All the on-the-set knowledge you need to know is covered. Emphasis is on practical application with usable tools and information to help you get the job done. This is a complete reference to the knowledge and skills required to shoot high end digital films. The book also features a guide to the Sony DVW in-camera menus, showing how to set them up and how they work – a device to save you time and frustration on set.

2001 • 208pp • 106 illustrations • 246 x 189mm • paperback
ISBN 0 240 51614 1

Paul Wheeler is a renowned cinematographer/DoP and trainer. He has been Head of Cinematography at National Film & Television School (UK) and still runs courses on Digital Cinematography there. He has been twice nominated by BAFTA for a Best Cinematography award and also twice been the winner of the INDIE award for Best Digital Cinematography.

Also by Paul Wheeler:
Practical Cinematography, 2000, ISBN 0240 51555 2
High Definition and 24P Cinematography, 2003, ISBN 0240 51676 1

For more details visit www.focalpress.com

To order your copy call +44 (0)1865 888180 (UK) or +1 800 545 2522 (USA)
or visit the Focal Press website: www.focalpress.com